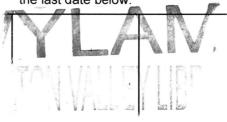

IN ACTION
WITH THE SAS

by the same author

The Cruellest of Tests (*The Book Guild Ltd*)

IN ACTION WITH THE SAS

A Soldier's Odyssey from Dunkirk to Berlin.

by

ROY CLOSE

Pen & Sword
MILITARY

First published in Great Britain in 2005 by
Pen & Sword Military
an imprint of
Pen & Sword Books Ltd
47 Church Street
Barnsley
South Yorkshire
S70 2AS

ISBN 1 84415 286 3

A CIP catalogue record for this book is
available from the British Library

Typeset in 11/13 Sabon by
Phoenix Typesetting, Auldgirth, Dumfriesshire

Printed and bound in England by
CPI UK

Pen & Sword Books Ltd incorporates the imprints of Pen & Sword
Aviation, Pen & Sword Maritime, Pen & Sword Military, Wharncliffe
Local History, Pen & Sword Select, Pen & Sword Military Classics and
Leo Cooper.

For a complete list of Pen & Sword titles please contact
PEN & SWORD BOOKS LIMITED
47 Church Street, Barnsley, South Yorkshire, S70 2AS, England
E-mail: enquiries@pen-and-sword.co.uk
Website: www.pen-and-sword.co.uk

Contents

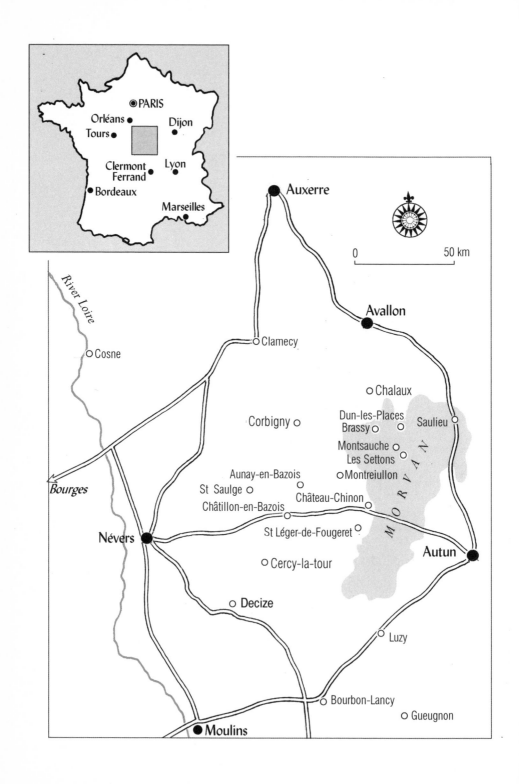

NORTH SEA

Groningen

Oldenburg

Lorup

Emmen

CANADIAN
FOURTH ARMOURED
DIVISION
April 1945

Cloppenburg
Meppen

Osnabrück

SAS
COLUMN

AMSTERDAM

NETHERLANDS

Arnhem

Munster

Rotterdam

R. Neder Rijn

R. Ems

R. Waal

Nijmegen

Emmerich

Cleves

G E R M A N Y

R. Maas

Venray

Eindhoven

Horst

Geldrop

Venlo

Düsseldorf

Ostend

Antwerp

R. Rhine

Gent

May 1940
Actions

PANZERS

Cologne

Ypres

Dunkirk
Poperinge

Courtrai

BRUSSELS

B E L G I U M

Liege

St.Omer

Lille

R. Meuse

Bethune

Mons

SUPPLY
COLUMNS

Bastogne

LUXEMBOURG

F R A N C E

0   50   100 km

Peace is declared an' I return
To 'Ackneystadt, but not the same;
Things 'ave transpired which made me learn
The size an' meanin' of the game.

I did no more than others did.
I don't know where the change began.
I started as a average kid,
I finished as a thinkin' man.

Rudyard Kipling: *The Return*

Introduction

It would make a good start to these recollections to claim that I had forgotten they were there and came across them 'by accident' this number of years later. Alas, it would not be true. I knew they were up there. In the attic in a box. Yellowing pieces of paper, two tatty scribbling pads, a couple of cheap notebooks and a slightly better quality hardback notebook only partly filled. They all contain scribbles made during my almost seven years in the Army during the Second World War and its immediate aftermath. Some of them record events in which I was involved. Others attempt to describe one's reaction to other events and one's emotions at various stages of service life. They are the rambling, immature thoughts of a young man whose early adolescence had been dominated by the inevitability of war and whose early manhood was ordered by the demands of the worldwide conflict that followed.

Reading them now, I see again the clear conviction many of my generation then held, not only that a war was inevitable, but also that we should fight it if we were not to be ruled by a brutal foreign dictatorship. We harboured no doubts. Yet there were strong contrary views – perhaps held largely by those who had personal experiences or memories of the ghastly First World War. There was much grumbling about the dangers of being dragged into another conflagration with unforeseeable consequences. It was worth, some thought, giving in to Germany's demands for 'living space' to avoid a senseless struggle. The Press, like the country, was divided. There were many anti-war demonstrations, accompanied by much debate about our readiness for war. The previous Labour Government had introduced a disarmament policy. The Conservative Government of

Neville Chamberlain seemed so intent on the pursuit of peace by appeasing Hitler that they seemed reluctant to introduce at the same time an adequate re-armament programme that would strengthen our forces. When something of a re-armament programme began it was slow and seemed half-hearted. Rumour abounded. Some said, 'Ah, there's a lot going on behind the scenes'. Others sought to assure us with the nonsense that 'Germany is not as strong as she claims; her equipment is made of ersatz material and her tanks are made of wood'. Many thought that if war came we would find ourselves dangerously under-equipped. They were right. When we went to war in 1939 under our treaty obligation to Poland we were poorly armed – surely a crime against our Servicemen and women. For some years our weapons and equipment were inferior to the enemy's. It took time and cost many lives and limbs to catch up.

So it was that many of us who saw the approach of the inevitable joined the Territorial Army, as I did in 1938, or its equivalent in the other services. There was nothing noble about this. Self-preservation, rather. We wanted to choose, if possible, the Arm in which we would prefer to serve and to get some early training to give us a better chance of coping with what was coming. As it turned out our freedom of choice was limited in a way we had not expected. It was conditioned by such practical matters as which Arm or Service had a Drill Hall where you would have to go for training that was not too far from your work place or from your home. It was usual to go for training on 'Drill nights' on the way home from work.

But these details affecting our personal preparedness did not lessen our recognition of the real significance of the struggle we were engaged in. I see that in my notes, trying to describe the highs and lows of our military existence; during the tense periods of action and the long, frustrating periods of inaction not only were we utterly sure that the future of our free, democratic society depended on the outcome, but we were equally certain that afterwards things had to be done to repair the grave shortcomings of our society. And we wanted a say in that reconstruction. We had seen the gross inequalities of our pre-war 'system' and realized that men and women from all walks of life – the privileged, the rich, the poor, the employed and the unemployed – stood side by side, often in the same fighting units, and on the 'home front'.

My comments on some of these issues in those shabby pages reflect the way many of us thought about those things at that time, when there was much dissatisfaction. They also reflect discussions we had about them in our many idle moments, and about those great issues of morality, God and L-I-F-E, much as we might have done in different circumstances at college or university. I see now how naïve and simplistic many of those thoughts were, especially our aspirations for political changes. Many years later, when working in the field of economic development alongside successive Governments of different complexions, I saw at first hand the complexities of government. I saw in both the erroneous belief that the road to social contentment and prosperity is paved with yet more legislation and how well-meant intentions are thwarted by the 'law' of unforeseen consequences. But then we were young and immature.

For years after the war I wanted to have nothing to do with these jottings. Part of me wished they weren't there, yet I did not want to destroy them. There was an immediate post-war period when I and, I suspect, many others wanted to set the war aside. Not forget it; that wasn't possible. There were unpleasant memories to be suppressed, frightening dreams to be exorcised, and the war's legacies were everywhere to be seen and felt. But put it aside. The scars would soon heal because it was irrelevant to what we now had to do: find a way of earning a living, get married, find somewhere to live, raise a family, all in an environment of acute shortages, rationing and lack of housing, and cope with the sudden change from the laddish, brutish, couldn't-care-less culture to a more normal, caring relationship. This was a life style we had not thought about for years. It was not an easy transition to make. It took time to get used to, to feel part of the civilization we had fought to protect. Some never did.

Thus it was several years before I took my first 'post-war' look at the yellowing bundle. I felt both intrigued and embarrassed. Intrigued that I should have bothered to scribble so much. Why? Recognition that one was living through unusual, significant times? Perhaps, but certainly not with any sense of writing a 'journal' of historic events. Perhaps just the need to do something to keep the mind occupied in boring times. I don't know why. But as I went to them from time to time over the years I found, trying to ignore my embarrassment at their youthful lack of awareness, that they reminded me of things I had put at the back of my mind and said something about times swiftly fading from many minds. Thus it was that after I retired and had time to think back and reflect – retirement's passtime – I decided to enhance their status and promote them onto the shelves in my study, if only to use them occasionally to shake the kaleidoscope of memories that is the privilege of old age.

As I did so I realized that fewer and fewer people today know much about that period, especially among the new generations like my own middle-aged children, busy making a living, and *their* fast-growing offspring so absorbed for the time being, understandably, with electronics, computers, computer games, surfing the web, making friends, doing exams, seeking their own personalities. Yet perhaps someday they might be interested.

Now, 60 years on, we see clearly that those times *were* a landmark in our history; crucial for the survival of our country as a free nation, a survival gained at a heavy price. That price was not only the lives of Service personnel and innocent civilians whose sacrifice was total, and the horrendously life-changing disabilities and disfigurements of the wounded and injured, but also the shattered family relationships and searingly memorable experiences of all who were directly involved. Those experiences did something to us all, though I'm not sure what. Perhaps lumbering us with the yoke of a boring past. Perhaps life-dominating memories from a relatively short but vivid phase in our existence. Yet making us realize that a freedom so won must never be compromised by latter-day 'newspeak' politicians lacking, or ignoring, any historic perspective.

So I have, with yet more presumption, decided that – whatever they represent – my jottings may be worth editing and putting together as one man's impressions of those times. Using the notes as a prompt, I have tried to recall as honestly as I can the details they evoked as I read them, surprising myself that so much came welling up from those dark recesses of the mind, unrecalled for so long. I have honestly tried not to let the intervening years be the father of exaggeration. Here and there I have included conversation as quota-tion, but, of course, at this distance in time I cannot be sure that the actual words are the same. But the sense of them is, and recalling them thus has saved me from repeating endlessly a boring 'as far as I can remember', yet I ask you who chance to read this to bear that phrase in mind throughout.

4

1

Mobilizing the Unready

This will not be a story of great heroics. It will not be a thrill-a-page adventure story. There are lots of those around, as well as genuine accounts of gallantry. But in almost seven years of war there were for most of us, I surmise, long periods of inaction and boredom. Purposely I have not tried to diminish them. They were part of the war as I experienced it. Certainly there were periods of intense excitement and strain which I will try to describe, but I want to convey also how we tried to cope with those periods of boredom. It is a simple story of how we, ordinary citizens, responded to the threats that dominated our early lives and the demands that the course of the war put upon us. While many performed deeds of great gallantry, most of us just did what we had to, coping with tensions, controlling our fears, trying to behave well in action, believing we must destroy a great evil and preserve our democratic system, warts and all. So it's the story of one individual who, when circumstances required, put down his clerk's pen, took up a weapon and, like many others, spent six and a-half years in uniform. It's nothing spectacular. Just my memory of the way it was.

This time the whole population of the country was involved, determined to defend our freedom. We played separate parts. Some fought. Those who worked on the land, who made armaments, warships, warplanes and ammunition often worked until they dropped from exhaustion. They and others suffered fearsome bombing in their homes. And, of course, families were split up for the safety of the children whose upbringing was then warped, perhaps for life. For years personal relationships were threatened with instability. Yet those pressures also forged a unity of purpose, the like of which has not been seen since and, in the Services, comradeships that have endured.

So often I have wished it were possible to convey to the generations who now enjoy the freedom that was won that it must not be given away in pursuit of an ambition that cannot be realized because of those who wish to force centuries of differing history and separate cultures into a single mould, instead of moving towards voluntary co-operation in a globally interconnected world. Sadly, beliefs that united us then seem to be eroding.

I can offer two excuses for the immaturity of these jottings. At the time, obviously, I was not only young but also uneducated. I was born and lived for ten years in a very modest district of North London the pervading atmosphere of which I can recall today – sugary fumes from a nearby sweet factory mixed with the smell of coal gas from the equally nearby gasworks. Mother, Father, brother and I lived downstairs, though my brother and I slept upstairs in the unheated 'spare room' next to the two rooms where Grandmother and Grandfather lived. In those days milk was collected in jugs from a three-wheel portable urn the milkman pushed along the street. In the summer we tried to keep milk and butter fresh by standing the jug and dish in water outside in the shade with a wet cloth over them. No refrigerators, a small gauze-covered cabinet for a larder, no cling film, no aluminium foil. Coal was delivered from a horse-drawn cart and emptied by a powerful coalman wearing a leathery hood over his head into the cellar through a hole in the front doorstep which Mother whitened daily When she wasn't doing the housework or preparing meals or washing our clothes, taken from a coal-fired 'copper', on a corrugated washing board, or shopping among the market stalls that in the winter were lit by snorting gas flares, or darning and mending, she would, when the weather permitted, clip the hedge in the tiny front garden, or, on her knees, the small lawn at the back with an old pair of shears.

Looking back and remembering the love and care that marked my – our, my brother and I – upbringing, though we were not short of 'rows', all the more disturbing when between parents because they were such brutal intrusions to our world, I see it was a God-loving rather than a God-fearing house. Christianity was at the core of our family beliefs, though less obviously in my Father, who, however, when later trying to persuade me to become a Mason, in which he reached a fairly high rank, emphasized his belief in its religious

6

significance. Mother, Grandmother and Grandfather were religious people. Mother and Grandmother were the nearest to being saints on earth than anyone I shall ever know.

Mother was the most tolerant, the most understanding and loving of people. Yet she had had a terrible early life, one of four children of an often absent soldier father who beat his children when he was home, but who was badly wounded at Gallipoli in the First World War. I suspect he drank through frustration. He had been a medical orderly during the war and wanted to be a doctor. Her mother was a sick woman who struggled to bring up a family on the meagre allowance her husband allocated from his army pay. She died when my mother was very young. Perhaps as the youngest, my mother felt especially close to her, seeing her struggles. I know she adored her because once or twice a month she would take me by bus to the cemetery to tend her grave. She bought a few flowers at the cemetery entrance and placed them in a jam jar by the headstone. Always before we left she would kneel in silent prayer. She, her sister and brother were brought up by the oldest brother. His responsibilities had, it seemed, made him a severe man. He frightened me when we used to visit him and my aunt, but he was a caring, upright and very moral man. Mother was a devoted follower of the Salvation Army, as was my grandmother. Often we were visited by fellow Salvationists.

My paternal grandfather was every kind of nonconformist in his time – Methodist, Presbyterian, Congregationalist, total immersion Baptist. He was an engineer, probably unqualified, working for a company that made plant for the gas industry, but he must have had a searching mind. I have a lovely, leather-bound family Bible given to him by his mother for his seventh birthday! She had lost both her husband and her oldest son in that same year. In the Bible I found references to passages in the gospels which had interested him. Even at that young age it seems he was looking for answers to those un-answerable questions of purpose and destiny which he chased for the rest of his life.

Having carried out some research into the family genealogy, I now appreciate that he was probably strongly influenced by both his father and grandfather who were local dignitaries in a very non-conformist chapel in Somerset which was supported by villagers who were discontented with the lack of services provided by the parish church. The chapel was said to have links back to the Dissenters. For a long time the members of the chapel worshipped in a schoolroom led by the headmaster who had established a small private school 'for all denominations and none'. In the 1970s all but two or three of the congregation had died and the chapel was converted into two houses by developers. The marble plaque on the wall honouring my great-great grandfather, his second wife, who was a donor to the Chapel, and my great grandfather was destroyed by the builders. Their graves are somewhere in the back gardens of the residences!

Grandfather and grandmother had come to London from Somerset where our modest forebears, peasant farmers and church-wardens, had lived in the same village near Glastonbury for about three hundred years, going there from Boston in Lincolnshire in the early 16th Century. They were born and bred country lovers, but, presumably in search of work, they came from Somerset to live near a gasworks in North London! On Sundays I could hear my grand-mother playing hymns on an old upright piano upstairs, and I knew, because sometimes I used to go up and sit on the floor in their living room, that they would then sit down and read their bibles.

One of the 'treats' I remember was to be taken by 'Grandad' on a Saturday, or Sunday, afternoon for a walk in the country when he would point out trees and flowers and birds, a lot of things I did not then understand. These expeditions involved bus rides which were very exciting, partly because it was a rare experience and because we often had to hurry, me sleepily on his shoulders in 'flying angel' posi-tion, to catch the last bus home. The places we went to are now covered in arterial roads and ribbon housing which you pass quickly through to get out of suburban London.

As I said, my grandmother, like my mother was a saint, a quiet comforting person I could run upstairs at any time to see. She always had a twinkling kindly smile and whatever she was doing there was always time to sit on her lap and talk, or she would have a little book handy from which she read. She was also my confessor. If I had done wrong, a not infrequent occurrence, and had to tell someone she was the one. She never scolded me, but quietly advised me to go down and 'own up'.

From today's relative opulence it is difficult for anyone to imagine that kind of life – small coal fires in one room; no fires in the bedroom unless you were ill, draughts, chilblains, gas mantles for lighting, radio only if you made your own 'wireless set' until you could afford to buy one and parents sitting at the kitchen table with available money before them planning the week-ends' purchases. Sometimes there was a joint of meat for Sunday lunch, but chicken was a rarity, a great luxury, a 'special treat'. It was a time when you closed the curtains if someone down the street died, a time when you stood still on the pavement and bowed your head if a funeral cortege went past.

Those were the days when a visit from the postman was an event. It did not happen very often. 'Postman,' my mother used to say, 'I hope its good news,' approaching the doormat with some apprehension, because often it wasn't. More likely a death of a relative. But sometimes a postcard from a relation on holiday at a popular resort: Margate, Southend-on-Sea, with a photo of them in their Sunday best on the pier.

I didn't know it at the time, but there was a period when my father was unemployed. When he came out of the Navy after the First World War he started a small business with a partner supplying parts for office typewriters. His partner absconded with the funds. It was only later, when I knew about this, that I realized I had agitated to do things involving expenditure when funds were non-existent. There is a big disadvantage in the philosophy that 'we mustn't worry the children with this'. It would have been better to have been told, and coped together with the disappointments, than later to carry the guilt of having behaved badly. But that was not the attitude those days and one cannot blame parents for conforming to the mores of the times. We children were protected from the embarrassing truth and life seemed quite normal.

We were aware that there was another kind of life in what we called 'up West'. Another 'treat' was to be taken by bus 'up West' and walk around looking at the bright lights and staring into the shop windows, seeing people get out of chauffeur-driven cars and go into hotels, then go to Lyons Corner House in Oxford Street and buy 'something special' to take home for supper.

When I was about ten we moved 'up market' into a terrace house in one of the ribbon developments along a new arterial road. I think it was then that we began to get pretentions. We had a saloon car. (Our first had been a second-hand Calthorpe with two seats inside and a 'dickie' outside where I and my brother sat.) Father was getting on.

I had been to a Church of England infants' and elementary school. Saints Days and Empire Days were holidays. The Headmistress was a rather large, waddling, bespectacled lady with a kindly eye and a friendly disposition. We were allowed to stand in the playground to watch through smoked glass panels a total eclipse of the sun and to watch the Graf Zeppelin fly over. Although my first school was C of E, Sunday school, every Sunday afternoon except on a fine afternoon when one or two of us 'diverted' ourselves to some nearby 'gardens', was in a Methodist Chapel.

I then went to a secondary County School. Scholastically I was a failure. 'Must do better.' 'Wastes his time.' 'Does not use what he's got,' were the kind of remarks in the School Reports I had to hear read out to me by my parents. 'You've got to concentrate, my boy,' said my father. 'Do try, darling, you can do it,' said my mother. But I was more interested in sport. First eleven cricket, first eleven soccer (sometimes) and swimming. I won the swimming and diving championships in my last year. I liked history, English literature, geography, geometry and arithmetic, but obviously not well enough to gain a General Schools Certificate, let alone a Matriculation. So I left school before going into the sixth form and with my Headmaster's recommendation that I should go into the Post Office: 'It will be safer for you'.

So it was from that background that in my first job as a clerk in a stock jobbers office I, my brother and one or two friends, convinced by Hitler's continuing threats to 'seek justice' for Germans in neighbouring countries that we were 'in for it', went one lunchtime to a recruiting exhibition for the Territorial Army to find out what we should do to get some training before it all started. We looked at the tanks and decided they looked flimsy; we looked at the anti-tank guns and decided they were inadequate. Finally it was all decided for us. A recruiting sergeant came up to us and said, 'Well gentlemen what do you want to join?' We did not know. 'Where do you live?' We gave him various addresses south of London. He looked at a list he had in his hand. 'Can you all drive?' Yes we could. 'Well go and join the Royal Army Service Corps in Croydon. They need drivers.' That was how we made our choice! We became Trooper drivers in 509 Company, 44th Home Counties Division.

Our 'drill nights' were on a Friday. We worked in the City of London and lived some 15 miles from Croydon. In those days of impending crisis 'T.A. drill night' was accepted by most employers as a reason for leaving work early. So on Fridays there was a scramble to get home and find out which father was prepared to lend his car for transporting several sons to the drill hall. It was a request that was seldom refused. After all, it was for an honourable, patriotic cause.

10

While I suspect most fathers did not mind, they could well have been apprehensive about the drive back, which, as they probably guessed, involved a number of less honourable pub stops.

In the summer of 1939 we went to a T.A. camp down in Kent. It was meant to be part of our training, but I can only remember that it was all good fun and very much a game of soldiers, unspoilt by the threatening clouds. We were from different backgrounds, but we were all volunteers from a particular locality and we got to know each other and, more importantly, learned to trust each other. It was a friendly atmosphere. Many of the officers had been to school with some of the troopers who lived not far from the Drill Hall. Our spirits were high and we developed a great camaraderie. It was there that I made firm friendships with 'Bill' Pearson and 'Freddy' Brittan, friendships that lasted long after the war as our families grew up, until their sad deaths.

The call to arms came on 31 August 1939. All reservists were mobilized and voluntary organizations asked to stand by. Instructions had already been given on how to black out houses and all other premises. It was an offence to show a light during the hours of darkness. Air-raid sirens had been installed in all towns and villages. Air-raid shelters – some for the garden, some for under the dining-room table – were distributed. Stirrup pumps for extinguishing incendiary bombs were also provided. Gasmasks had already been issued to the whole population. The evacuation of children from London and other large cities began. It was all quite efficient; a democracy was waking up; its young citizens were preparing to go to war, while others were taking jobs in factories making arms and equipment, and in essential work in coal mines and steel works.

To state it thus is to ignore the family and personal dramas that it all entailed. Think about it. Labelling young sons and daughters with their names and sending them to destinations, some in this country, some overseas, and waving them goodbye – for how long? For some it was an adventure, but in reality it meant a separation and a prospective loss of family love at a critical time in young lives. It meant worry and stress for parents. When would they meet again? Some children, whose parents were killed, never saw their parents again. But in other cases new friendships were formed. My mother and father took two evacuee girls whose school had moved nearby from London. They kept in touch until after they had married and raised their own children.

As far as I and my brother were concerned, when the call came we collected the kit we had been issued with, including our 1920 rifles, endured a tearful farewell from our parents and went, in someone's car, to the Drill Hall. A few hours later we were trying to find a way of getting back home because the Military Command had not found anywhere for us to sleep. 'Come back tomorrow,' they said. Looking back, that experience, when the German war machine was poised to invade Poland, which they did the following day, together with the recognition that we were inadequately prepared, set the disorganized tenor of our early war.

After we were mobilized we were sent first to Kent where we had comfortable civilian billets in Maidstone. When, nervously, we met our hosts, who had no choice in the matter, we were surprised that they were so friendly and welcoming. Then we were sent to the West Country, to Somerset. This time we were stationed in a public building, the Corn Exchange in one of the county towns, a large bare hall with a concrete floor which I remember well because rows of us slept in it on rather thin straw palliasses.

I remember two particular incidents. First, one morning when we were woken as usual at 6 a.m. and failing to get the man next to me moving, I found that he was dead. He had died from a heart attack during the night. The second was when someone discovered that one of our number was a professional singer. He had sung in the chorus of the Royal Opera. One evening as we were getting ready to 'bed down' someone asked him to sing. Without accompaniment he sang 'Largo al Factotum' from The Barber of Seville. The exuberant chatter from our visit to the pub subsided and gradually we, such a mixed crew, either sat down on our beds or stood where we were and quietly listened. When he finished there was a pause, then applause from everyone and embarrassed shouts of 'bravo'. He had reminded us of a more civilized existence which we would meet rarely again in the coming months – years?

The Division was spread over Somerset and Dorset and our job was to supply the various Divisional units 'in the normal way'. I should explain that in those days the Company was divided into three: HQ, Echelon One and Echelon Two. The two echelons performed the same tasks on alternate days. One echelon would go to railhead, or roadhead, and pick up supplies in bulk, then break that bulk down to unit requirements ready to deliver to the units at specified rendezvous the following day. Meanwhile the other echelon would be out delivering to the units and collecting numbers and requirements for the next day when it would go to collect the bulk, break it down into unit requirements and deliver. A logical system, which ensured regular supply to the fighting units, though in action, as we discovered later, the rendezvous was constantly changing and often under fire. But at that time in the peaceful West Country we had no vehicles, and the infantry, artillery and engineers did not have all their weapons or other equipment. We spent the first weeks scrambling round to commandeer whatever vehicles could be found: builders' trucks, delivery vans of all kinds.

Gradually things got better and we got our Bedford three-ton covered trucks and the officers got their little Austin staff cars. We did the RASC job quite happily. Less happily, we did quite a lot of square bashing to remind us we were soldiers and not just delivery men. We did field training, field tactics, firing on the range, all of which I enjoyed. It was more like proper soldiering and I felt that the more we knew about these things the better it would be for us. Which was the way it turned out. That winter was freezing cold and we shivered in our greatcoats and balaclavas as we guarded such important military installations as a railway siding in Yeovil! The evenings were spent drinking a lot of rough cider which sent us cold-proof to the concrete floor of the Corn Exchange. I haven't been able to face rough cider since.

This was the period of the 'phoney war' of 3 September 1939 to 10 May 1940. We were at war but the serious fighting on the Western Front had not broken out. The German Army and Air Force ferociously and brutally invaded Poland on 1 September, in whose hopeless cause we declared war on Germany on 3 September. That gallant nation was overrun and surrendered in October. But from September into the New Year the Netherlands, Belgium and France, hiding behind the concrete 'impregnable', interconnected fortifications of the Maginot Line, just waited. The British Army was confined to the French side of the Belgian and Netherlands frontiers because those nations wished to 'preserve their neutrality', which, as we feared and as was proved, meant that Germany could have a 'free run' into those countries whenever they wished. There were reports of patrol activity on the Franco-German frontier, a few prisoners were taken, reports of aerial reconnaissance, a few bombs dropped, but little fighting.

The only way the Allies could have fulfilled their pledge to

Poland would have been to attack, but that would have been useless. The Dutch and Belgians, anxious not to 'provoke' Germany, would not have let us through. We all knew that the only way the deadlock could be broken was for the German Army to invade the Low Countries and France. Until that happened the British Expeditionary Force could not take up defensive positions in Holland and Belgium. We could only wait. It was a hiding to nothing. At the time many voices were raised that the 'phoney war' was a duplicitous arrangement between the Allies and Hitler. It was a time of rumour and propaganda.

The winter passed. The Division became properly equipped; we became more competent. Friendships were established with the kind and caring people of the villages and towns in which we were stationed. Looking back, it was impressive the way the voluntary groups – Womens' Voluntary Service and the like – with their canteens, offers of help, laundry, baths and so on did so much to provide a bit of civilized comfort for the troops. For occasional diversion we listened to Lord Haw-Haw, William Joyce, the English traitor who broadcast from Germany, with his call-sign 'Germany Calling, Germany Calling', and he told us how we were getting on with our preparations. In fact it was from him that we first heard that we were about to cross the Channel to join the Expeditionary Force. This was at the end of February or beginning of March 1940.

Just before we prepared to embark I and two comrades were told by the Sergeant Major that we had been picked out to be the Echelon's Light Machine Gun Team. We would be responsible for protecting our convoys against ground troops and against enemy aircraft like Stuka bombers and Messerschmitts. We were given a 1914 Lewis gun, taught how to deal with the various stoppages to which it was prone in action and taught how to strip it, clean it and reassemble it. We were then sent to Aldershot for firing practice. It comprised shooting at slowly rising balloons set up from behind the butts of a rifle range, which was meant to train us to fight off the Stukas and the Messerschmitts while in convoy. We were given a 15 cwt truck with a metal tripod screwed to its floor into the top of which we had to place a lug hanging from a band clamped round the barrel of the gun. It broke the second time we used it in action. From then until we reached Dunkirk we took it in turns to fire from each other's shoulder. My youthful petulant criticism of our 'powers that be' for their failure to prepare us for war was inflamed by this personal example of our total inadequacy. We were comprehensively outgunned.

The Division set sail at the end of March from various ports along the South Coast. My abiding memory is standing on deck in the stern one night watching the faint twinkle of a light from a largely blacked-out coast recede in the distance and hearing someone ask, 'I wonder when we shall see that again?'

Our echelon landed at Cherbourg and were sent straight to a camp just outside the Port. It was pouring with rain. The site of the camp was certainly not chosen by a trained Boy Scout. The mess tent was on a bit of a slope and the sleeping tents were just below, in the path of the water streaming down from the mess tent. The food was an example of the worst that an Army cookhouse could do. There were so many complaints that the officer in charge called a meeting in the mess tent to which he brought the sergeant cook. (Though there are many origins to this story, this one was, for me, *the* original.) During the 'what are the complaints?' session the Orderly Officer rapped his stick on the table: 'Stand up the man that called the cook a bastard.' No one stood up, but a voice from the back countered with 'Who called the bastard a cook?'

We were there for some days while we unloaded our vehicles. Then early one very grey and drizzly morning we set off in convoy. We did not all have maps but the officer in charge of the convoy showed us a route that would take us to Le Mans where we would have a break before proceeding to our destination, which was . . .? Well, for security reasons we would not be told until later! I do not remember how long it took us to reach Le Mans, but it was a long time. It was our first experience of marshalling a long convoy on an overseas route observing local rules of the road. I retain one memory of it. As we went through one village we passed a marriage procession walking in the other direction towards the Church. Our troops leaned out of their cabs and called 'Good luck', the linguists *'Bon chance'*. The bride waved, smiling. As we drove on one could not help wondering what would become of them. Yet it seemed to signal a kind of defiant hope, as did the many marriages in Britain at that time, entered into before the fiancé, or fiancée or both, went off to join their units.

At Le Mans we were told that we were heading for Lapugnoy, a village close to the frontier between France and Belgium. There was a factory on the outskirts – cigarette-making, I believe. Many of the workers were young girls, a large number of whom were Polish refugees. This was a great benefit to the troops. When off duty they would wait outside the factory entrance at 'clocking off time' and walk with the girls, never singly (local opinion, uneasy in any event, would never have approved and we had been warned not to offend) along the river (or was it a canal?) bank. Some of the bolder refugees, presumably those without much local background, agreed to meet their 'Anglais' boyfriends in the estaminet in the evening and brave the glares of the groups of resident males. Those of us who went there fairly regularly off duty would show off our knowledge (slight though it was) of the French way of life by ordering *pastis* or more daringly, the stronger *Amer Picon*.

Time passed without incident. Railheads and roadheads had been established and collection and delivery to the regiments were part of the daily routine. We had set up a sandbagged gun emplacement for our Lewis on the edge of the village, which we manned from dawn to dusk except during collection and delivery times when we took the gun on its mounting in the back of the truck for convoy protection. However, we were ordered not to open fire on enemy aircraft – sporadic reconnaissance flights – from the gun emplacement for fear of giving away the unit location!

Uneventful though our waiting was, we knew the real war would soon begin. The Russians, who had earlier invaded eastern Poland after its collapse under the German blitzkrieg, then invaded Finland. Germany occupied Denmark and invaded Norway in April. A British expeditionary force counter-invaded Norway and fought battles at Namsos and Narvik, but was forced to evacuate in early May. This news filtered through to us heavily embellished with rumour, particularly concerning large German forces massing on the frontiers of Belgium and Holland. We were on 24-hour alert.

It was at dawn on 10 May that from our gun emplacement we heard low-flying aicraft approaching fast from the north. Two Heinkels swept across the village, machine guns blazing. They were so low we could clearly see the pilots. We immediately opened fire, heard a similar response and saw the tracers from the other echelon's gun firing at another raider. It was over in seconds. They had appeared, straffed and flown on. As we watched, composing ourselves after this brief introduction to 'action', we heard a rather dull explosion and saw a column of black smoke in the distance.

'Bombing' we thought. We learned later that it was one of the aircraft that attacked our two locations. We had shot one down! Naturally both echelon's guns claimed the kill, but that did not stop us getting a 'dressing down' for disobeying orders by opening fire!

We did not need telling that the Germans had invaded the Low Countries. The phoney war was over. The real one had begun.

2

Dunkirk: Chaos to 'Miracle'

It was several days before the Division began moving into Belgium. At first we were able to use the rail and roadheads we had already established and supply the regiments from Lapugnoy. Rumours abounded; official information was scarce. Apart from those that warned us that German troops were infiltrating our lines dressed as nuns and that German parachutists were everywhere, some of the rumours – that the Wehrmacht was advancing, that the 'line' was fluid – were correct. But our 'information' that a large counterattack was about to be launched was not. We moved up and the Division went into action. Almost immediately the fluidity of the line was apparent because the rendezvous with the the units we were supplying kept changing.

A scrappy piece of paper written by pencil indicates the situation as I experienced it then.

24th May. Left Lapugnoy through Moreslede and Zonnebeke to deliver to Division near Merris. Division heavily engaged. Returned to railhead to reload. Back to Zonnebeke. Left on Friday for Oudenarde, difficulty finding delivery point. Heavy fighting at Oudenarde. Division took a hammering. Roads clogged with refugees. Straffing and bombing. Spent night in farm somewhere. Moving on Saturday.

Monday to Dikkebusch again and delivery near Merris on Monday (27th?) Roads bad. Refugees very frightened. Getting straffed. Dead and wounded. Plenty of shooting at Messerschmitts and Stukas (downed an Ms.?) with the old Lewis. Nothing but rumours: breakthrough here – or there;

German paratroops behind us (?); Fifth columnists dressed as priests!! (?) etc. etc. Back to farm. Bombed by Stukas – miraculously no casualties. Tuesday, delivery to Division near Fletre. Straffed on way back and Stuka bombing (Hit a Stuka; went off in smoke). Military Police told us Panzers had broken through the lines – have to make for Dunkirk. (Where's that?)

Later I was able to fill in some of the details from memory, which I then extended when unexpectedly running across a former member of the Company when I joined the Parachute Regiment in North Africa. He also had gone off to the Parachute Regiment. These are our combined memories of that time.

We moved up with the division from Lapugnoy to make our first delivery. The German Army had invaded and the battle for Holland and Belgium had begun. We were to deliver to a rendezvous near Merris, as mentioned above. Apart from the sudden and brief air raid on Lapugnoy on the 10th this was to be my first experience of being under direct enemy fire. The LMG truck was travelling second in the column behind the OC's little Austin staff car as we made for the delivery point. We noticed some of our artillery camouflaged in some trees and then passed some infantry lying in shallow trenches and behind bushes. I remember thinking quite absurdly, 'Must be an exercise . . .' Suddenly with a loud bang and a rattling shower of gravel, earth and sizzing bits of shrapnel, the truck shifted sideways and stopped; a big hole had opened up in the road close to the cab. Then another on the other side in the verge. In the back of the truck Ron Holmes and I, manning the Lewis, had managed to hang on, but I thought our driver, 'Ginger' Grummit, might be hurt. An exclamation of 'Fuckin' 'ell' from the cab reassured us. The front had advanced and we had driven through our front line (no one had tried to stop us) and were under enemy shell fire!

The OC was quickly out of his car signalling for the column to turn round and go back, which we did very quickly as shells continued to fall, fortunately missing all our vehicles. From then on there wasn't a day when we were not under fire, mostly when straffed by Messerschmitts or bombed by Stukas as we went up to deliver to the hard-pressed infantry and artillery, almost always caught in a great crowd of very frightened civilians, men, women, the very old and very young children, all streaming away from the front, unnerved by the rumours they had been fed. Some in vehicles,

19

but most on foot or with bicycles, carrying in cases or sacks whatever they were able to bring from their homes. Some shouted warnings about 'the Boche', pointing back up the road. It was chaotic. We had to force our way through to get to our troops, calling on them to get out of the way, while keeping our eyes skywards waiting for the inevitable attack.

It became a daily occurrence – roads crowded with these refugees fleeing from the advancing enemy, cars with mattresses and luggage strapped to their roofs, people pushing wheelbarrows or old prams containing their few goods, others dragging cases or bags, all blocking our way forward. The straffing and bombing were also daily. At first it was scary seeing a couple of Messerschmitts flying towards you just above the trees with the guns in their wings flashing and rattling out their deadly message, or looking up to see a flight of Stukas circling to begin their screaming drive and watching for the release of the bomb. But after the first experience there was just no time to think about consequences. We were too busy firing, changing 'pans' on the gun and preparing for the next raid.

The casualties, dead and groaning wounded, in the ditches after each raid were pitiful to see. The memory of the open wounds, the scattered body parts and the little child crying beside the mother's body never leaves me. (It was during this, my introduction to action, that I first experienced a strange clarity of vision, seeing everything clearly and vividly and, I think, fairly calmly. I found this happened each time I was in action. Perhaps it was my own kind of funk pacifier?)

In those actions I know we scored some 'hits'. We quickly learnt that the best tactic was to put up a field of fire (unfortunately, with our WW1 Lewis gun, not a very concentrated one) in front of or below the attacking planes, through which they would have to fly. But they flew so quickly through the 'curtain' that they were not badly damaged, except on two occasions, one when we were fairly sure we downed a Messerschmitt and another when we probably got a Stuka. The Messerschmitt came straight and low down the road, firing indiscriminately. We shouted a warning to the refugees and put up our field of fire. He flew through it and, as we tried to follow him round, we saw smoke coming from him as he broke off, banked round and flew back the way he came, getting lower and lower, leaving a dark trail as he disappeared over the horizon almost at ground level.

On another occasion a Stuka, one of a flight of three, came

screaming down towards us and again we set up a field of fire in front of him which he had to dive through. Just as he released his bomb, which exploded behind us, he belched a lot of smoke, wobbled and flew off very low. We were too busy to pay any more attention to him, but our chums down the column told us afterwards that they saw him go below tree level, then heard a loud explosion and saw black smoke rising from behind the trees. Naturally at the time we counted these as definite 'scores' and were much encouraged by them, as were our comrades in the column who until then were pretty scathing about the amount of protection we could give them!

How we escaped injury in these raids I shall never know. Reflecting afterwards, it seemed unjust that some of us got away with it, while others did not. But there's no fairness in war. We were lucky. Apart from being unscathed standing with Ron in the back of the truck operating the Lewis when under attack, there was an occasion when we were caught by a Stuka attack out in the open out of the truck and there was nothing to do but dive into the nearest ditch. Lying there, we could hear the amplified screech of their dive and then a series of approaching explosions in the adjoining field and a trembling of the ground where we were stretched out. Clutching the earth as firmly as I could, I heard the voice of Nobby Clarke, who had been a stockbroker, muttering, 'I'm going a bear on this. Definitely not bullish, old boy.' The Stukas flew away and we stood up. We were luckier than we had thought. There in the ditch just between the two of us sticking up from the earth were the tail fins of a bomb. Thankfully it hadn't exploded.

Ahead of us the fighting was fluid and our rendezvous were frequently changed at the last minute, but always coming back towards us! One day the Battalion failed to meet us at the RV. It was near Oudenarde and we heard that the Division was heavily engaged and having a bad time. Our column took shelter in a wood while we waited to hear about a new RV. We rested by our vehicles and listened to the rumble of the battle, which seemed to get nearer. We wondered when we would hear the next rumour about 'a break-through'. It came with some authority, from the Sergeant Major who rode up on his motorcycle. 'LMG team in yer truck. Breakthrough to the north. You've got to go back there and cover the withdrawal of the column if they come this way. We're still waiting for orders. Follow me.' He led us up the track in the woods to a clearing. 'Here you are; leave the truck under trees ready to chase the column when they are clear. Get yer gun down and make your position there . . .', pointing vaguely towards the clearing, 'and hold on until I come for you'! He roared off back down the track.

I think we stood looking at each other for a few minutes and listened to Ginger's string of very disrespectful expletives. It wasn't the best of briefings, but it was to the point. Nor was it the best of defensive positions. It was in the open. We needed cover and we needed a good field of fire towards the wood at the farther side of the clearing.

We saw there was a low ridge running across the field. We decided to settle for that. I took the Lewis and tried to make myself invisible behind the ridge in the centre. The others took their rifles – Ginger close to my right to help put new 'pans' of ammunition on the gun when required, Ron on my left. It was a hot sunny day. There were lots of irritating flies; we watched and we waited. After a short period of silent tension we relaxed and started chatting in stage whispers about our earlier lives, about what we thought about the war and a little about our beliefs. 'Ah! about time too,' said Ron as we heard our vehicles starting up back in the woods and the sound of them slowly moving off. But almost immediately we saw a large flock of birds rise from the trees ahead of us. Safety catches went off; we stared fixedly ahead. We could hear the muffled sound of a motorcycle. 'Patrol,' whispered Ron. We heard the motorcycle more clearly and heard shouting from inside the wood in front; the foliage between the trees began to move. I'm afraid we didn't wait to see the whites of their eyes. I opened up with the Lewis and the others gave rapid fire from their rifles for a couple of minutes. This was followed by moments of complete silence. Then we heard the motorcycle again, but receding. This was not very courageous on our part but if we were to be confronted by a German patrol we did not want to attract enemy fire onto our ridiculously exposed position. We waited nervously, knowing that 'they' would probably return in greater strength. Fortunately a few minutes later we heard the more familiar sound of a motorcycle coming up the track behind us. It was the Sergeant Major. 'Right, in the truck double sharp. We're on the move. Follow me.'

We found the divisional transport waiting for us in another wood a few miles away. It was at these meetings that we had news of the progress of the battle. It had got worse as the days passed. On this occasion, when they were heavily engaged in the fighting round

Oudenarde, it was particularly bad and the drivers and their loaders looked tired and drawn. 'We've taken a lot of casualties,' one of them said flatly.

It was the next day, or the day after, that we had to meet the battalion transport in a farmyard which, again, we found to be rather exposed. Our transport had to line up along the road to await their turn to drive in, quickly transfer the supplies to a battalion truck and get out. In spite of protests from the farmer, we parked our LMG truck by a barn in the yard and watched the skies as the delivery proceeded – at record pace, I might say. It was not long before we spotted a flight of Stukas flying fairly high. It looked at first as if they were going to miss us. Then we saw the leader waggle his wings as he turned towards us; the others lined up behind him. We shouted the 'take cover' warning. The farmer, who, having given up his protests, had stood watching our activity with his wife, grabbed her by the arm and ran indoors. Drivers and their mates grabbed their rifles as required by 'air-raid drill' and prepared to take aim. The dive began, directed straight at the farmyard. We waited and then opened up. The first bomb landed at the far edge; the next lifted one of the battalion trucks in the air and turned it over; the third destroyed one of the barns. Seconds later it was quiet again. No one had been hurt! To shouts of 'Hurry it up' we reloaded and watched the skies.

We went straight back to draw more supplies ready for the next delivery. It was getting more hectic. In the circumstances the theory that we should draw from the railhead, carry out repairs and maintenance while the other echelon delivered, then deliver next day, was out of the window. The infantry, artillery and engineers needed more supplies, and quickly. We had to get some to them. We were told that on the following morning we would meet the divisional transport somewhere near Flêtre. We would be given the RV map reference later. The position was certainly 'fluid', as communiques would put it.

We set out early. It was clear the battle was going against us. Our convoy was soon brought to a halt by a flood of fleeing refugees. Again there were cars with matresses strapped to the roof, pony carts, barrows and prams stacked with some belongings, little children crying, all streaming away from the fighting. We tried to get them to keep to one side of the road, but they would not. They were all round us. Terrorised, they were understandably concerned only to get away. Some of them pointed to the direction from which they came, the direction we were going, and shouted, '*Allemandes. Beaucoup Allemandes*'. I'm afraid that at the time we were less sympathetic than we should have been. Our concern was to get through. Ahead of us was a slow-moving horse-drawn French unit of some kind, also in the way. In the back of the truck we searched the skies, the gun resting on one of our shoulders. The tripod lug had snapped in an earlier action. Because of the weight and the shattering noise in our ears, we had to keep changing over.

We knew it would be only a short time before it would happen. It was too good an opportunity for the Luftwaffe to miss. And surely they came. We saw them ahead, flying as usual down the road just above the trees. We heard them at the same time and shouted warnings, waving our arms to the terrified refugees. We could see that the attack was going to be a disaster. Those in cars or small lorries were hooting and shouting at those on bicycles and those on foot pushing carts and prams who were milling all round our vehicles. Those who heard our warnings ran for the ditches and the fields beyond. Others saw them running and followed. Those in cars seeing the rush for the fields opened their doors, looked out and abandoned their vehicles, leaving them on the road. But the ditches were wide and open and there was no cover in the fields.

There were three attacking planes in line. All our drivers and their companions were out of their cabs with their rifles. We opened up with the Lewis. It was difficult, firing over Ron's shoulder, to change the elevation as the first came over us and then switch back to the next one. All around us people were hit, some as they ran, falling with a cry, others as they lay unconcealed. As always it was swift and merciless. The shouts, the cries, the roar of the aircraft, the rattle of their machine guns, the more punctuated sound of our gun with tracer bullets curving up and the crackle of rifle fire down the column were followed by a relative quietness broken by the pathetic moans of the wounded, the crying of little children and the squealing horses from the French unit writhing on the road. Casualties lay everywhere. It had all been so easy for them.

We had been lucky again. Only two of our trucks had been hit and only one man wounded, in the leg. As much as we wanted to we could not stay to help. We had to distribute supplies from the damaged trucks among our other vehicles and we had to push obstructions out of the way so that we could get up to the Division. As they worked, some of our drivers rushed over and gave their Field

Dressing packs to the injured. This was strictly against the rules. To give away your Field Dressing even to a comrade meant that you had no protection if you were hit. But that is not the way of the British soldier.

It was some time before we were able to carry on, threading our way through the dreadful aftermath of the unprovoked, unnecessary attack. The OC went on ahead to contact the Division, confirm the RV and to reassure our battalions that, though late, we were on our way. We were due to meet at a crossroads about five miles away. When we got there we met instead complete chaos again. Refugees from three directions were converging on the road we were on, pouring past and around us heading south to the French frontier. We halted at the side of the road and waited. There was no sign of our OC. After some minutes we saw a Military Police sergeant on a motorcycle weaving his way towards us. 'What are you doing here?' We explained that we were waiting to deliver. 'No chance. The Panzers have broken right through. 44th Div have had to pull out. We're evacuating. You have to get to Dunkirk.'

'Where's that?'

'Over there,' he said, waving his arm towards the west.

'What about our RV with our OC?'

'Wherever he is, he'll have been told the same thing. Now get on. I've got to find as many as I can and I don't want to be here too long.'

We passed the order down the line of the convoy and turned the truck on to the road to the left, pushing through the crowd surging towards us. We moved slowly, stopping frequently to wait for the other vehicles to follow us round. They too had to negotiate their way through the terrified throng. We could hear the sound of the battle to the north, causing the refugees to hurry, half-running as best they could with their loads, shouting and pushing past the slower ones. It was a very unhealthy situation. We were just waiting for another air raid. Up in the back of the truck we tried to watch the sky all round, shifting the weight of the gun from shoulder to shoulder.

The Stukas came first. They were quite high when we first saw them, but there was no chance that they would miss seeing us. Their target was the crossroads we had just left, but some of our vehicles still had not made the turn. The gun was on my shoulder this time, and as the planes went into their dive Ron shouted, 'Left a bit. Down a bit', so that he could get the right aim. It was difficult keeping a grip on the shuddering barrel and, with the staccato rattle in one's ear and the terrifying scream of the diving planes, hard to crouch, stand and twist as Ron wanted. They dropped their bombs straight down the middle of the road. We could see yellow-orange flames, the fountains of earth, cars turning over, handcarts and bicycles flying in the air. The planes flew through our field of fire. Some must have been hit, but they showed no sign of serious damage as they banked, climbed and flew back the way the way they came, presumably to refill their bomb racks.

The serious damage was on the road they had just flown over. There they had left silent, limp, doll-like bodies, screaming and moaning wounded, and, among those who had been spared, those whose fright had given way to anger, to pointless shaking of fists and the shouting of insults at the departing *sales Boches*. Looking back across to the other road we could not tell whether any of our vehicles had been hit. Fortunately most had been further back. As we watched we could see another Military Policeman on his motorbike stopping at each of our trucks shouting some instruction. He came up to where we and a few others were stopped. 'It's no good. You're not going to get through with that convoy. The roads are jammed and you're making more congestion. Drive your vehicles into a ditch; shoot up the engines and tyres. Start a fire if you can. Take all weapons and ammo, and see if you can get there on foot. Good luck.' Ginger was the first to react. He came out of the driver's cab with his usual pertinent summary of the situation: 'Fucking 'ell, Corporal.'

We got our weapons – rifles and the Lewis – and ammunition together, fired several rounds into the sump and the engine block, tore out the electric wires, bayoneted the tyres, punctured the petrol tanks, soaked our kit in petrol and set it ablaze. With the crews from the nearby vehicles, about nine or ten of us set off down the crowded road. Looking back we could see flames springing up from some of the other vehicles. We had a rough idea of the direction, but we had no idea how far we were from Dunkirk. We had no map. I think it was about then that the dreadful realization hit us that we were not involved in a withdrawal or a regrouping preparing to make that promised counter-attack, but that our whole army was in retreat and had somehow to be rescued.

My memory of the next twenty-four hours is both vivid and dull – vivid of certain episodes, dull about the depressing walk through jostling refugees of all ages and conditions, keeping an eye on the sky. Everything we were carrying, and reluctant to lose, was getting heavier. There were frequent air attacks, some ahead of us, some behind us, and the Lewis went into action many times. But we felt vulnerable on the road in the midst of such a target. After one of the attacks when we found the road ahead completely blocked we decided to break away and cut across fields. As we crossed the ditch to a field sloping down to a small river we were halted by a shout, 'Corporal.' I looked back and saw a Medical Orderly waving from beside an ambulance. 'If you're going across there could you give us a hand getting these men across?' There were, as I remember, four stretcher cases of wounded. 'It's suicide sitting here with them,' the Orderly said as we helped lift them out.

Between us we carried them all over the field to the river which fortunately was quite shallow and we were able to wade across it. Beyond that field and another we came across a road, inevitably packed with refugees and vehicles, but less crowded. Miraculously the vehicles included those of a Field Ambulance Unit. Again, miraculously, they had room in their ambulances and a truck for the stretchers we were carrying. The Orderly, who thanked us for bringing them, was quietly crying: 'The trouble is some of them are not going to make it.' I had seen some of the terrible wounds they had suffered, when the blanket slipped off one of the stretchers. 'But we can't leave them and we shan't get away. Our war's done.'

We walked on, determined to keep to fields and along hedgerows. We had not gone far when behind us we heard the now familiar roar of aircraft engines and the scream of diving Stukas. The road we had just left was under attack. We stopped and looked at each other. It was Ron who expressed what we were all thinking: 'Fucking bastards. Those ambulances.' We could only hope they were not hit.

Crossing roads, keeping between roads, avoiding all buildings, we made slow progress. But it was progress. Coming to one road, we broke our rule about not travelling on them. We came across an artillery unit of three twenty-five pounders hauled by their trucks. Grey-looking gunners were sprawled fast asleep in the trailers. Quickly in agreement, the LMG team decided to take a ride. We were tired. However, others of our party decided not to. I remember lying uncomfortably across a gun barrel and falling fast asleep. I woke, conscious that movement had stopped and conscious of much shouting. It was getting dark. A sergeant gunner came running past. 'Get off there mate. They say there are Panzers ahead. We're going to deploy for action. I'd make myself scarce if I were you.'

'Can we help?' I asked. He looked at the Lewis and our rifles. 'They won't be much use,' he replied. 'Best get on.' They were busy unlimbering the guns as we left the road and made for the fields again. I don't know how far we had gone. It was dark and we were having difficulty finding our way and avoiding the inevitable obstacles on our cross-country route. We had heard no sounds of battle behind us and assumed the action had not taken place. There was no point in going back, but we were tired. We decided to rest and felt our way into the shelter of what appeared to be a small copse. We just lay down and fell asleep. I woke to the sound of lowing cattle. Through the early morning mist I could see two of the beasts, but, more worrying, not fifty yards away was a farmhouse.

As quietly as we could we collected our weapons and retreated through the small wood into the next field and resumed our trek. We now had no doubt about our direction. Way ahead of us we could hear the noise of battle. Flights of German aircraft were pounding their target on the horizon, columns of black smoke rising into the air. The rumble of exploding bombs rolled towards us. 'Christ,' said Ron, 'Dunkirk.' We stared at it, wondering. For us it was still a long way off and we could not tell what was between us and the port. Had the Panzers already got there?

We started off again and after about an hour we saw a village a mile or so away being bombed. We gave it a wide birth, keeping under cover as much as we could. But it was now getting difficult avoiding buildings and small hamlets, while woods and hedges were getting scarce. The terrain was getting flatter and more open. Then on either side of a road we had to cross we saw a small group of houses. There was a strange quietness about them, so we lay down on some grass about a hundred yards away and watched. It looked as if some of the doors were wide open, but we detected no movement. Cautiously we moved forward, safety catches off. As we reached the road and walked slowly up between the buildings we could see in the rooms bottles of wine, glasses, even bread, on the tables, but no people. The place had been abandoned, and hurriedly.

After a very brief discussion about the danger of booby traps, we reasoned that if the Germans had been in to set traps they would have taken the wine. Later we wondered whether our reasoning had been sound, but at the time we were weary, hungry and thirsty. We had not eaten for over twenty-four hours, so we fed on French bread and wine while discussing how long it might take us to reach

28

Dunkirk and guessing what we might find when we got there. It was Ginger who suddenly shouted, 'Listen. Listen.' It was the unmistakable metallic grinding, grating, squeaking sound of tracked vehicles. Ron went to the door and peered out. 'Three tanks coming straight up the road. Not ours.' When we had entered the house we had investigated a cellar under the stairs. Very quickly we left the table and descended into the darkness; we had neglected to check if anyone was there, but there wasn't. Through a grating we watched, scarcely breathing, as three Panzers clanked by. As soon as they were gone we ran out of the house, round the back and across the fields in the direction of Dunkirk again.

It was hot. There was now little cover for us and, although we tried to jog across open ground, we were too exhausted to keep it up. We just chanced it. I don't remember how long we had walked before we saw ahead of us a crowded road, but this was crowded with retreating British troops, not in formation, different units, different regiments, some in shirt sleeves, some with tunics undone, rifles slung, helmets pushed back on their heads. It was not an inspiring sight, but I suspect that, like us, they had been through a confusing, ill-informed experience and had walked a long way. Yet within this motley column there were some small units, perhaps part of a platoon or a company, who were in formation, marching in step, under an NCO. They were bad for our consciences, but good for our morale. We joined this dispirited stream of Britain's Expeditionary Force. We were a target, but the enemy were too busy with the port of Dunkirk and, as we discovered later, with the beaches.

We arrived at the outer defences. It was either 29 or 30 May. A Military Police officer stood between two lines of trenches on either side of the road, manned, as I remember, by a Guards Regiment mostly in shirtsleeve order. 'Keep rifles and ammo, you'll need them on the beaches. All other weapons and ammo to the rearguard,' he said. And so we handed over the old Lewis, which we had cursed for its inadequacy (as we cursed those who gave it to us for their lack of foresight), yet were sorry to let it go. We handed it to one of the guardsmen. He reached up. 'Thanks, mate,' he said. 'Good luck,' we replied as we heeded the M.P.s 'Come on. Move on. And watch the sky,' – well-meant unnecessary advice. I was several yards down the road before the import of that brief exchange came to me. Why the hell was he thanking us? He was probably going to save our lives and if he survived he'd spend the rest of the war as a prisoner!

We were still a mile or so from the town. Air activity ahead was intense. The columns of black smoke which we had seen from a distance emitted the odour of burning oil. Along the way the stench of death from the rotting carcasses of cattle and horses was over-powering. Human bodies were being collected up and laid in a line. To this day that combination of fuel oil and rotting flesh invades my nostrils from time to time. I shall never be rid of it. We walked past some buildings, one of which had been turned into a small Field Ambulance station, outside of which were some stretchers carrying bandaged wounded. At the far end was a Naval Officer who directed us away from the town. 'The beaches here are too crowded. You won't get off from here,' he said. 'Make your way along the beach to Bray Dunes.' Until then we did not know what was meant by 'get off from here'.

But we soon saw as we went down on to the beach to begin the treck through the sand to the far end, to Bray Dunes. It all looked the same: more beaches packed with troops, dispersed, as much as possible, into groups. Down at the water's edge khaki queues stretched into the sea, the front ones up to their waists. Out at sea were a variety of vessels – a destroyer, a large civilian craft and a paddle steamer from some holiday resort, and what looked like some trawlers. Another destroyer stood farther out. Closer to the shore were a number of smaller boats, mostly river craft. They seemed to be waiting for a higher tide so that they could come closer in. The lines of troops in the water were just waiting, quite quietly. All the time I was on the beach at Dunkirk I never once saw any of the troops waiting to get taken aboard one of the craft push or shove a comrade out of the way. I saw people hurrying, running, but no panic.

But within minutes of our reaching the beach the quiet was broken by the inevitable raid. We heard the drone of the planes as we heard the shouts of 'Take cover'; helpful, but sand does not provide much cover. Those at the back of the beach dived into slit trenches or shallow holes they had dug for themselves. We went down behind some dunes. But there were hundreds exposed on the flat foreshore. Some of those lining up at the water's edge turned and ran for the dunes. But some of those at the front of the lines, nearly waist-deep in the sea, stayed. They were not giving up their places at the head of the queue, no matter what. We were heartened to hear the defiant sound of anti-aircraft fire from some Bofors guns along the dunes and from all the Naval and other craft offshore. As we dived down

30

we heard the whistle of the bombs. They fell along the shore, sending up showers of sand. It was a short but intense raid, followed by a minute or so of silence before the cries of the wounded and the shouts of 'Stretcher, stretcher'. Medical Orderlies seemed to appear from nowhere. They collected the wounded and took them off to the ambulance station behind the dunes.

We went on, keeping close to the dunes. On the way we met some of the lads from our Company who had got there before us, but not my brother or Bill or Freddy. The former decided to come along with us to Bray Dunes. It was hard going in the sand and we were tired. We stopped by one of the Bofors guns and asked if they had any water. We had emptied our bottles on the way to the port. 'Here you are, mate,' one of the crew said as he handed me his water bottle. 'Have some of that. There's a water tap back there. You can get your bottles filled up.' I gratefully took a swig from his bottle. I coughed and gasped. It was Brandy. 'Bloody hell!!!' 'Do you good, mate,' he replied. The gunner nodded approval as I handed the bottle round. They were forewarned and drank more circumspectly. We found the tap, filled our bottles and moved on.

There was another raid before we reached Bray Dunes, Messerschmitts now, flying in low from the east, guns blazing. This time everyone opened up on them with their rifles. It was not very effective, but it helped our morale. They flew along the water's edge targeting those waiting, vulnerably, for the small boats. Many of the waiting troops scattered and many did not get up from where they fell. The British Army was disorganized, utterly vulnerable and powerless on open ground, and at the mercy of a relentless enemy.

It was early evening before we found a place where we could dig ourselves in among the dunes. It was not very safe, but we had no intention of getting caught on that open ground even if it meant not getting away until later. But how long would that be? How long had we got? There were rumours even on the beaches. 'They've got to the outskirts,' some said. Certainly the town was now under continuous fire. 'That's shell fire as well as bombs.' It's hard to remember now how many air attacks there were as we waited and wondered. There were intervals of quiet, of course, but the raids were more or less continuous – high-level bombing, Stuka dive-bombing, Messerschmitt straffing. It was strange that in those intervals little was said about our chances of escape, but we did attempt to understand the gravity and the consequences of our defeat.

'What will happen now?' I remember Basil, one of our Company who we had met again on the beach, asking. 'All that equipment gone. We'll never stop them coming over to invade us.'

'Yes we will,' said another. 'There must be reserves at home. And there's the Navy to stop them,' nodding out to sea where the destroyer and other craft were waiting for the tide. 'Anyway, this will bring the Americans in,' forecast another. We were not exactly defeatist, but we were not very convincing either. Yet I do not remember anyone saying, 'We'll never get away'. It was just a matter of 'When'.

Magically, that evening small groups of troops appeared carrying tins of corned beef, hard biscuits and a large billy can of hot tea, with some mugs which we shared. That also was a morale booster. There must have been a Field Kitchen at the back of the dunes. A sergeant with them nodded to where groups were still standing in the water. 'They've got a nerve waiting to get out to that destroyer. Yesterday evening another destroyer out there loaded up ready to set off for Blighty. In the middle of the night she blew up. There one minute, gone the next. Poor bastards probably thought they were safe. We could see another vessel farther out burning, and heard the shouts of the men in the water. Wasn't anything we could do. Must have been torpedoes.' It was all very much a matter of fact. They moved down the beach with the rations. The information did not encourage us to join the queue.

We slept fitfully and uncomfortably that night. We could hear the raids on the town. Next morning the raids began early, the first at first light. Those forming the queues at the water's edge kept breaking to throw themselves down on the beach. But it was a hard choice. They were as vulnerable there to Messerschmitt bullets as in the water, and later to the bombs. More people came up to the dunes, which were certainly not spared Luftwaffe attention, but at least there was some comfort in digging yourself a hole of some kind. The raids became intense, probably more at the far end of the beach and on the town. There was growing anger among the troops, who were feeling helpless and undefended. Much of the anger was directed at the RAF. Where were they? Where were our fighters? The enemy were having a free run! There had been an occasional skirmish high up, but no show of strength, no attacks on the formations of bombers or on the Stukas who attacked us so frequently, and the Messerschmitts seemed to fly in at will.

It was not until much later, back home, that we understood the reason – the need to preserve what strength there was for the forthcoming Battle of Britain, which we might not otherwise have won. But of course there at that time that did not enter our minds. We spent the whole day jumping into and climbing out of our shallow trenches, running down to help wounded, running back again. In quiet moments we wandered round to see if there was a place which would give more shelter and we watched carefully the progress the small boats were making in taking groups off when the tide was right. What a heart-warming sight they were. But we still waited, preferring not to stand out in a much more exposed position until we could see a chance of a quick getaway. Nevertheless the inexorable pounding and machine-gunning from the air began to sap our morale. Apart from those who could loose off some ineffective shots from their rifles, there was nothing we could do about it.

That night was no more comfortable than the previous one. The raids on the town were more intense. We could see the flames lighting the night sky. Next day was more of the same. We were told that Dunkirk was now surrounded. As we watched the shore line, we noticed that fewer small boats were returning after they sailed off to ferry their cargoes to larger boats or to set of across Channel. In between raids I sat wondering about Roddy, my brother, and other close friends such as Bill, Freddy and Doug, with whom I had joined the T.A. They had been at railhead when the breakthrough occurred. Perhaps they too were on the beach somewhere.

That afternoon a Naval Officer appeared to tell us, and others, that there was now little chance of getting away from Bray Dunes. They were concentrating the evacuation on Dunkirk. 'Better get back there,' he said, 'as quick as you can. Time's getting short.' We set off the way we had come two days before. It was a slow plod again, interspersed with the inevitable dive for cover. We found ourselves joining a procession. The word had gone round 'Get back to Dunkirk'. Progress got slower. We could see a variety of boats lying off the mole under fairly constant attack. The Navy was putting up a marvellous barrage of anti-aircraft fire.

We were being directed towards the mole, on which there was a long line of waiting troops. At the far end of it two vessels (minesweepers as we discovered) were moored alongside a destroyer. One difficulty was that the mole itself was now under fire and one shell had blown a hole in the middle of it. Someone found a ladder and placed it across the gap. We had to crawl along the ladder on all fours, one at a time. It was a slow business. As I shuffled towards the gap I saw two lads, trying to hurry across at the same time, fall into the shallow water below. 'Slowly, slowly,' someone yelled. On we went slowly, but those far back in the line could not understand the delay and were pushing forward. It was the only time I sensed the possibility of a breakdown in discipline. Fortunately it did not. Meanwhile the end of the mole and the ships moored there were under fierce air attack. The destroyer and the minesweepers were throwing up everything they had.

Once across the gap we were hustled on by Navy personnel. 'Come on, hurry. Get aboard quickly. No time to waste.' Some made for the climbing nets up the side of the destroyer, others for the open decks of the minesweepers. Ron, Ginger and I clambered over the side of the nearest 'sweeper and made for a space just in front of the bridge. The boat was commanded by an officer of the RNVR. He had the best line in continuous foul invective I have ever come across. Somewhat to our amusement, we saw he had an old Lewis gun mounted on a tripod in one corner of his bridge. Between running to the gun and firing into the air shouting, 'Take that you bastards,' he came to the edge of the bridge yelling such well-meant encouragement as 'Come on lads, pile in. It wasn't your bloody fault. Those other fuckers caved in,' which was not very complimentary to our allies, 'never fucking well told us. Just let us get on with it. You did your best lads. You did your best.'

It was getting dark. The bombing was very heavy and, looking back, we could see German artillery fire landing all round the mole. They had certainly got the range, even though, as far as we could see, they only made the one hit. Our skipper, with the gun at his shoulder, suddenly stopped firing and, looking up, shouted, 'Jesus Christ, look at that fucking lot.' High up, coming in from the north-east, was a large formation of bombers. 'We're fucking well getting out of here. Cut the cable. Cut the cable.' One of the crew ran to the stern and started hacking with an axe. 'Stand well back.' At the same time the order 'Full ahead' came from the bridge. As the last blow fell on the cable the boat surged forward, almost with a jerk, and the free end of the cable thrashed wildly in the air like a serpent in its death throes, fortunately missing everyone. A single blow would have been fatal.

We were clear of the mole and the other boats in a few minutes. We saw the other minesweeper pull away. The destroyer was still taking troops on board and another vessel came alongside her. Several of us squeezed our way to one of the gunwales to look back at the desperate sight of the port of Dunkirk burning against a back-cloth of flame and a huge pall of black smoke. We eased our way back and sat wherever there was some space, buttoning our tunics, if we still had them, against the chill sea air. Relief at getting away from what had been a pretty daunting experience began to give way to a kind of depression.

Gradually the chatter stopped. Just our thoughts remained. What had happened to Roddy, Bill and Freddy? They had been at railhead; perhaps they were already away, surely not back on the beach. Now we were on our way back, a thoroughly defeated army. Some time later, when there was time to reflect, I remember wondering if one's only military experience was – after all we had heard about our armed services when young – to have taken part in the greatest defeat ever suffered by the British Army. Surely the war was not going to end like this? Live under a Nazi regime? We still had a Navy. What about the Americans? Would they come in? What about . . . ? With the spray from the rising and descending bows blowing over us, I fell into a deep sleep.

It's hard to say now whether, as we pulled away from the mole and got clear of the bombing before we fell asleep, our mood was one of depression or relief. I suspect at the time it was relief, but the realization that we had been so comprehensively defeated hung like a black cloud over most of us. What we did not know at the time was that we would get another chance – thanks to more effective arms and equipment to new, confident Service leaders and to the help and subsequent decisive intervention from across the Atlantic – to turn the defeat in that battle to later comprehensive victories that eventually won the war.

3

Regrouping: 'The Few' Win Time

I did not wake up until I heard shouting and felt the shudder of the boat mooring alongside the quay in Dover harbour, a quay alive with Army and Navy personnel and the ubiquitous Military Police. Troops from another boat were shuffling into three ranks and being marched away. For such a ragbag-looking lot, some with tunics undone, some without tunics or caps, the re-imposition of some military discipline by the M.P.s was clearly a priority. Medical orderlies were helping walking wounded and carrying stretchers. It seemed incongruous that this scene of our routed army should be blessed by a lovely sunny morning: I think it was 2 June 1940.

As we, a motley bunch from different regiments and divisions, came down the gangplank from our beautiful, never-to-be-forgotten minesweeper and waved goodbye to the fearless, oath-rich skipper, we too were lined up on the quay and marched to a waiting train. As we were loaded, the blinds were pulled down ('Not to be pulled up until you are told') and the doors locked. We were too tired to question the need for all this. In any case we had been in the Forces long enough to know that you always obeyed the last order. But after a bit of reflection it did seem that the 'authorities' were keen, probably rightly, to conceal as much as possible the scale of the disaster. We were asleep by the time the train moved off.

The next we knew was a knocking on the door as it was unlocked and a voice calling, 'OK blinds up. Tea stop'. We looked out onto a platform from which lovely-looking WVS (Women's Voluntary Service) ladies – angels in uniform, we thought – were dispensing mugs of hot tea. By their sympathetic expressions as they handed out the mugs, they seemed ready to hug us all. Certainly we were ready

36

to hug them. Sadly it was not to be. But they also handed out plain postcards and pencils. 'If you want to let your nearest know you are safe we'll post them for you.' It was a wonderfully thoughtful and, for us, a very comforting gesture. I think we all took advantage of it. Unfortunately in my case the card never reached my parents and by the time I was able to telephone them they were desperately worried.

It was not a long stop. We handed back our mugs and the written postcards, and stayed for as long as we were allowed gazing at this heart-warming cameo of caring Britain on the platform of a country railway station. Along came the M.P.s and locked the doors again. 'OK blinds down' and we left for . . . where? We did not know, and frankly were too tired to be greatly concerned.

We stopped once more. The doors were unlocked and we were allowed out onto the platform – at?? – to 'stretch your legs'. Hot tea and corned beef sandwiches were handed out. Three or four M.P.s were patrolling the platform. They were very friendly, offered us cigarettes and asked sympathetically, 'Had a bad time mate?' But they would not tell us where we were. As with all railway stations during the war the names were removed, as were road signposts. The idea was to avoid aiding invading enemy paratroops. It was probably a good idea. It certainly kept us in the dark, but at the time I do not think it bothered us much.

As soon as we had finished we were told to get back inside. The doors were locked again and the blinds pulled down. We were fast asleep within minutes. It was evening before we stopped and were ordered out. Buses were waiting. We were told we were in Rugeley in Staffordshire. The buses took us out of the town and up a hill to a pithead where tents, a cookhouse and a mess tent awaited us. The cookhouse and mess tent were particularly welcome. The sausages and baked beans could not have been bettered at the Ritz. We were told to use the pithead showers, then collect blankets and a straw palliasse and find a tent. We were also told that in the morning we would be issued with pennies so that we could use the telephone box at the bottom of the hill to ring our families. As there was only one telephone box we should line up outside it in an orderly manner.

When I got into to the phone box towards the end of the morning, I prayed that my father would answer my call; my mother was a kind and loving person, but very sensitive and nervous. I was relieved to hear him answer, but horrified to learn that the postcard written on that railway platform had not arrived. It never did! Anticipating my concern, he immediately told me that my brother and my old friend Bill were safely back. Being at the railhead when the breakthrough occurred, they got to the beaches earlier and 'caught' an earlier 'ferry', but they had not known where I was. We were more fortunate than some; family and friends were safely home. It was an emotional moment, a cause of relief all round. Father must have made some sign to my mother. I could hear her sobbing in the background. It wasn't a good time to talk to each other. What we would have said was quite understood.

I cannot remember how long we were at Rugeley. We drilled in the mornings and afternoons, which at the time we thought was bloody stupid, but which I and, I'm sure, many others subsequently recognized as a necessary maintenance of discipline in defeat and a boost to our deflated morale in showing us we were still part of an organized army. I recall more happily the evenings spent swilling beer in the local pub with the overwhelmingly friendly and generous miners and their families.

It cannot have been more than a few days before we were ordered to Oxford by train where the scattered Division was to re-assemble and be addressed by the Divisional C.O. We marched from Oxford station by a roundabout route to Port Meadows. We would have welcomed marching through the town for no other reason that it would have been shorter, but presumably it was thought bad for morale to display our defeated army to people at large.

When we arrived at Port Meadows we were marshalled on to a part of the meadow and told to sit until the other Regiments arrived. The weather was fine but what seemed at first to be an enjoyable occasion of reforming the Division was transformed into a very sad one as the various units arrived. We heard them marching down the track from the road, 'Left, right, left, right; right wheel,' and about twenty men of that regiment marched in and took their places. Again: 'Come on, pick 'em up; left, right, left; right wheel; quick march' and about thirty of that regiment took their places. And so it went on. We had been badly mauled.

I heard only a part of the C.O.'s address. The breeze carried his voice away. In any case my attention was on what was left of a T.A. volunteer force. But I did hear his remonstration of those who had scratched 'BEF' on their tin hats and sought public sympathy. 'We are not heroes,' he said. 'We have nothing to be proud of. We have been defeated. We have to learn from it, re-train and go out and win next time.'

38

Our own Company next paraded in the playground of a school. It was the first time the two echelons had come together since we moved into Belgium. It was a Regimental parade with the officers, the Regimental Sergeant Major and CSMs. As we waited for the RSM to bring us to attention for the officers to march on, it occurred to me, and evidently to many others, that we had not seen our officers since the Panzer breakthrough. We were on our own on the way to Dunkirk. They too had got there, but we had not been conscious that they had tried to find us. The chaotic conditions probably made that impossible, but I suppose we were feeling aggrieved. By some mass telepathy, for we had not discussed it, we all sat down on the parade ground in protest.

There followed a few minutes of confusion. The officers stopped parading on the flank of the square and stared incredulously. The RSM, momentarily stunned, drew himself up and, his face scarlet, yelled, 'Parade! Parade . . .!' No one moved. He then seemed to realize that what was in military terms a very serious situation had to be defused quickly by other means. He shed the officiousness of his rank, stepped forward and said quietly, 'OK, lads, you've made your point. Stand up.' We stood up and the parade was conducted in the normal manner, though with some very worried faces in the commissioned ranks. Some of them we never saw again. They went, we assumed, to other units. Certainly we would have had no confidence in them.

From Oxford we were moved to Sussex, not far from East Grinstead. We were stationed in and around a charming village with a very good pub. We were in upper-middle-class country. Most of the houses, old and not so old, were large and in their own grounds and the pub was noted in better times for decent pub food. But here in wartime the village was on a war footing. The people could not have been more welcoming. If in the pub we outnumbered the locals, they showed no resentment and many of them offered us warm friendship. On the opposite side of the street a shop had been turned into a WVS café and shop – bacon and beans, bacon and egg, egg on toast always available when we could sneak in for a snack. On a notice board there were always offers of hospitality – radio evenings, musical (records) evenings and, most welcome, offers of a hot bath. That was a luxury few of us could refuse. Those WVS ladies had got it right; they had guessed correctly what we needed most.

It was there that I enjoyed one of the most pleasant, if brief, interludes of my wartime experience. Three of us responded to an advertised offer of a musical evening with hot bath and snacks. It was an invitation from the charmingly cultured, middle-aged daughter of a very successful businessman with a large estate just outside the village. Margaret had her own house in the grounds. She was naturally musical; she sang in choirs. We were told in the village that she had a well-trained, beautiful voice and had wanted to be a professional singer. She had a large collection of classical records, some of which she played while we enjoyed a supper provided from her meagre rations, following a hot bath. She talked about the music in a way I had never heard before. I learnt a lot. We became very friendly; she would use her scant petrol allowance to run me home (to Surrey) to see my parents when I had a 48-hour pass! In doing so she met my parents and also became friendly with them.

I recall one evening when we had dinner (in battle dress and heavy ammunition boots) with her rather stern father and gentle mother. After dinner her father asked if I would like a game of billiards. I was already feeling far too inadequate to confess that I had only played once or twice. After I had missed a couple of shots he glowered at me and said something like, 'You haven't done much of this have you lad?' 'N . . . No,' I said and straightaway ploughed my cue into the baize cloth! 'Good God,' he shouted, threw his cue down and stormed out. It's an understatement to say I was embarrassed. When I returned to the lounge I wanted to leave, almost to run away.

Her father had not reappeared, but Margaret had guessed that something 'untoward' had happened and suggested we went for a walk in the grounds. When, miserably, I told her, she laughed and said, 'Oh, he can be an old bear sometimes. Don't worry about it.' But I did worry about it and still do. Not surprisingly I never went to dinner with her mother and father again, but did spend many more happy evenings with Margaret in her house. I doubt whether in the whole of my Army career I had bathed so often.

I still wonder about another brief interlude with Margaret. On one occasion when we had a weekend pass she asked me if I would like to go to an orchestral concert in Tunbridge Wells, which she would drive me to, then back for supper, stay the night and back to duties next morning. Of course I said yes. That night my room was next to hers. After we said good night I sat on the edge of my bed and wrestled with my conscience. I was young, lusty and uncouth; she was more mature and from a different background. She had shown me great kindness. So I decided I should not abuse her hospitality by acting like a base licentious soldier. But, unable to sleep, I went to the window – it was a wonderful, warm summer night – and leant out to look at the sky. 'Can't you sleep either?' I heard. She was leaning out of her window. 'No,' I said. We exchanged a few more words then went to our respective beds. In retrospect I think I may have misjudged the situation.

I was told later in the war that she had married a Canadian officer and had gone to live in Canada. I hope she had a happy life. She played a big part in my development.

Our short stay in Sussex was an enjoyable and restoring period. We had worried how we would be regarded locally. We, the army generally, put a lot of effort into demonstrating that we were still a disciplined and effective force, not a defeated rabble. It was gratifying that we made so many friends. Our confidence and self-belief returned.

Yet in the background all the time was the dark threat of the expected German invasion. Anti-invasion measures were evident everywhere – railway stations without names, signposts stripped of their names and directions, concrete pill-boxes across expected routes from the south coast to London and other important towns, tall poles erected on open spaces that might provide landing places for parachutists and gliders, making every field like a hop-field. The blackout at night was strictly controlled. Barrage balloons surrounded important installations. Notices everywhere warned us about security: 'Keep Mum'; 'Careless talk costs lives.'; 'Be suspicious of strangers'.

The news constantly referred to the massing of German troops along the north coast of France and the concentration of invasion barges in Calais and Boulogne. South coast residents had been evacuated and coastal defences were strengthened. There were occasional air raids and aerial dog fights but not of the intensity that we knew would come. We were required to mount guard day and night on every building we occupied. As we were under strength this was a great strain. We did four or five night guards a week and the 'day off after guard duty' was cancelled. We were all very tired and I narrowly escaped a Court of Inquiry for falling asleep while writing a letter home in the guard room while in charge of the guard on our Headquarters.

The re-grouping and re-forming of the Army was gathering pace and increasingly troop formations were seen moving south to invasion danger points. And that was where our Division was sent next, to Kent.

There our Company occupied two large country houses not far from Canterbury. The Division was deployed across Kent and East Sussex behind the coast in a second line of defence. One echelon, and Company Headquarters, were at Chilham Castle. My echelon was at Chartham House, thankfully a few miles from H.Q!

It was about this time that General (as he then was) Montgomery took command of the Corps (Was it 21 Corps? I forget.) and a new vigour and positive attitude swept through all formations. Even down at our level we could see it and feel it. Officers were summoned to great conferences with the new Corps Commander and came scurrying back to impose more demanding early morning P.T., which now included them, and to set up new, more extensive training programmes. Some of our more middle-aged officers were posted elsewhere and new ones, younger, some newly commissioned, arrived, clearly imbued with the new zeal. Symptomatic of one of Monty's favourite dictums, 'put everyone in the picture', we began to get more information and briefings.

It was also the time when we began to get new recruits to make good our numbers. They were an early intake of conscripted young men from all backgrounds, fresh from a short basic training. We made a great effort to make them feel at home in a volunteer T.A Company with some war experience, drawn mainly from, for want of a better description, the 'middle class'. But they needed more training, so, in the extensive grounds of Chartham House, three camouflaged Nissen huts were erected under the trees and the Company Training School was established. I was genuinely surprised to be made a full Corporal and told I was on the staff of the new Training School to instruct in parade ground drilling, map reading, arms drill and 'personal hygiene', a combination of responsibilities that caused some confusion among the trainees.

My promotion came at a time when in a generally inactive period I felt depressed and it led to some moody introspection. This was the note I made at the time:

'The thought of being given new responsibilities by this promotion is refreshing and challenging in this boring existence. We are just waiting. There is so much waiting in warfare. Waiting for what? The next action? Sometimes we are too long in one place, too long doing one job and it gets boring. There seems no end to this pointless existence. No end to a war we seem to be losing. The news is only of defeats. Why aren't we, here, helping more? Training,

training! Nothing but training! Are we doing any good? If we win, will we be able to do any good after the war? I'm depressed. Is it because our existence seems to be without purpose? Yet the purpose is to get in and win. Why aren't we helping?'

Such were the occasional moods when, in a frustrating period of inactivity, one's contribution to the war effort that was being fought elsewhere, with people of one's own age being maimed and dying, seemed, and was, negligible.

Yet while we were 'enjoying' this repetitive, boring life in the beauty of a Kentish parkland, between fields of wheat, hop gardens and apple orchards, the beginning of a deadly battle for survival in which none of us on the ground could assist was evident. Aerial activity was increasing – channel convoys attacked, increasing number of dog-fights. We all knew that Germany could not invade us unless she had control of the skies. That battle, the Battle of Britain, had to be fought first. And when the heavy raids, with huge formations of bombers high in the summer sky, began – attacks on airfields, ports, defence installations, and then cities and towns – the most crucial of all battles was joined. Was there ever a more fateful summer in our long history?

For us on the ground that deadly crisis seemed unreal. The weather was perfect; the green countryside basked in sunshine; crops were ripening. We went about our business of training the recruits, slowly replacing the equipment lost at Dunkirk and preparing ourselves for battle, probably against the first foreign army to set foot on our shores since 1066, as a precedent that didn't bear thinking about. We knew we were still badly equipped for the task.

Yet it was high above us in the clear blue sky, day after day, that a complex tracery of vapour trails and the occasional scream of engines straining to perform the miracles demanded of them were the signs that the fatal fight between the attacking air armadas and our defending fighters was being waged. Yet we, who had lost our first battle in Belgium, could do nothing to help. We watched. We wondered. We hoped. And, in our own ways, prayed. We watched planes spin, often burning, out of the sky; sometimes a parachute opened. One of theirs or one of ours? We cheered if we saw one with German markings go down. If it was one of ours, we prayed for the pilot. If a white canopy appeared and floated down we cheered again.Great deeds of heroism were being performed for us up there and all we could do was watch and hope.

43

In the evenings we gathered round the radio to hear the 'score'; so many enemy bombers shot down; so many of our fighters lost; so many of our pilots safe. How long could this go on? Had we enough fighters and pilots? These were the anxieties of all in Britain at that time. I think it is impossible to describe the relief, the joy, the gratitude we felt when, following that wonderful, historic day in September when the skies were suddenly clear and silent, we realized that we, they, that small band of aerial heroes, had won. Without doubt that was the first vital step on the long road to eventual victory, though we could not see so far ahead at the time. And we guessed there was a lot more to come, which in the event were the murderous night raids on our towns and cities, on our civilian population, in the pattern of the raids on Poland, Holland and Belgium.

But what happened in September 1940 was Germany's first defeat of the war and our first victory. More significantly it was won, as were Crécy, Agincourt and other great victories, by the fewer in number. Winston Churchill's ringing description of that victory: 'Never in the field of human conflict has so much been owed by so many to so few', perhaps a little devalued by subsequent repetition and inappropriate adaptation, expressed the nation's gratitude and defiant mood. And that victory won by 'the few' undoubtedly did more than turn back an invasion, it restored our confidence in our ability to defeat what had been thought of as an invincible military machine.

Yet, for our part, we just went on training and taking part in exercises that were meant to train us and the Home Guard to resist the German invasion when it came. But most of us realized that, after the successful Battle of Britain and the reported withdrawal of German invasion forces across the Channel, it would not now happen.

It was at this time that my dear friend Bill took an initiative that helped halt our intellectual atrophy. He decided to form an economics study group. We sent for a correspondence course from the 'Henry George School of Economics' a very left-wing organization whose main tenet of economic faith was that economic prosperity depended on the nationalization of all land. We 'clubbed' our finances and sent for the books. We met regularly. Weekly? Fortnightly? I can't remember. But between times we had to read chapters set by Bill and then discuss them at the meeting. It was a good discipline and jerked us into some mental activity.

I don't think we took the Henry George proposition seriously, though most of were very 'leftish'. We saw the need for improvements in education, 'welfare' (as we then called it) and in economic performance. We believed that the pre-war 'system' had not worked. The depression of the thirties and its high unemployment eased only when, much too late, the nation began to re-arm. Constant yielding to Hitler's demands and the consequent inadequacy of our arms and equipment when we went to war had shamed us. With youthful zeal we wanted to play a part in improving 'things' after the war. By trying to influence, perhaps join, political parties we wanted to help formulate 'enlightened' economic and social policies that would right the wrongs we had seen. Revolution by evolution: we were clear that it was democracy and freedom we were fighting for. To our newly exercised minds, it was a serious, exciting aim, not a lot of idealistic nonsense!

Again thanks to Bill, we used this to improve our knowledge of classical music. My own musical appreciation had begun patchily and in a very limited way at home when I was very young. My parents, who were far from well off at the time, had bought me a rather tinny mechanical gramophone with a sound-box and a metal needle, together with a couple of records of extracts from *Carmen*, which I played over and over again. And my father had taken me to Alexandra Palace to hear great organists of the time – Custard and Cunningham – play on that magnificent instrument. Many years later, during our brief wartime stay in Sussex, my visits to Margaret's home had advanced my knowledge of the classics. Now, in that crucial period of 1940/41, but which for us was an interlude, Bill had discovered that the Dean of Canterbury, Dr Hewlett Johnson, known as 'the Red Dean' because of his declared belief in communism, provided gramophone classical musical evenings in the Deanery every Sunday.

The Dean was a most distinguished-looking man. Tall, fine features, with a high forehead framed by white hair, he was an eloquent defender of the Soviet system and all that went on in Russia, as expressed in his book *The Socialist Sixth*, the proportion of the Russian land mass to the world as a whole. He had visited the Soviet Union and believed that what he was allowed to see was a true representation of the miracle of the Russian revolution. We lived to see the error of that belief and saw what was an atheistic and brutal society. He did not live to see the heroic success of Soviet arms, which

45

he would have admired, as we all did. But nor did he see the disintegration of the communist dream in Soviet Russia. What a disappointment that would have been for him. He was lucky enough to die with most of his illusions intact.

These were contented but unsettling days, because we realized that elsewhere people were in the thick of it. We blessed our luck, but knew it was unfair. It was in this period that, perhaps under the influence of the discussions in our 'economics group', I questioned again my personal convictions. Was it enough just to be concerned about the conditions I had become aware of before the war? I remembered seeing as a boy groups of miners from the Welsh pits walking along the gutters singing, as only the Welsh can, and holding out their hats for pennies. 'Why are they doing that?' 'They haven't any work.' 'Why?' I remembered being confused, again as a boy, by the General Strike. The public seemed determined to beat it and cheered sailors who were driving trains. But the trade unions were determined too. There was relief when the strikers were defeated. But I recalled hearing people saying, 'Something must be terribly wrong for them to do that'.

I also recalled the shame many of us – mostly, but not exclusively, the younger generation – felt later, during the years of appeasing Hitler and Mussolini, when we allowed them to use the Spanish Civil War, in which, as we saw it, a rebel army attacked an elected Government, as a 'dress rehearsal' for the bigger war they were planning; when we allowed Hitler to grow stronger as he invaded more territory under the pretence of defending German 'rights'; when, having failed to resist his ambitions at the outset, we still failed to prepare for the inevitable and so went to war outgunned and poorly equipped.

Naively, a lot of us were relieved when the war started, because we thought we could now stop 'Hitler's games' and destroy the Nazi/Fascist systems. Well, in the end we did, but not until our forces and the civilian population had suffered so much. How many lives would have been saved in Poland, Holland, France and at Dunkirk if we had resisted Hitler in his occupation of the Rhineland in 1936? This is how I, naively, tried to express those feelings at the time:

'Our recent discussion emphasized that criticism without constructive suggestion leads nowhere. Perhaps a majority of people would now agree that we need changes, but unless there is a plan for new policies, plans for industry, for social security, for education, for eliminating slums, their views will not be heard. There must be an overall objective so that we can say, "There, that's the kind of society we want". Without such a declared aim by a united pressure group, or opposition, the government of the day will plan inadequately to avoid the difficulties and modify the Beveridge recommendations. The danger is that we are not kept fully informed. Argument must be based on up-to-date information in order to prepare proposals for a comprehensive policy for change.' (In those days the phrase 'joined-up policy' did not occur to me.)

'Sometimes it seems that one is fighting just for green fields, a lake with mountains beyond, a cottage surrounded by fields and woods, the right to go down to the inn or the pub and get a bit tight and curse the Government from top to bottom. But surely we should be fighting for something more idealistic; more comradeship in civilian life, as it has become in wartime; less class distinction; better education for all; more opportunities for children; a better understanding between nations. But what right has one to say that one is fighting for any of these things if one is not *fighting*. How damning the phrase "To thine own self be true" if you are not.'

A new, interesting interlude occurred at this time. While we were stationed in Kent Bill and I met, on the way to one of our visits to the local pub, a Dr Bill Mair. He was a Captain in the Royal Army Medical Corps, operating from a hospital not far from the village. Bill and I were walking down the road to the pub. We noticed him in front. He probably heard us talking and turned round. 'Hello', he said with a soft Scottish accent, 'are you bound for the pub?' We saluted smartly and said we were. 'Come along then,' and the three of us fell in step and continued our way, but Bill and I were embarrassed: two rankers walking alongside a Captain! Unheard of in those days! We hoped none of our own officers were in the vicinity. We would have been rebuked.

It sounds silly now, and would certainly have been ridiculed when later I was in the S.A.S. where rank was observed formally when necessary, but informally at other times, without losing the essential discipline. When we reached the pub we said, 'We go into the Public Bar, sir,' expecting him to go into the 'Saloon'. 'So do I,' he said. So we did and we spent an evening talking – about everything.

That was the first of many interesting evenings we spent together in discussion and in disputation. We discussed education, the war, the evil of Fascism, life before the war, what we hoped for afterwards. Not far from the local pub was a huge disused gravel pit full of water. On the way back from our drinking/talking sessions we used to go there, strip off and swim up and down, still arguing our points of view. Bill Mair was a most unusual, kind and thoughtful man. A most unlikely trio, we spent happy evenings together that summer, drinking wartime watered beer, locking our intellectual horns, Bill and I, perhaps pretentiously but satisfyingly, – swimming in that gravel pit. This is my note at the time:

'Recent discussions with Bill and Bill Mair have been so stimulating and so wide-ranging. The first evening we met on the way to the pub here at Chartham (Bill came over from Chilham). He was in front of us and turned to introduce himself and suggested we walk to the pub together. He said he had heard us talking about the need for a better education system after the war, which was something he too felt strongly about. We were embarrassed because he was an officer and we were a couple of 'squaddies'. That combination did not often engage in serious conversation, especially in a public bar.

'We discovered he was a doctor and a psychiatrist working at the mental hospital on the outskirts of the village. He was the son of a crofter in the Highlands who had gone down to Edinburgh to get himself qualified. And we were discussing the need for more education opportunities! When we left the pub he asked us if we would like a swim. He knew of a flooded disused gravel pit so we went along, embarrassed again to be walking along the village street in conversation with an officer. How he laughed when we confessed to him. "Och, what rubbish," he said. I think he is the least rank-conscious or class-conscious person I have ever met. We stripped off and swam up and down the gravel pit deep in conversation. We met again and again, generally in the pub, and we talked about politics, economics, sex – how to cope with it in the army – philosophy and religion, generally finishing the evening with a swim.

'The discussions on religion have been very meaningful to me, and I think to Bill also. We do not know what to believe in this war. I have been brought up in a fairly religious household. I went to a Church infants' school. Later I went to a Methodist Sunday school. Mother and grandmother were Salvationists. God was never far away. Yet later, full of intellectual pretensions, I read and talked myself into being an agnostic, as Bill is. I know that when we were under fire in Belgium I was frightened but refused to pray because I felt it was pointless to ask for God's protection when I wasn't sure he existed. Later, after the German breakthrough when we suffered a lot of straffing and bombing and I felt very frightened, I prayed fervently! I survived both occasions. So where was I? Which attitude could one trust? These meetings and discussions have made a wonderfully elevating period full of good friendship and intellectual satisfaction. Yet, yet, it has shown something else. How ignorant one really is. So much I don't know. So much to learn. When? Where?'

So, anachronistically, that was a peaceful phase in the middle of war. It was a time when we were able to reflect, let our thoughts take flight, test ideas on each other, seek comfort in philosophy, in poetry, and think about some kind of better post-war world. Yet we still could not entirely ignore our concern that we were able to indulge in these pleasures while others were fighting, being maimed, getting killed. Because of that concern it was also an unsettling time as well. Unsettling too because this brief period of 'further education' had induced some salutary introspection which revealed great gaps in our knowledge and experience. Deep inside I certainly felt uncertain.

I see in my notes of that period that I returned to the theme that was worrying me. 'To thine own self be true,' the poet said. But how can you when you don't know what one's 'own self' is? Is it a born condition? Something conditioned by upbringing, environment? Something you *think* you are? Something you *wish* to be? It's difficult when 'one's own self' is an unformed thing.

It was during that tormenting period that I tried for the first time my amateur hand at 'creative' writing. This story tries to describe an incident I had observed walking across fields one evening on a short cut to the 'local'. I thought it illustrated the restrained longings of young people away from home, probably for the first time, which contrasted with the usual image of the 'brutal and licentious' soldiery:

'It was the first fine spell for some time. The sky was blue with feathery clouds moving slowly. The sun was reflected from the green of the leaves on the trees and the grass, and was absorbed by the brown earth. They could feel its embracing warmth.

'Down in the field at the foot of the hill a Land Army girl in brown overalls, yellow scarf round her hair, walked her monotonous way slowly up and down the furrows scattering seed right and left with either hand from a shallow tray suspended in front of her by straps across her back. Dust from the seed clung to the front of her overalls.

'On the green of the hillside a group of young soldiers sat talking and laughing, a few drawing on their cheap cigarettes. With time off from the nearby camp, they had walked across without purpose except to enjoy their period of freedom from boring duties.They were stripped to the waist, their coarse khaki trousers were tied round by broad belts or braces.

'In the centre of the group two of them were having a boxing match encouraged by the shouts of their comrades. Moving quickly in spite of their heavy 'ammunition' boots, they circled first this way then that, watching each other before coming together in an exchange of blows. The blows left red blotches on their sweating bodies, unheeded as they danced away and clashed again, their eyes bright with the enjoyment of their fine physical condition, and occasionally they smiled as they caught a comment or jibe hurled by friends. When this pair decided they had had enough they grinned, shook hands and went and stretched out on the grass, bodies glistening, recharging their energy with deep gulps of clean country air while another pair replaced them in the circle.

'The sun was moving to the west as the Land girl began plodding up the hill, empty seed tray under her arm, towards the farm just over the crest. She was hot and tired from her labours. Not far from the group of carousing soldiery she stopped to wipe her forehead and poke wisps of hair back under the scarf. The blouse under her overalls was stained under her uplifted arm. One of the soldiers noticed her and drew his friends' attention by shouting and pointing. They all joined in with remarks and improper suggestions which, if she heard, she ignored. She smiled and walked slowly towards them and sat a yard or two away. The boxers, who had ceased their activity when they heard all the shouting, laughed and set to again with a vigour clearly intended to impress this unexpected fair spectator. Two of the guffawing group detached themselves and went and sat beside her and exchanged hesitant 'hellos'. Crude shouts followed them. One offered a cigarette which she accepted with a smile, while the other searched for matches.

'She drew deeply on the cigarette, exhaled and then sank slowly back on the grass, arms above her head gazing up into the shining blue. The jokes and suggestions gradually stopped as they gazed at the reclining female figure, heaving breasts hidden beneath the blouse and overalls, yet in their minds quite revealed. They gazed, some licking dry lips, their piercing eyes trying to penetrate to the beauty their imagination had already reached. The object of their attention, lying still, with eyes closed, and apparently oblivious of the young men around her, was also taunted by thoughts. For she had noticed more intently than she had shown the half-naked, fit young bodies and the glistening muscularity of the boxers. But she and her admirers were all conscious of the barrier between her thoughts, their thoughts and reality.

'She sat up, drew deeply on her cigarette again and then crushed it into the grass beside her. She stood up, picked up the seed tray and with a brief, smiling 'Thanks. Goodbye,' she set off up the hill. A chorus of subdued 'goodbyes' followed her as they stood to watch her go. At the top of the hill she stopped, turned and waved. A little forest of hands responded accompanied by shouts of 'Bye' as she disappeared down the other slope. The soldiers, quiet now, looked at each other a little shyly, gathered up their shirts, put them on, got into their tunics and made their way down the hill back to the camp.'

My life as an instructor at the Training School was one of continuous activity in a very regimental regime intended to give the recruits a more intensive introduction to military discipline, as well as to the knowledge they needed and the procedures they were expected to follow. They were from many walks of life and from different parts of the country. The concept that our Army should comprise a number of County Regiments in Regional Divisions was long outdated. The tragedy of local losses on a huge scale in the First World War ended it, but it persisted, for obvious reasons, in the Territorial Army. In order to do 'peacetime' training you had to be from the locality. In common with many other units at this time we had the task of integrating different backgrounds into our company. It turned out to be surprisingly easy. We got on well with each other and new friendships were made, probably because of the realization that we had a common interest and accepted the common cause, rather than because of any great intellectual understanding of what was required. They were a cheerful lot and had already learned to carry with them at all times the first essential for life in the Services, a sense of humour.

Across the years amusing incidents come readily to mind from the tedium of the training regime. As I said, our recruits were from a variety of backgrounds. I recall some: a small, dark costermonger, a burly docker, a trainee accountant and a young man from a stock-broker's office. As instructors, there was myself, two other corporals and a Staff Sergeant in charge. The sergeant, a tough Lancastrian with deep-set penetrating eyes, had been brought in from another part of the Corps to run the Centre. He was a regular soldier who had seen more service than all of us put together. Now he could no longer serve overseas and his mission, as he saw it, was to lick us 'part-timers', as he called us, into shape to behave as if we were regulars. He quickly earned the nickname, never to be uttered in his hearing, of 'Blitz'. He roared at the recruits on the parade ground; he swore at us corporals in private for our inadequacies. Yet he earned everyone's respect. He was a breed apart from us. He was one of the non-commissioned officers who were, are, the backbone of the British Army.

The fact that I lectured on such different subjects as map reading, personal hygiene and weapon training seemed to confuse some of the recruits, particularly those who had, as they say these days, learning difficulties. For example, classroom lectures on map reading prior to going out into the countryside to demonstrate the practical value of reading a map correctly focused on recognizing a map's shorthand for important features.

'The hatchings for an embankment, on which you could be visible, go this way, while those for a cutting, in which you would be concealed, go the other. Important to remember the difference. Trees shown on the map like little Christmas trees are evergreen, keep their leaves all the year round. OK for concealment of you and vehicles in the winter, but they do not provide the best cover. Those shown with a bushy top, deciduous trees, give better cover, but not in the autumn and winter when they shed their leaves. Bushy-topped trees are deciduous and lose their leaves in winter. OK?'

In personal hygiene I had the responsibility, at the age of 21, of explaining to that mix of recruits, dockers, street traders, stock-brokers, all older than me, some of the fundamentals of service life. One was how and where to dig a loo and make it reasonably comfortable to sit on by supporting tree branches across the pit, and how to be sure you concealed all traces when you moved on. Another was to advise them how to avoid venereal disease, explaining what to look out for in cases of crabs, gonorrhoea or syphilis. This was always followed by a reminder never to indulge in sexual intercourse without protection:

'What's sexual intercourse, Corporal?'

'F***ing.'

'Oh. Same as what we do.'

Then followed a stirring call for self-restraint as the best way of avoiding trouble.

'Why endanger your health for the sake of ten minutes of pleasure?' I asked.

'How do you make it last ten minutes, Corporal?'

I could not advise.

The real difficulty came when we faced the Commanding Officer's visit for 'Passing out day' after three weeks of training. That was an occasion when we applied a liberal quantity of bullshit – the substance that, despite its consistency, lubricates the military machine – to show not only that we had trained the recruits well, but also that they had learned well. To be sure that no one would be embarrassed in the forbidding presence of the C.O. I decided to 'plant' some questions with the most vulnerable of the recruits and rehearse them beforehand. For our barrow boy trader, who, though not the most literate of the bunch, had a quicker mind than most when it came to working out a price and telling you how much change he should give, I said I would ask him to tell me what it was when I pointed to a bushy-topped tree on blackboard. All he had to say was 'Deciduous tree, and it's leaves drop off in winter, so you can't use it for concealment at that time.'

Came the day. The C.O. came into the room. Several questions were satisfactorily asked and answered. Then came our barrow boy's turn.

'What sort of tree is this?' I asked, pointing to the board.

'A de-syphilis tree, Corporal. You shouldn't try to hide under it in the winter'!

'True enough,' the General murmured as he walked out

After a few weeks' duty at the Training School I was asked whether I would accept a Commission if recommended after further training. I was surprised and had many doubts, not least an anticipated feeling of insecurity in leaving comrades from TA days and leaving a familiar environment. Against the doubts, I felt there was an obligation to accept the responsibility offered and hoped I could be trained to discharge it fully. With much trepidation, I accepted.

I was told to report to a Pre-Officer Cadet Training Unit (OCTU) course at Brighouse in Yorkshire. We, aspiring subalterns from many different units in the RASC, lived for the next few weeks in a disused woollen mill being lectured on the subjects I had just been teaching to new recruits, being drilled on a makeshift Parade Ground in the routines I had been giving our recruits, being instructed in vehicle maintenance in the way we had been taught in our T.A. days. More appropriately we learnt about the methods of 'man management' and carried out a number of 'Field Exercises'.

The memory of that part of my military life is dim. Much of it was already familiar to me through the good fortune of having been a soldier in the T.A. and through being an instructor at the Company Training School. There was little new in it. I felt I was just 'going through the motions'. It made little impression except as a staging post on the way to OCTU.

4

Frustration in North Africa

OCTU was at a well-known school just outside Bristol, Clifton College. It had been taken over by the Army for the onerous task of turning aspiring, nervous Cadets, formerly elements of the 'brutal and licentious soldiery' into 'temporary officers and gentlemen'. This required, as a start, crowding grown young men in dormitories hastily fitted with wooden two-tier bunks, who washed at low-level basins and squatted at appropriate times on low-level toilet seats, challenging the capacity of the school's sanitary system.

Again I remember little of the detail of our lives there, only a mental scrapbook of images and incidents: lectures on Military Law, disciplinary procedures, the organization and use of I Groups (Information Groups), O Groups (Order Groups) and the formulae for the logical handling of many conceivable war situations. But, as we already knew, there were many situations for which there were no formulae, only calm common sense. We had TEWTS (Training Exercises Without Troops); Field Exercises, for which we were given at different times the roles of convoy commander, officer in charge of railhead or roadhead depots, Don R (despatch rider marshalling the convoy) and we practised the drills for handling, loading and unloading ammunition, petrol and food, separately, to get them to the front quickly. Necessarily there was much practical map-reading. And a lot of drill.

I also recall the time we spent at the end of the day on 'spit and polish', blancoing our equipment and cleaning the brass on it. Cleanliness and smartness, we were told, were essential for good discipline, for a soldier's self-respect. It was a boring pastime, but I for one needed no convincing of its value as I remembered the scene on the quayside at Dover when we disembarked from the Dunkirk beaches and saw the pride on the faces of those who, having endured that experience, formed themselves into three ranks and marched off in step, compared to those with tunics undone shuffling along in a dispirited fashion.

The time we spent on the parade ground was also part of the process of implanting the need for discipline. We were drilled under the oath-ridden, fierce, relentless command of the OCTU's Regimental Sergeant Major. He was one of those priceless, experienced senior Warrant Officers who are the knowledgeable disciplined strength of our Army, whom all soldiers love to hate while wholeheartedly admiring them and appreciating their value. I think we accepted, without liking, his drill periods, and by the end of the course he was admired and respected.

At the inevitable end-of-course Passing-out party in the Mess, we queued up to buy him a drink and joke with him. Equally inevitably one of the Cadets (now a responsible Subaltern?) spiked his drink. I was in the toilet when he came in and said, 'Excuse me, I have to vomit.' He did. 'Sorry about that,' he said 'There's always some silly young bugger who will do that to me but they will never get me drunk. If you are coming out you can buy me a pint and whoever played their stupid little game can watch me drink it.' He pulled his tunic jacket straight, smoothed his hair and, very upright, marched out ahead of me. I bought him that drink, a pint of bitter. He turned with his back against the bar, raised his glass and, pausing as he raised it to his lips, looked round smiling, then drained it without a pause. I don't know who started it, but in a second we were all applauding him.

I recall one exercise at the start of which a fellow cadet sadly lost his life. He and I, mounted on motorcycles, jointly had the responsibility of marshalling and guiding a convoy of three-ton vehicles to a given map reference in the country where we would practise dispersal and concealment. While the convoy was assembling we decided to have a quick ride up on Clifton Green to get used to our allocated bikes. We were approaching a fairly sharp curve when the bottom of the greatcoat I was wearing covered the air intake to the carburettor, causing my bike to falter. As I bent down to pull the coat away I heard a shout and looked up to see my colleague failing to negotiate the bend. He mounted the far pavement and rode straight into a brick wall. I heard him shouting until he went over the handlebars to hit the wall with his helmeted head. When I reached him I could see he was dying. By the time I was able to get help, he was dead. There followed an unscheduled and unhappy lesson in military Courts of Inquiry, procedures for burial with Military Honours, and my harrowing responsibility, as the only witness, to explain the circumstances of the accident to my friend's grieving parents when they attended the funeral.

I remember warmly the friendships we formed in that short period of our soldiering. There seemed to be a kind of unspoken understanding that we, from our different backgrounds and experiences, were embarked on a venture requiring self-discipline and the exercise of whatever qualities of leadership we had or had acquired in fulfilling given orders and safeguarding the lives of the men who, like it or not, had to trust us. Light-hearted and superficially happy-go-lucky though we were while there, I'm sure we realized we were about to shoulder a daunting responsibility. To that extent, as well as honing our proficiency, OCTU did its job.

One particular relationship led to an unexpectedly lasting friendship, but not quite the way it started. I met Geoff in a railway platform refreshment bar on a blacked-out station during a long, interrupted train journey to Bristol from London. In those days rail journeys were extremely unreliable. What has changed, you may ask. But the reasons then were different. The routing, the timing and availability of trains depended on the priority given to military requirements: raw materials for factories, delivery of armaments, movement of troops.

The train I was on had already been diverted to somewhere in the Midlands when it was stopped and all passengers had to get off and wait (no one knew how long it would be). With others, I found my way to the cold, poorly stocked 'refreshment' bar with its few curling sandwiches and half-a-dozen hard-looking sausage rolls. Against the bar was another soldier from the RASC looking at a glass of the watered-down beer. We introduced ourselves. He was slightly older than me, on the way to the same OCTU. We spent the next hour drinking the beer and exchanging backgrounds, in the process of which a good friendship was established.

The OCTU rules permitted married cadets to have 'sleeping out' passes at certain weekends if they could find accommodation locally for their wives. Geoff found a small two-roomed flat and so it was that one weekend I met his wife. Several of us had foregathered in a 'local' for a Saturday evening 'session'. By tradition they were hard-drinking sessions, relief from the training regime. It was then that we were introduced to Joanne. I was captivated immediately. To me, an exuberant but very gauche cadet, she was someone from another world. Of striking appearance, tall, dark-haired, slender, with a good figure, she was attractive and sophisticated with a charming but confident manner. She drew attention without trying. Later I discovered why. She came from the glamorous world of modelling and show business. I think we all returned to our celibate bunks that evening thinking 'lucky Geoff'. That impression of marital bliss was dimmed when much later that I discovered there was a rift in their relationship.

On another weekend, when again we gathered in the local, Joanne invited three of us to join Geoff and herself for a supper. We took bottles back with us and continued our high-spirited drinking while she busied herself in the partly curtained-off kitchen. The room was small and the dining table was a card table round which she asked us to seat ourselves somehow. Without fuss she miraculously produced five plates of sausage, eggs, bacon and baked beans. It must have taken most of her rations for a week. Full of beer and bonhomie, we huddled round the table and tried to find space for our plates of her generous and delicious offering. Unfortunately my plate must have been right on the edge of the table. When I cut into my first sausage it tipped up and the priceless contents went flying, partly landing in my lap, partly flying over my shoulder. I looked round and saw to my shame baked beans sliding off the wall.

It is an understatement to say I was utterly humiliated. Sadly the ground did not swallow me up, as I wished. I can feel now the embarrassed silence, but within a minute, which seemed an age, it was broken by wonderful Joanne cheerfully saying, 'I didn't think much of mine either. I was going to do the same with it.' It was completely disarming as well as soul-saving. I could not have been more grateful. The silence turned to peals of laughter as everyone offered gifts from their own plates. As I mumbled repeated apologies to Joanne I hoped she saw the gratitude in my eyes. From then on I was ready to worship her.

We remained friends long after leaving OCTU and going our various ways. Whenever possible I met her when I had a bit of leave from my different postings. There was an age difference which never seemed to matter. I think she saw in me a distraction from her problems with Geoff. She was vivacious, yet attentive and patient, and from her I learned much that guided me later. She was a strong influence at the time and I know that in her company I matured. Even after the war when I had become engaged to my future wife, the three of us met from time to time, often when we were staying with my fiancée's family in the country.

I was commissioned in 1942. While I waited for my posting to an 'operational' unit I was sent as an 'umpire' to oversee part of a training exercise in which a group of Home Guards were to repel an invading force of newly recruited 'regulars'. My job was to assess the adequacy of the Home Guard's strategy for defending their sector. The exercise, involving Police and Fire Services as well as the troops, was to take place between 1400 hrs on the Saturday and 1800 hrs on Sunday. I went early to contact the C.O of the Home Guard. His H.Q. was a Nissen hut behind a large country house in Surrey. A retired regular officer, he proudly showed me his 'battle board' indicating his dispositions and the expected line of the 'enemy' advance. It was winter and the Nissen hut was heated by an enclosed stove in the centre. I thanked him for his explanation and went off on my motorcycle to grab a sandwich and a beer in a pub, saying I would be back just before 1400 hrs. As I was riding back at about 1350 I noticed a column of smoke rising from the direction of the house and the Home Guard headquarters. When I arrived the Nissen hut was burning furiously and the C.O. was running pathetically to it with a pail of water.

'I'll ring the Fire Brigade from the telephone box at the end of the drive,' I called. When I got to the phone and was connected through the 999 emergency system I told the Fire Service that the Home Guard H.Q. was on fire. 'Oh no,' the voice replied, 'you don't catch us like that. The exercise don't start until 1400.' I failed to convince them that the emergency was genuine and when I got back to the H.Q. there was nothing left but a stove standing in smouldering remains and a heartbroken C.O. He recovered and used runners to communicate with his troops and went down and commanded them on the ground. For all that I gave him points for initiative in an emergency.

Later I was sent to Tillicoultry in Scotland, a place I had never heard of, to join an RASC artillery supply unit being prepared for overseas duty. Of course they didn't know where they would be sent. That would become clearer, they said, from the kind of equipment they would be required to have! Our headquarters and billets were in a disused paper-making mill. However, that stay did not last long. We soon moved to Bothwell Park, just outside Glasgow, where we were billeted 'under canvas' in the Park. There followed another period of training with the inevitable field exercises. But it was boring. Why were we not told where we might be going? Or when? Inevitably the answer was 'security', which was fair enough, but it was not enough to dispel the persistent feeling that we were safe and relatively comfortable, while others were in the thick of the fighting. It was a comparatively easy life.

I did not enjoy this part of my military life. The C.O. was a former cavalry officer of the old school. Unexpectedly, he was not a great disciplinarian, except on occasions when he apparently thought he should have a 'blitz', and he was quite easy to get on with. But unfortunately I did not get on well with my fellow officers. Some were reservists, mobilized. Some were younger from an Officer Training Corps school background and called up. None, apart from the Royal Artillery liaison officer who had been in France and Belgium in 1940, had seen any action, and, it seemed to me, not keen to see any. Conversation in the mess was complacent and out of touch with what was going on elsewhere. I was relieved when I was posted to another unit and back to Yorkshire.

This was a small unit commanded by a Captain with me as his fellow officer. We were being brought up to strength with postings from other units, some experienced troops, some a bit 'raw', and being equipped for an overseas posting as Corps support troops somewhere, though it was fairly obvious we were going to a warm climate.

Fortunately we, Dick Gardner and I, got on well together. Detail bored him and he left it to me to ensure the unit obtained all the stores and equipment needed for our future (undefined) role, while he took charge of the training. Although I would have enjoyed the training role, having spent time as an instructor before I was commissioned, I was quite content to play the administrative role because it put me into contact with interesting groups of middle-level 'Brass' and taught me a lot about military administrative procedures and how to benefit from them. Off-duty we had many happy, if argumentative, drinking sessions. He was tolerant of my dogmatic 'leftish' views.

When we were ordered to move (the destination was Algeria to join First Army) Dick was told to sail immediately with the main part of the unit, while I was to take charge of the 'rear party' and move the vehicles and heavy equipment up to Scotland to sail from there. We were sent to Glasgow to load, board and sail from Greenock. Inevitably there were delays; the designated ship hadn't docked; other material to be loaded hadn't arrived. During this time I lived in a billet in Greenock and fed in a Mess under an elderly Colonel from the Scots Guards. He was a very proper soldier, completely lacking a sense of humour. After dinner in the Mess it would have been a deliberate insult not to have lingered over the port to hear accounts of his life in the army and endure his continual complaints about the falling standards of behaviour and the neglect of military tradition. ('The merging of Regiments, and reinforcements, conscripts an' all, coming from outside the County or region, you know'.)

I remember one occasion when we walked from the Mess to the dockside to check on progress with the loading, he resplendent in trews and glengarry, shoulders back, head high, swinging his swagger stick. As we made our dignified way to the docks we were followed by a group of young lads shouting, 'Ach ye tartan-legged bastard'. I was embarrassed for him, but we proceeded and he chattered away without pause, apparently deaf to the insults being hurled from behind him. It was admirable and, of course, right; the kids, deprived of any reaction, soon tired and ran away.

Some days later we, myself, my sergeant and six men, boarded the cargo boat that was to take us, a contingent of Royal Engineers and a hold-full of vehicles, equipment and stores to our North African destination. It was late afternoon as we slid quietly in a line of three or four other vessels down the Clyde to join, as darkness fell, a convoy that stretched far into the gloom. My sergeant and I, our men and a few of the Royal Engineers, all wearing the obligatory life jackets ('You must have them with you at all times' was the instruction from the bridge) lent on the rails and watched quietly, juggling with our individual thoughts about what and who we were leaving, and trying to guess about what we were heading for, until we were ordered below.

The voyage took a long time, though I cannot now recall how long. Looking out each day at the ranks of vessels on either side of us, ahead and astern, we and they seemed to be scarcely moving in the endless grey-green swell. A case of keeping pace with the slowest, we thought. But gradually the sky brightened and the sea became bluer as we moved sedately, vulnerably, we sometimes thought, down through the Bay of Biscay. We avoided boredom by sessions

61

of P.T. on deck, playing a kind of football game and sitting chatting, quietly speculating. There was great excitement one morning when through the mist we saw the rock of Gibraltar. It looked majestic, so grand and secure. Even though few, if any, of us had seen it before, it meant a great deal. We knew that for centuries it had guarded our trade routes to the Middle and Far East. We pointed and waved. For a while we felt close to home again.

On the starboard side we watched the North African coast take shape. The distant reddish-brown ruggedness of Morocco, with white buildings scattered along the hillsides, emerged from the mist. As we moved closer to the coast and the hot sun rose in a clear steely blue sky, we could see the shape of fortified buildings, perhaps old castles, in prominent positions, and the white houses grouped in the foothills into, we assumed, villages. For me, naively, it was a romantic sight; it brought to the imagination colourful sheikhdoms, Moorish architecture and sweet-smelling secluded gardens. It seemed far removed from the demands and strains of a world-wide war. Of course, as I learned later, it was not that far removed. Morocco and Algeria were, as now, cauldrons of political intrigue and religious unrest.

That evening my sergeant and I were on deck, leaning on the rail staring at the coast, now dim in the fading light. We weren't sure whether we were still looking at Morocco or Algeria. Whichever it was, we were fascinated by our inadequately informed romantic view of Mediterranean Africa. It was then that the vessel on our starboard side, that is between us and the coast, erupted in a sheet of flame and black smoke, settled back in the water and slid, within seconds it seemed, below the surface. We looked at each other with the same realization in mind. We had broken the convoy's rules; we were on deck without our life-jackets. Not a word was said; we just turned and dashed for the companion way and as we did so there was another loud explosion on the port side and across the deck, one vessel away, another was burning. Half-way down the companion-way we heard a third explosion and the boat rocked.

When we returned to the deck and took our emergency positions there was another gap on the starboard side. The U-boat had got a position on the shore side of the convoy and was taking pot shots. He had already scored three direct hits. By this time two destroyers were circling and dropping depth charges. As they did so the convoy moved sedately on. Looking back we could see a lifeboat from one of the stricken vessels carrying waving sailors and we saw one of the boats moving out of line towards them.

Later that evening, when the 'stand down; go to your cabins' order came from the bridge, my sergeant and I and a number of others found corners on deck out of sight of the bridge and settled down, now wearing our life-jackets, for a night's sleep that would be safer, we thought, than down below.

Next morning we arrived off Algiers. The sea was calm, like a sheet of blue-coloured glass. An early mist dispersed as a large yellow sun rose into the sky, spreading its embracing warmth. We anchored offshore and waited for clearance to enter the port, disembark and unload. Behind the jumble of the port area, white buildings climbed the hills beyond, standing in sharp relief from the brown of the rock and soil. We spent that day and part of another waiting to move in.

Late next morning we docked just before midday. We were in French North Africa as part of the British First Army. Dick, with a dozen men, was there waiting on the dockside to take over the vehicles and stores as we unloaded. As we were supervising the unloading he told me that the unit was, temporarily, until we were moved forward, split into two parts. He and the main part of the unit were already installed in a farm on the edge of Algiers. I was to go with my rear party to another farm, a vineyard, east of Algiers just beyond a place called Maison Blanche.

The authorities had requisitioned two buildings on the vineyard. A small two-roomed whitewashed outhouse was my 'billet'. One room had a small table and chair. In another I settled my 'issue' camp bed. My twelve men, including three N.C.O.s, occupied a much larger storehouse, in front of which was an area for our vehicles. We were several hundred yards off the main east-west coast road that ran along the north coast of Algeria.

It was not until next morning that I was able to take stock of my surroundings. I was awakened early, at daylight it seemed, by a bell which, I discovered, called the Arab workers to work on the vineyard. That bell, hanging on a wall opposite my billet, was rung by a kind of supervisor or manager, to indicate when work started, when there was a break and when work finished. They worked a very long day.

The door of my billet opened on to a large plantation of vines. In front was a large concrete cistern from which was water drawn off, almost every day I was there, to irrigate the vines. The Arab labourers scraped channels in the dry, brown soil to the parts of the vineyard requiring the water. As they bent their backs to do this they kept up a kind of monotonous conversation, almost a chant. It was an everyday noise that to me became an essential part of this new, strange environment. From my door, looking over the row upon row of vines, I could see through the heat haze the distant Atlas Mountains.

It was a strange phase of my military life. As a contribution to the war effort it was useless. We were told that we were waiting to be moved up to Tunisia as part of a Corps Headquarters. Meanwhile we were to get ourselves acclimatized, continue drilling and carry out movement exercises! We certainly needed to acclimatize. It was very hot and oppressive and we were plagued by flies and mosquitoes attracted in their thousands to a nearby open rubbish dump, but who seemed to find us more interesting. With the wind in a certain direction the sickly, putrid stench from that dump pervaded our location. We survived only with the help of copious quantities of DDT spray. We tried to keep activity to a minimum in the heat of the day. At night sleep came fitfully in the heavy, airless heat, alive with the whining swoop of mosquitoes.

At first life there was fascinating because there were new things to observe. We had seen the fine houses of the French colonists and the official buildings in Algiers along the coast. Later we became aware of the poor living conditions of the Arabs in the face of which their apparent cheerfulness was remarkable. But overall the scenery was breathtaking. The sun rose as a huge orange ball from the sea and sometimes the early morning landscape took on a mysterious splendour with the ruddy brown hills at the back of the coastal plain seeming to stand waist-deep in mist, while their peaks reflected the rising sun. Slowly the silvery skirt slipped off and for a time they stood starkly bare until the sun rose like a yellow disk high in the sky and drenched the plain in unrelenting heat, sending the hills in retreat behind a shimmering haze. Then the stifling sirocco from the desert beyond the hills would blow across the plain, throwing the dust and dirt on the vineyard into swirling spirals, banging and rattling the shutters on the farm buildings and my billet.

I had one regular visitor to my whitewashed outhouse. She was the colour of creamy coffee with black oily-looking hair hanging in ringlets to her shoulders. She wore a short coloured frock which always left one shoulder bare. She was beautiful with lovely eyes,

64

dark pupils set in shining white eyeballs, inquiring, placid and silently pleading. When I was there she would walk slowly to the open door and stand at the threshold looking down as her bare foot made circles in the sandy soil. Then she would look up smiling, eyes shining, and come and lean on the wall just in the entrance. Never any nearer. I doubt whether she could have been more than five or six years old. She was the child of one of the Arab women workers in the vineyard. The woman was always working down by the cistern, on her knees hacking away the earth with a small hoe to make gulleys for the water to flow down through the vines. The first time she came to the door I looked past her to the woman I correctly took to be her mother. She had knelt back on her heels and was frowning. I came forward a little, careful not to frighten either the child or the mother. I smiled at the mother and nodded in what I hoped was a reassuring way. The mother looked, then smiled, first at the child, then back at me and nodded before getting on with her task. So it was every day I was in my billet. Nothing was ever said. We had no contact, never tried to speak. I never gave her anything, but we were great friends. I could not believe, and still cannot, that such beauty, innocence and simple happiness could come from such hardship and poverty.

I still cannot think of our stay in Algeria without feeling the stifling sweaty heat, smelling rotten garbage and hearing the low buzz of flies, the screech of attacking mosquitoes and hot sleepless nights. Having more spare time than we should have had, I filled the idle hours with renewed scribbling. From my notes I see that one evening, when the day's heat had not diminished with the passing hours, I wrote along the following lines:

'Today as always the sun shone brightly on the plain. The rich brown soil was baking. Between the rows of vines the Arab women and boys bent their backs as they scooped the soil away with their short-handled hoes, making the furrows that allowed the life-saving water from the cistern to flow to the vines. The sun sparkled in the flowing water. The sweat dripped from the Arabs but their chanting chatter never ceased, nor did the shouting of the supervising agent of the French patron. Beyond the vineyard the plain stretched to the distant mountains which changed shape as the sun moved across the sky casting different shadows and highlighting different peaks. At the end of the day the sun dipped behind the headland across the bay and as it did the mountains came nearer and

65

then from behind them the huge pale moon ascended majestically. As the light of the sun faded, the moon climbed higher in the darkening sky and as it became smaller it cast a bright silvery light over the whole plain.

'That night I sat at my small table reading by the light of a hurricane lamp with a DDT spray before me, ready for frequent use. The air was getting hotter and more stifling. I could hear the rustling of the wind outside blowing through the fruit and palm trees, and in my billet the hinges and latches of the closed shutters rattled. Suddenly there was a rush of air as the wind became a veritable gale. I went to the door and opened it, surprised by the strength of the wind. It was as if a blast from a hot oven hit me in the face. I could see leaves from the pomegranate and fig trees swirling across the face of the moon and the clusters of bamboo bowed to the force of wind. Yet still it blew harder The noise from the trees and from the clattering shutters was almost obliterated by the wind itself, and I could see dimly an advancing wall of dust blown up from the vineyard. I quickly went inside again and closed the door.

'That night was as hot as the day had been, but more oppressive and airless – doors and shutters had to be kept closed. Flies and mosquitoes were everywhere. (We had no mosquito nets.) Constant use of the DDT spray virtually poisoned the air. I sat at my small table reading by a paraffin lamp, sweating. The furious clatter of door and shutters was incessant. I did not sleep that night. I simply lay on my camp bed sweat pouring from me, as I tried to suck in some oxygen from the stifling atmosphere. Then, just as dawn broke, the wind subsided and all became still. More for air than anything else I went to the door and took in great gulps of fresh air. In the thin early morning light I could see the inevitable mist shrouding the distant foothills. And around my billet and the adjacent cistern were piles of blown leaves and dust, but best of all was the cool air, cool, fresh and sweet. I filled my lungs again and again. Then I paused, surprised, as I saw first one, then another, and another large drop of rain fall onto the dusty earth. There was no pattern to it; a useless scattering at first until suddenly the heavens unleashed a veritable torrent that poured from the rooftops, spluttered up from the soil and sent water rushing down the channels dug the day before. The rains had come.'

After that I found in one of my books of poetry a verse that expressed all that so much better!

Come the dawn,
White mists enshroud the morn
And thoughts, on wings of memory borne,
Come tumbling into a mind that's torn
From slumber's dreams. There form
Mosaics of peace.

It was while I was trying to get used to the strangely colourful yet increasingly boring life in Algeria that I became very ill with jaundice, an illness that afflicted many of us at the time. I have never, before or since, suffered an illness which made me feel so suicidal – bilious, depressed and suicidal. I lay in the field hospital for a week or two I think, sweating, periodically delirious and wanting to die. Eventually I recovered from that, but was left very weak. So I was sent to convalesce at a 'rest camp' in a resort west of Algiers called Castiglione, a fascinating little town on the Mediterranean coast where Colonial French and Arab seemed to have come to terms with each other, more at least than in Algiers. It was hot and dusty, but the busy palm-tree-lined main street had shops and stalls selling colourful textiles, fruits and vegetables, pottery and awful-looking meat and was thronged with Frenchmen and attractively dressed women, Arabs and troops like me on sick leave. It had a large sandy beach where the same mixture of people sunned themselves and swam. It was far removed from the hardworking, divisive environment of my vineyard beyond Maison Blanche.

Anyone who has had jaundice will know what I mean when I say that for the first few days of my stay there I felt utterly weak. I just walked to the beach and sat looking at the glass-calm blue of the Mediterranean. I think it was on the second day that I was conscious also of an additional quite breathtaking sight. She stood at the water's edge, tall, statuesque, nut brown, with long dark hair reaching down her back to her waist. Her swimming costume was a faded blue and probably, I thought, rather old because it was not a close fit. It was very loose at the top where her firm breasts pushed it out, revealing their seductive curve at the side. At her hips it was pulled high as if short for her, barely covering her brown buttocks and showing attractive long thighs. She stood motionless, feet in the gently lapping water, her head raised towards the blue sun-filled sky as if in supplication to a god. Then slowly she waded into the sea until she was at a sufficient depth to dive into the almost motionless blue. She

67

emerged a few yards farther on and with a lazy crawl stroke made for a raft anchored a hundred yards or so from the shore. In one movement she hauled herself aboard the raft, brushed her wet hair from her face and stretched out on the raft, submitting herself to the sun. Even from that distance I could see the enticing curves of her body. I was contentedly enjoying the evocative scene when a voice interrupted my teasing thoughts: 'Come on sir, I don't think you're up to that yet. You'll have to get better first.' It was the medical orderly. Furious at the interruption, I turned to him. He saw the look on my face. 'Ah-ah, don't say it. It's medicine time. Come on,' and he led me back to the camp. But, weak though I was, I am sure that Aphrodite was the key to my subsequent rapid recovery.

Though the time in Algeria was memorable, it became increasingly depressing. The harsh reality was that, as a part of the British Army, we were in limbo. There was no indication of when we would move up to Tunisia. The men's morale was declining fast. It was difficult to keep them occupied. We pestered a local charity run by the resident French to find a couple of footballs. We accepted their offer to come and give us a concert, which to the disappointment of the troops turned out to be a concert of chamber music. We organized 'passion wagon' trips into Algiers, issuing strict instructions not to attempt to go to the well-known brothel in the Casbah which was out of bounds to both UK and US troops, and frequently raided by the Military Police of both. Needless to say it was always well-attended and the best war stories one could hear at the time were how 'a' or 'b' managed to escape arrest when the brothel was raided.

An occasional bright interlude was provided by a friendly American Captain. His 'outfit', engineers, had set up camp a few miles away. One morning he drove into our compound in a typically American confident and relaxed manner. 'Saw your vee-hicles from the road,' he said, 'so I thought I'd come and make contact.' We introduced ourselves and chatted about what we had each been doing in the war. This was his first overseas posting. He invited me over 'to meet some other guys' the following evening.

It was then that I realized how well the Americans were equipped. Their tents were huge, all with floorboards and beds. The mess hall was an enormous marquee, floorboarded, with tables and chairs. There was a large PX store on site and an open-air cinema. Whenever I visited him it was a generous drinking evening. When he came to see me, he would bring his PX bottles. One day he told me that Bob

Hope was coming to give a concert and invited me and all my men. When we got there forty-eight hours later a huge stage, complete with amplifiers, lighting and tiered seating out front, had been erected. American troops must have come from miles around. There were many hundreds of them. The show was hilarious – wonderful one-liners from Bob Hope with much-appreciated digs at authority and top brass. His accompanying lead singer was the well known and attractive Frances Langford who appeared in a very flimsy and revealing costume that brought roars of delight from the G.I.s and, more mutedly, us. The show went on with encore after encore. My men caustically commented: 'Beats chamber music any day'.

Our only periods of excitement were the occasional rumours and alarms about possible attacks from German parachutists, presumably intended to be a bit of a diversion from what was happening to the Axis forces in Tunisia and the Western Desert. Whenever an alarm was given we had to set up road blocks and mount patrols. Nothing came of these rumours except a test of our ability to respond to a situation. Sadly, however, on one such occasion an American vehicle crashed through a road block and came under fire. Not the first or last case of 'friendly fire'.

These isolated incidents did nothing to assuage my increasing boredom and frustration. I reflected again on the importance of the fight against Naziism and Fascism, a 'just' war, as I believed. I also reflected again on what I wanted the post-war world to be like: fairer, less poverty, more education opportunities, employment opportunities for all, a national health service, all the aspirations expressed in the Beveridge Report. It seemed to me that if one felt deeply about these things, as I did, one could not argue for them, 'agitate' or work for them unless one had shown they were worth fighting for. So, I asked myself, what I was doing about it? The honest answer was nothing. Since the blitzkrieg that devastated the Low Countries and France, destroyed the British Expeditionary Force in 1940 and sent us to the beaches of Dunkirk, I had not faced the enemy. I *had* to do something about it, but what?

A chance meeting that helped to convince me that I had to do something more active was with a young, debonair Naval Officer. His name was Christopher Dreyer. He had been on our convoy coming out from the U.K. I had met him down at the docks in Algiers when I was supervising the unloading of our vehicles. He was unloading Motor Torpedo Boats (MTBs). He commanded a flotilla of three and had already been decorated for his exploits against enemy convoys in the Channel and for his work in the Dunkirk evacuation. (I learned after the war that he came from a distinguished Naval family and his promising career was ended by ill health.) It was the Dunkirk experience that we had in common. Now he was required to attack enemy shipping in the Mediterranean.

When we met later he said he was testing his MTBs prior to going operational. Would I like a ride? Of course I would. It was a most exhilarating experience as he put his boat through various manoeuvres and speed tests. As we docked after one such run, he said, 'Well, you go and knock the shit out of them on land and I'll do the same at sea'.

Of course I was not about to do anything of the sort and I worried again about my inactivity. Then, while I was wrestling with my conscience an event occurred that led to a decision that changed my life. Not only my life in the Army, but also my future. In itself it was not of special importance, but for me the consequences were long-lasting.

I was asked to take some documents to the camp of the Parachute Regiment up in the Atlas Mountains and hand them personally to the Commanding Officer. We, my driver and I, set off in a small Austin staff car early one morning, armed with a map and a map reference, hoping to get well on with our journey before the heat of the day. It was a long trip, increasingly hot and dusty. The 'main road' into the mountains was quite good, but from then on it deteriorated and the by-road into the Para camp was not easy to identify.

When we arrived, after the inevitable yet thorough identity check, we were welcomed and shown to their respective messes for food and drink. The C.O. was equally friendly. Having thanked me for the documents – he did not say what they were about – he said there was no point in my going back until the following day. It was almost nightfall and, although the road back was not enemy territory, at night it was at the mercy of marauding brigands, as he described them. 'So join us in the mess tonight and relax with us. Your driver will be well looked after by my batman. Have a look round tomorrow morning, then you can be on your way.'

That evening was one of the happiest I spent in North Africa. Those officers of the Parachute Regiment (I cannot remember which Battalion) observed all the formalities of British Army Mess procedure but in a very unstuffy way and their relaxed friendliness to me was heartwarming, their hospitality almost overwhelming. I was given a camp bed in a large tent, but when I got to it I was not in a condition to note much else. That experience and my observation next morning of the confident, buoyant, self-disciplined attitude of all ranks, keen to get back into action, showed me what I had to do. Before I got far on the road back to Algiers, I decided to join the Army Air Corps' Parachute Regiment, as it was then known.

Within a few weeks of applying I was interviewed and accepted. I think they must have been short of 'recruits' – lucky for me. A couple of weeks later I was on my way back, by sea, to the U.K. for parachute and battle training.

5

Battle School with the Paras

I sailed home on a freighter converted to troop-carrying. It was not very big. I can't now remember how many of us were on board. Perhaps twenty or so troops and about ten officers. People going back for a variety of reasons: sickness, 'walking wounded' needing further treatment, people being re-posted. I shared a cabin with three other officers. One was a gunner, a captain who was, unhappily, escorting a subaltern in a County Regiment back to the UK to stand a Court Martial for surrendering when what was left of his platoon were surrounded in the battle for the Mareth Line. The other was a captain in a Guards Regiment (again I can't remember which) who had been badly wounded. He had been shot in the thighs and groin and had had his penis shot away. During the day he worried about how he would tell his wife and how she would react; during the night he often woke us all with his screaming.

We were, of course, sailing in convoy and the life-jacket and boat station drills were as I had experienced on the way to Algeria. Remembering the U Boat attack on the previous occasion, I was much more diligent about following the rules. However, the voyage was without incident. I think I was absorbed with a feeling of excitement at my change of direction and with some apprehension as to what the future might hold. I also spent a lot of time talking to the wretched subaltern and the more wretched Guards captain about the fighting round the Mareth Line, the German defensive position intended to prevent the British Eighth and First Armies from joining up, thus completing the destruction of the Axis forces in North Africa. So for me the time went quickly. We watched once more as we sailed past the rock and as we moved into the Bay of Biscay, felt the change from Mediterranean calm to Atlantic swell and the change from sun to cloud and rain.

It was a grey morning when we first looked out from the deck on to home soil. An overcast sky shed a steady drizzle as we slowly moved up the Clyde. Overhead, seagulls shrieked, circled the vessel and swooped over the grey-green water where the bows formed small waves topped with white foam. As we moved slowly onwards the river banks closed in on us and through the mist we saw our first homeland people. A few stood on the banks watching our silent progress, but as the banks moved closer to us, clusters of houses and factories appeared, wet slate roofs reflecting the grey light. We moved past clanging, banging, riveting shipyards. Blue-overalled men and smocked women came to the banks' edge and waved. The troops waved back enthusiastically, shouting messages to the women and whistling, some of whom responded by lifting their skirts, kicking up their legs and making crude gestures with their hips and arms.

I was given a week's leave before being required to join my new Regiment. It was mid-December 1942 and the weather was atrocious when I set off for the Parachute Regiment Training depot near Chesterfield in Derbyshire. Train delays and the lack of taxis at the station made me two hours late in reporting. Not a good start. The sight of the camp through the swirling rain, a random collection of brick huts connected by concrete paths to a central mud-covered road, was depressing in the extreme. All of that seemed irrelevant when I reported at 'reception' and felt immediately the brisk, encouraging efficiency.

I was ushered, as smart in full kit as I could be after the journey, into the Course office to meet the Course Commander. His briefing was direct and to the point: 'Training starts tomorrow morning. Report in fatigue dress. You'll take a platoon of troops through the training with you. They'll look to you for leadership and help. So you won't be just getting yourself through the Course. You have to get to know them, find out what they're made of, and they'll find out what you're made of. Later you may have to go into action with them. The training is very physical. We aim to get you very fit. You'll probably feel very tired at the end of each day. There's plenty of nourishing food here, nothing elaborate, but good stuff. Living conditions are a bit rough, but you'll get used to it. After 1 January you'll go to Ringway for pre-jump training and then your jumps. If you pass all this you may get a bit of leave, but it may be embarkation leave. There's a war on. Good luck.'

A sergeant met me outside and conducted me to one of the huts in which there were about a dozen iron bedsteads with mattresses, pillows and folded army blankets, each with a narrow cupboard alongside. 'Sort yourself out, then report to the Quartermaster's stores, sir,' he said, saluting on his way out. All but two of the beds were taken by other officers, so I took one at the far end. I introduced myself to the officer next to me, a very young-looking, very blond, very slim individual, and to the one opposite me, who, by contrast, was short, stocky and dark-haired. That was how I met Ed (Mike) Mycock and Tom Bryce and formed a relationship that lasted for the rest of the war and, in the case of Ed, way beyond.

The visit to the Q.M.stores was to choose a red beret that fitted, draw a Parachute Regiment hat badge and Parachute Regiment buttons for our dress uniforms. That evening we dined in the sparsely furnished Officers' Mess, another hut, everyone rather subdued and tentative in their new relationships, sank a few drinks and went back to our quarters to sew, rather proudly, the buttons of our new Regiment onto our uniforms.

The parade next morning was taken by the Officer Commanding Parachute Training Company. He gave us an inspiring address about taking pride in being members of this new Regiment and reminding us that parachuting was just a different way of getting into battle. The Regiment's reputation would be built not on parachuting but on how well it fought in battle. We were then allocated to our platoons and smartly moved off by a drill sergeant to begin our training.

In those last days of December we were subjected to the most demanding physical trial I have ever experienced. It was tough, at times exhausting, and we grumbled. Yet in a strange way we revelled in it, because we were being constantly tested – and winning, even though there were times when I thought it would be better to give in. We got up early in the morning, had long sessions of physical training, climbed ropes, throwing heavy medicine balls at each other, running for miles wearing our ammunition boots across the Derbyshire countryside, beautiful if only we had had the time and inclination to admire it. We did team exercises with pine logs about the size and weight of telegraph poles; we did long fast marches; we ran five miles in full battle kit including rifles; we scaled cliff faces and we abseiled down them. We had to do all these tasks within a time target. As light relief we had hours of 'square bashing' under a drill sergeant who kept shouting 'Smarten it up you lot. Put some swank into it. Bags of swank. You're in the elite Regiment of the British Army. For God's sake show it.'

We must have had a week or ten days of those non-stop physical activities before we went on to battle training. Whereas the fitness testing had been arduous, the battle training was arduous and exciting. The battle course, of the kind now familiar to most people through film and television, was in a wooded area. Everything was done at the double. We ran from one obstacle to the next and had to negotiate each one as quickly as possible, keeping ahead of the colleague following behind. We scaled a large, swaying climbing net stretched between trees, rolled over the top and down the other side; we climbed a rope to get to a cable stretched between two more trees and hauled ourselves along it upside down by our hands with feet locked over it; we scaled another cliff and abseiled down it; we crawled through ditches, drain pipes and under barbed wire while a member of the training staff fired live rounds from a Bren gun over us, a great inducement to keep low.

We did all this in platoon strength. It was no good you getting through it successfully if the rest of the platoon were stragglers. You won points only if you succeeded together. Next day we did it all again because we had to be faster. This time, breathless, we had to go straight from that to the rifle range to make sure we could still shoot accurately after the physical stress of the battle course.

The following day, Christmas Eve, we were faced with the first of a number of tests which had to be passed before we went to do our parachute jumps. It was a fast route march of several miles in full kit and we had to complete it, as a platoon, in the required time. Back in our huts at the end of the day Father Christmas was a long way from our thoughts. By contrast Christmas Day was fairly relaxed. A later reveille, no drills, plenty of beer before serving, in the tradition of the Army, the men with their Christmas dinner, much bonhomie back in our own Mess over dinner, which was followed in the evening by a rather riotous party which we came to regret next day.

We were told that on Boxing Day we would complete the required 'passing out' tests, a decision which we regarded as sheer sadism on the part of our instructors. For me it was the day that almost ended my career in the Paratroops before it had begun. Immediately after breakfast, with a large piece of lead rolling round inside my head and with a throat feeling like the Sahara desert, we were set to perform exercises with the ruddy telegraph poles and medicine balls. That was bearable – just. Then in full kit we went on a short route march at the double. I can't remember how long, but long enough to have most of us gasping and retching.

The next indignity was where I came face to face with one possible exit from the Regiment. We, in full battle order with rifles, had to carry a colleague, also in full battle order with rifle, on our shoulder, fireman's lift style, at the double down a slope for fifty yards and back up the slope, another fifty yards, also within a given time. My sergeant and I paired off to do this together. He carried me, gasping and swearing he never wanted to be in the bloody Parachute Regiment anyway and it was all a dreadful mistake. But he completed the task in time.

Then it was my turn. I carried him down the slope, not easily, but at least I did it. It was coming back up the slope that was my nemesis. The previous night's party soon took its toll. Within a few paces I was struggling for breath. The world around me was pink and distorted. Nothing was real. Life was just a searing pain in the back of the throat.

I had almost come to stop when I heard the drill instructor's voice shouting, 'Come on, Sir, you're going to miss the time limit. You'll have to do it again.' That was it. I decided to give in. Anything would be better than the rasping pain in my throat and the weight I was carrying in my head. 'It's no good,' I grunted to my sergeant, between heaving steps, 'I'm giving up'. 'No you're not,' he shouted back from behind me. 'You're going to finish,' and he started prodding his rifle into my rear end. I was being goosed, but it worked. I took a deep breath, staggered up to the 'finishing line' and sagged to my knees, dumping my sergeant unceremoniously on the ground. I could not even gasp out my thanks – it was his success – though I did later, profusely.

'Well done, sir,' I heard the drill sergeant say, 'but hard luck. You were out of time. You'll have to do it all again.' I had just enough energy left to pull myself up and rather aggressively look at him and say, 'Now look here . . .' He smiled. 'Just joking, sir. You were inside the time.' I was close to becoming a murderer.

'Right,' he called, 'fall in, platoon order, and double along to the gym for the next test.' There were times when the continuously cheerful 'get going', 'can-do' attitude of the drill sergeants and the

P.T. instructors was irritating in the extreme. Of course, we recognized how invaluable they were in the Para training programme and for the most part we had a friendly, mutually understanding relationship. We knew they had to push us very hard and that when they pushed us to the edge of endurance, as they did, it was to increase the chances of our survival in future operations. They knew we struggled and were driven by pride and determination to fulfil the responsibilities we had accepted when we volunteered to join the Regiment. But there were times when, figuratively speaking, we could have slit their throats. That Boxing Day, when, irrespective of the Christmas Day indulgence, we had to pass successfully the torturous tests they had devised, was such a time. But in truth they were fine men.

The reason we were required to 'double along to the gym' was to engage in three rounds of boxing with a knock down counting against the victim, but points for the perpetrator. Having changed into shorts and gym shoes, we had to squat round the boxing ring so that we could be paired off for our contests by the drill sergeant choosing people of roughly the same weight and height. As all this was being explained, I hatched a plot with my sergeant. 'We'll squat at the back of the platoon,' I said, 'and then we'll go in together on the understanding we don't hit each other hard.' It was agreed. So we sat, watched and cheered as pair after pair enthusiastically clouted each other until the sergeant called, 'Anyone not been in yet?' We put up our hands. 'Yes, I had noticed,' the evil man said. 'Sergeant, you go in with the Drill Corporal. Sir, you come in with me.' The best laid plans. . .!

As I stepped into the ring, boxing gloves fitted, I thought I saw a challenging glint in the drill sergeant's eye. Had he a purpose in mind, I wondered briefly before the bout began. The next couple of minutes showed that he had. I thought I knew something about boxing, in theory at least. Len Harvey and Gene Tunney had been among my boyhood heroes and I had whacked a punchball in our garage. But in that ring I completely failed to locate my opponent; he was everywhere or, more sinisterly, I suspected there was more than one of him. Blows came in from every angle as I tried to find him and measure him for what I thought would be my telling right hand but failed.

In the second round it was much the same and the dripping sweat made seeing him even more difficult, so in exasperation I swung my right vaguely in his direction – miracously he was in that direction. I felt a connection and the rain of punches ceased. Shaking my head, I looked and there he was on the floor looking up with rather glazed eyes. Then he shook his head and looked at me. 'Good shot sir.' He scrambled to his feet. 'But you're going to be sorry!' And I was. How I stayed upright in that and the last round I shall never know. That evening, with the news that we had all passed our tests and were to be sent for parachute training, there was much celebration regardless of the excesses of Christmas evening, though we had a strong suspicion that we were going to be passed anyway. 'They' were just urging us on.

Within a few days we were off to Ringway (now Manchester Airport) for our parachute pre-jump and jump training. But it was in that brief interval that a small unusual event occurred that might have had a bearing on later decisions. One afternoon I went into Chesterfield to have a look round. I visited the church with the twisted spire and then found a second-hand book shop. Whenever I had a bit of money in my pocket during the war, and had the opportunity, I would buy a record (old 78 speed!), a picture or a book. So here was a chance to buy a book. I was a bit 'into' history at the time and in scanning the shelves saw a hardback book entitled *So Victoria*. I picked it up but when I opened it I saw it was actually *For Whom the Bell Tolls* by Ernest Hemingway!

Someone, somewhere in a book binding company had made a dreadful mistake. I did not mind. When I drew the error to the attention of the shop manager, who apparently had never opened the book, he was embarrassed and said he would withdraw it. I told him I wanted it, so he let me have it for one shilling and sixpence! I had been a great admirer of Hemingway since reading *A Farewell To Arms* and some of his short stories, as I had of Steinbeck, both of whom, I thought, in my untutored way, were creating a new, more vigorous style of writing. Within a couple of days I had read it. It fed my admiration of those who resisted the Fascist insurgent General Franco in the Spanish Civil War and it started me thinking again about the effectiveness of guerrilla warfare.

6

Feet and Knees Together

Since 1943, when I did my parachute training, thousands of our soldiers have been through that training, a great many have been to war that way (after all just 'a different way of getting into battle') and many have graduated to greater things – high-altitude jumping, dead drops and so on. And we now have many Parachute Clubs for people who do it as a sporting activity. Undoubtedly techniques will have changed and many people now will regard parachute training and parachuting as very matter of fact. But 1943 was in the early days of the deployment of parachute troops in this country. Germany and Russia had seen, and proved, their potential earlier. The Parachute Regiment of the Army Air Corps was young and growing. It was all fairly new then and the following is how one young but by now fairly experienced soldier reacted to the process. No doubt today's experienced parachutists will scoff, but it is based on what I wrote at the time.

It was cold and bright at Ringway that January, but, surprisingly, considering its location, not wet, which we were glad of when it came to our parachute jumps. Although, truth to tell, we were too excited to worry much about the weather. But before we could proceed to those jumps we had to go through several days of ground training. The first requirement was to learn that all commands had to be obeyed on the shouted word 'Go', even on the parade ground. This was because when it came to jumping you jumped from the aircraft on that word 'Go'. It seemed necessary to get us so conditioned that we obeyed it automatically. From then on the parade ground, the gym and the training hangers echoed all day long to a barrage of that one shouted order. In fact it *did* become second nature to react instinctively to that command to the extent that if we were on an evening 'pass' in Manchester and saw a member of the Regiment standing on a bus or tram platform we would shout 'Go' and chortle mercilessly as we watched him throw himself off into a parachute-landing position.

This landing position was the next thing we had to learn. We would, we were told, have to get in position on our descent, arms bent on either side of the head holding the 'rigging', to hit the ground with our feet and knees close together, knees slightly bent so that we could push our hips to one side or other and roll over onto our shoulder, the best way to avoid injury and be ready quickly to release oneself from the harness and get into action. This was known in para language, fairly obviously, as landing 'side left' or 'side right'. But here again repetition and frequent practice was needed to ensure, having made the split-second decision as to which side, to do it correctly. So we spent hours jumping from the door of a mock fuselage or releasing ourselves from other training devices and going 'side right' or 'side left' according to the instructor's command.

These other 'training devices' were a series of ingeniously devised appliances set in a huge aircraft hangar, designed to get us used to heights from positions that had few safeguards, to give one confidence in the unnatural act of unhesitatingly launching oneself into space on the 'Go' and to induce a habit of landing side right or left at speeds dictated by the nature of the apparatus. Notably there was the cable stretched on an incline from the roof of one corner of the hangar across to just above the ground in the diagonally opposite corner. You had to climb a vertical ladder fixed to the wall on to a small unprotected platform at the top end of the cable (it was then that I realized I really hated heights), grab hold of two short handles on either side of a pulley wheel on the cable and push off so that you hurtled, swinging forwards and backwards down the cable, until one of the instructors standing near some coconut matting on the hangar floor yelled 'Go; side right'. The idea was that you then let go of the pulley handles and performed a perfect landing on the mat. The sight of hard concrete beyond the mat rushing at you encouraged you to do just that.

A particularly devilish device was called 'the fan' which, we were assured, defied gravity. It too had a platform up in the roof of the hangar, reached by another vertical ladder. The platform had a hole in it just large enough to jump through, representing the hole in the centre of the floor of the aircraft through which we jumped in those days. (There was no door exit from the old Whitley.) Above the hole was a wooden roller, similar to those above old water wells, round which was wound a thick steel wire with a belt on the end. At one end of the drum was a handle for winding up the wire; on the other were the blades of the fan set at right-angles to the drum.

The idea was to strap on the belt, sit with feet dangling through the central hole and launch yourself through it in the approved parachute exit position – feet first, arched back, head up – and drop straight down to the hangar floor in the belief that as you fell, dead weight, the increasing speed with which the drum turned as the wire unwound would cause the rotating blades to meet sufficient air resistance to slow your descent just before you hit the floor to go into your landing position. It was, of course, absurd and dynamically impossible. The strange thing was that it worked, to the relief of the feeling of impending doom you had on the way down.

Then there was the tower, a tall steel structure outside, perhaps forty or fifty feet high. I can only remember it was a very long way up, from which an open parachute was suspended on a kind of crane arm. On another unprotected platform just below the open but slack parachute silk you strapped on the parachute harness and, holding the rigging in the approved manner, swung out and waited until the 'chute was released. This was a fairly painless exercise so long as you had faith that the 'chute would open properly. It gave one the feel of descending in a parachute harness and choosing one's landing position, though, as we discovered later, the real thing was sharper and faster.

During this part of our training and during the jumps that followed we developed, indeed were encouraged by the instructors to show, a lot of gung-ho bravado. We put a brave face on the nervousness we all felt and it stimulated our sense of camaraderie. In our platoon we adopted a call sign. Not a very original one, though it was before the TV programme, but it fed our comradely spirits. It was 'Hi-de hi platoon!' to which the answer, naturally, was 'Ho-de-ho!' We used it on ground training, but especially when we were doing our jumps. It was all part of the brash 'we don't care' attitude we needed to keep the adrenalin levels high, as were the songs we were taught by the staff.

81

One song in particular fell into this category. It was sung to the tune of 'John Brown's Body 'and dwelt on the consequences of a 'roman candle', the event of a parachute not opening. It describes how 'the parachutist's intestines were in the rigging and his brains were in his boots. Glory, glory, what a hell of a way to die'. It demonstrated, of course, the belief that that sort of thing always happened to the other chap. We sang it with gusto in the truck taking us to Tatton Park, close to the airport, for our balloon jumps, and later on the way to the airport for the aircraft jumps. It was also a way of trying to dispose of the secret nagging thoughts: 'Will I be scared? Will I funk it? Even if I'm scared, I won't funk it, will I?' In the end I suppose the fear of being a funk in front of comrades, as in battle, is the greater fear, and in the case of the Parachute Regiment so was the shame of being 'returned to unit' as a consequence.

So we moved to our jumping training. The balloon jumps involved eight or nine of us, called a 'stick', with parachutes on our backs, climbing into a basket, which had an aperture in its base that looked too small to get through, suspended below the balloon. The balloon, similar to the kind used as a barrage balloon in air defence, would then be raised to a height of 700 or 800 feet, which was thought to be the safest minimum height from which to jump. Why choose the safest *minimum* height? Because in action a descending paratrooper is completely vulnerable to ground fire. He cannot fight back swinging beneath a silk canopy. The less time he is in that position the better.

In the basket the stick, with an instructor known as the dispatcher who will see us out one by one on that well-rehearsed command, stand round the exit hole and as the balloon ascends and look round as if they are interested in the scenery; some look down as the ground rapidly recedes and wish they hadn't. At the designated height the ascent stops with a bit of a shudder and the first man to go (with each balloon and aircraft jump the order is changed so that the waiting time is changed) is invited to sit on the edge of the exit hole, feet dangling, hands on the edge, back straight, head up looking at the dispatcher. The art of exiting is first ensure that the end of your static line is firmly fixed in the basket; secondly on 'Go' to push yourself out into the hole, body straight, back slightly arched, head up. A strong push and an arched back are very important because it is essential that the parachute pack on your back does not hit the edge of the hole behind you, thus thrusting your face forward on to the opposite edge of the hole. A bad smack in the face will be the outcome when jumping from the basket, but much worse when exiting from the aircraft because the hole in the floor of the fuselage is a steel cylinder protruding like a dustbin from the belly of the plane.

Another aspect of parachuting from the balloon we were warned about, but could never accept with composure, was the problem of 'the critical moment', and in our ignorance accepted quite calmly, until we experienced it. It was the fact that when jumping from a balloon your static line releases your parachute, but you have to wait for the air to get into the canopy as you fall for it to open properly. In a straight fall from a balloon it takes a little time, 2.2 seconds, if I remember correctly. Whatever it is, it's the longest two seconds ever experienced. As you drop swiftly at an accelerating speed and you have, as you think, counted the seconds, you are convinced your 'chute is not going to open. You've got a 'candle'. That dread fear occurs at the critical last split second, but we called it the s . . . split second.

When we arrived at the dropping zone in Tatton Park jumping was already in progress. As we walked over to the store to draw our 'chutes we watched the descents made by those who had come earlier. It looked easy enough. As we climbed into the harness of our 'chutes we paid careful attention to the advice of the instructor; we needed no persuasion that it was important to get it right the first time, otherwise there would be no second time. 'Chute on our backs, harness tight, buckle secure and rubber crash hat on our heads, we walked with a bit of a swagger to 'our' balloon, feeling very much the part. We, with our dispatcher, climbed into the basket and took up our positions round the exit hole, keeping our eyes averted from it, and hooked up our static lines, hoping the others would not notice the number of times we gave the line an extra tug; just checking, you know. Then the shout to the man controlling the windlass: 'Up 700, nine down,' meaning we were going to a height of 700 feet and nine of us would be jumping out. Up we went, under control, of course, swaying a little from side to side as we rose. Meanwhile the dispatcher kept up a well-intentioned comment on the landmarks in the receding countryside in which none of us were interested. A sudden jerk told us we had reached 700 feet.

As it was our first jump and I was nominally in charge of the stick I was 'invited' to be No. 1. As soon as the balloon stopped, swaying slightly, and as all the forced chatter stopped, the dispatcher, obviously keen to get on with job, and I suspect keen that we should not spend much time thinking, yelled, 'Right Sir, take your position. Remember the training; sit with your legs down the aperture, hands gripping the edge.' I tried to do as he said as briskly as I could, as if I was used to this sort of thing, conscious that the eyes of the whole stick were on me. 'Come on, Sir. Straight back. Knees and legs, get them together.' I was pressing them even more tightly when I heard the command 'Go' and found myself, straight as a ramrod, falling out of the balloon with air rushing past me and dropping very fast.

There was a slight jerk which I guessed was the static line unfurling my 'chute, but I continued to fall very fast. Surely I had been dropping for more than the 2.something seconds! Yes, I must have! 'Oh God I've got a "candle"!'. Oh, dear God. Then I bounced and the speed of my fall was checked. Looking up I saw the lovely broad white canopy of silk. The canopy breathed, as is usual after opening, and I bounced again. But I was floating gently down, so exhilarated, high on the surging adrenalin, that I looked up and shouted an exuberant 'Hi-de-hi' and heard from the basket above and from others a resounding 'Ho-de-ho' in reply. Adolescent? Perhaps, but it was an essential part of the bravado culture we needed to adopt.

Suddenly I was enjoying this new exciting experience. Holding on to the web rigging of the 'chute, I looked around, admiring the countryside. I looked down at the green of Tatton Park and could see the various balloon stations. It looked as far away as when we were in the balloon at 700 feet. Yet I could hear the instructor on the ground shouting through his loud-hailer: 'Clumsy exit number one. Get your bloody knees and feet together. Adjust your swing.' Who was he shouting at? Not me surely. I did a jolly good exit and I'm in control of the webbing! Bloody cheek! I'm doing it, aren't I? I looked down again. Good God! The ground that had been so far away was rushing up at me at a very rapid rate. Quick! Position! I tried to judge the pace of drift, but was too late to correct it by pulling on the appropriate webs and I came in rather rapidly on an ill-judged side right and gasped as the breath left my body. I lay for a moment before hitting the clasp that released the harness. Not brilliant, I thought, as I rolled up my 'chute, but not bad. As I walked back to the truck waiting to take us back to the Mess, I looked up at others on the way down. 'That was a bad exit,' I thought, 'and he's twisting, got his legs apart. That will be a bad one!' Well, I knew about those things, didn't I?

That lunchtime the Mess was full of highly elated young Paratroop officers, competing with the exciting stories of their first jumps. It all seemed plain sailing from then to the completion of the six balloon jumps, including three night jumps. The Mess, incidentally, was beside a hangar in which young WAAFs (Women's Auxiliary Air Force) all of whom looked to us quite beautiful, worked at long tables packing parachutes. Attractive as they were, we had no difficulty in following the advice not to distract them in case it was your 'chute they packed badly under your flirtatious gaze. We used to walk past, wilfully staring straight ahead!

But our complacent optimism was for some of us to be misplaced fairly soon. We had been warned that everyone has a 'panic jump' sometime or other. That meant that there is an occasion when the bravado suddenly evaporates and the submerged fears come to the surface and you're scared, very scared. You get no warning. It occurs suddenly as you are about to jump. They said, if you are going to get one, best get it early so that, if you overcome it, you can get on with job, complete the course and earn your parachute wings. Of course if you don't overcome it and fail to jump you are immediately sent back to your parent unit. Although it was realized that no one refuses deliberately, it was considered essential to guard against the idea of fear spreading to the rest of the trainees.

My 'panic jump' was that afternoon when we returned to Tatton Park for our second balloon. Because I had jumped first in the morning I was now told by the dispatcher to be last. It was a dead-calm sunny afternoon and when we reached our designated height we were almost vertically above the balloon windlass. There was no drift and, as I sat in the hole after the others had jumped without incident, I looked down and saw the mooring cable thick under the basket and shrinking down to a cotton thinness as it reached the windlass below. Normally you don't see that connecting link because the breeze carries the basket in one direction or another. Suddenly to me it was a threatening hazard. I could not see how I could avoid hitting the cable as I jumped, without registering in my mind that the others had not hit it as they jumped. As I got into position on the edge of the hole, as directed by the dispatcher, I realized I was in a funk. I wriggled: 'Not comfortable, Sir?' he asked. 'No I'm not. It's the harness I think.' 'OK get yourself right' – he knew what was happening – 'You've plenty of time, Sir. Just take your time. Get comfortable . . . GO!!' It was automatic. It justified all the training. I went. I was out into the rushing air waiting, panic-stricken again, for the tug which would tell me I did not have a 'candle'. But that blessed dispatcher had not only spared me a ghastly embarrassment, but had also repaired my damaged morale.

On terra firma, after I had rolled my 'chute and after his basket arrived down, I went over to thank him. He had kept me in the Parachute Regiment. He took it very much as a routine matter. 'That's all right, Sir. We've seen it before. Most people get one sometime.' Though he thought little of it, that exchange did not adequately express my gratitude: I knew he had rescued me. Those dispatchers and instructors were absolutely magnificent. They were tough, determined, energetic; their apparent ruthlessness was applied with a lot of instinctive, gut psychology. They filled us with confidence and a lot of necessary aggression. They were on our side.

As we proceeded through the series of balloon jumps our confidence increased by leaps and bounds. As I see it now from a great distance, we became arrogantly confident in the Mess and went with an arrogant swagger into Manchester when we were given the evening pass that enabled us to look for relaxation, necessarily involving beer and attractive company. The Mancunians did not let us down. They were very tolerant of us. We made ourselves prominent in their pubs, which they could have resented, but did not. We drank lots of beer and boastfully sang our Para Regiment songs that conveyed the myth that we didn't care. In fairness the wonderfully friendly, unpretentious 'locals' encouraged us and cheered us on, and the ladies were very friendly.

But, back at the 'ranch' I noticed during our programme of jumps that one of my 'stick' seemed to be a very reluctant jumper. Did I have a potential 'jibber', a refusal that could raise doubts in others' minds? The possibility of a jibber had to be reported immediately so that he could be watched and if he did refuse to jump action could be taken quickly without fuss and without blame. No stain on the individual's record. It could happen to anyone So I had to watch this man's reactions to each jump. It was not a pleasant thing to have to do, and not easy. It had to be done without raising worries.

My first night jump from the balloon was appalling. I had no trouble exiting; that marvellous instructor had seen me over that trouble. But in the descent on a pitch-black night I did not know where I was, could not see the ground or the direction of my

86

approach. 'Never reach for the ground,' they said. 'Just relax'. Easier said than done when trying to find out where the ground was. I did reach for it and came in very hard on the left when I had prepared for a side right! I was convinced I had damaged my leg, but hadn't. It was several minutes before I got my breath back. 'What sort of landing do you call that?' inquired the instructor from somewhere in the darkness. I did not answer. I was glad I could not see him, and I expect he was glad too; after asking such an insulting question I would have hit him.

So we came to the aircraft jumps. The theory was that they were less scary than the balloon jumps. That is to say less scary for ordinary mortals who normally get very scared. Some idiots, like the instructors, actually enjoyed parachuting, whether from balloon or aircraft, and piled up a huge score of jumps. And today, of course, there are lots of mad people who do it for sport. But what we were trying to jump out of then without injuring ourselves were old Whitley bombers ('one hundred thousand rivets in flight formation', someone said) with holes in the floor of the fuselage from which hung something like a steel dustbin.

The intention was, as with the balloon, that you sit on the edge of the hole with your legs dangling in the 'dustbin', having already clipped your static line to the overhead rail, keeping one eye on the light in the roof of the fuselage which will turn green when it is OK to launch yourself, straight as a ramrod, into the 'dustbin'. You focus the other eye on the instructor crouching on the other side of the hole holding his hand in a kind of 'halt' positions, who will drop his hand and shout 'GO' as the green light comes on. The trick of the manoeuvre, as with the balloon, was to go so straight through the exit aperture. Failure to go straight through, without the chute on your back thrusting you forward, was more dire than in the balloon. Hitting your face on the steel dustbin was known as 'ringing the bell' because of the melodious sound it made. But the broken nose or split lips that resulted were less enjoyable.

The main difference between jumping from a stationary balloon and a moving aircraft, we were told, was that you experienced no 'dead drop' exiting from an aircraft. As soon as you were out you were in the slipstream which quickly filled your chute as soon as it was unfurled. No dreaded s . . . moment. But the downside was that, you were immediately swinging from side to side in a strong oscillation which had to be corrected by pulling on the parachute webs on the appropriate sides, if you could remember which ones did what, while you tried to get your bearings and estimate your speed and direction of descent.

It was during the 'plane jumps that my fears of having a jibber in my stick increased. Across this span of years I cannot remember his name. I shall call him Ken. He was a stolid sort of fellow, very quiet and seldom joined in the ragging or the boasting. But during the first three of our plane jumps, which I had grown to accept as something we needed to learn to do properly, but not to like, as some claimed, I noticed that whichever number in the stick he jumped there was a long gap between the man who jumped before him and his own exit. This would be bad in operations because the aim was to land as closely together as possible to give each other protection and to move off quickly as a unit. Why was he hesitant? He couldn't be having a 'panic jump' each time, could he? Was he likely to 'jib' on some crucial occasion? I remembered that in battle training he had always been the one we had to encourage along so that we completed tests as a platoon.

I remembered that he froze half-way up a cliff when we were scaling it by rope and I remembered that on the battle exercise carried out under live-round shooting he always had his backside dangerously high. So I decided to discuss my worries with the instructor/dispatcher. We decided that on the next jump we would put him as number one on one side of the exit hole and me as number two opposite him on the other side of the hole. (The exit 'dustbin' in the floor of the Whitley was more or less in the centre of the fuse-lage. Half the 'stick', or platoon, sat forward of it, the other half sat aft and each man shuffled, seated and pulling his clipped-up static line with him, towards the hole as his colleagues jumped alternately from the forward and aft edges of the hole.)

So, on the next jump Ken was nominated number one and sat imme-diately forward of the closed exit hatch. I sat, as number two, opposite him on the aft side. We took off from Ringway airfield and circled to gain height before making for the DZ (dropping zone) at Tatton Park. There was little light inside the fuselage, we just sat and waited, trying to imagine how we were making our approach. Then the cry 'running in' came from the dispatcher, meaning we were approaching the DZ, and proceeded to open the hatch covering the exit hole. Immediately the fuselage above the 'dustbin' was filled with a ghostly green light, the reflection from the countryside below. I had not noticed it on previous occasions as I had been farther back in the stick.

1. The beach at Dunkirk, May 1940, during a lull in the air raids.

2. The author's patrol in the Morvan region of central France, 1944. *Left to right:* Bill Craig, 'Boy' Borrie, the author, Dick Higham, Chris Tilling, 'Woody' Woodford, Johnny 'Barongelle', 'Smudger' Smith.

3. The 'liberation' of Châtillon-en-Bazois after a successful ambush, 1944. The author is beside the guns of his jeep with flowers on the back and surrounded by the people believing, mistakenly, that they had been liberated.

4. An interlude near base camp at Chalaux, Morvan, central France, August 1944. *Left to right:* Bill Craig, children from the village, Chris Tilling, the author, Paulette, who, on her bicycle, carried messages between the SAS and the Maquis groups Bernard and Camille.

5. The graves of the twenty-two male citizens of the small town of Dun-les-Places who were shot by the Germans in reprisal for Maquis and SAS activity.

6. Corporal Johnny 'Barongelle' with the cousin he went to find in Paris on an amusing 'out-of-bounds' visit to Paris before the entry of Charles de Gaulle in 1944.

7. Fraser Mcluskey,
wartime Chaplain to
the 1st SAS Regiment,
now the Very Rev. Dr.
J. Fraser Mcluskey,
MC, MA, BD, DD.
*(By kind permission of
Dr Mcluskey.)*

8. Paddy Mayne: Lt. Col Blair Mayne, DSO and 3 bars, Legion d'Honneur, Croix de
Guerre, CO Special Raiding Squadron 1943, CO 1st SAS Regiment 1943-45.
(By kind permission of Mrs Fiona Ferguson, née Mayne.)

9. The author *(centre)* and Major Harry Poat, *(right)*, second-in-command, 1st SAS, listen to Major Bill Fraser's account of an operation, Antwerp, 1944.

10. Ahead of the armour, temporarily surrounded and under fire in a forest near Coppenburg during the advance into Germany in 1945. Paddy Mayne is leaning against a tree on the right.

11. The well-tended cemetery of the Maquis Bernard in the forest above Ouroux, Morvan. The graves are of Maquisards killed in battle and the crew of an RAF bomber shot down in the area.

12. The SAS Brigade Memorial at Sennecy-le-Grand, bearing the names of 515 members of the British 1st and 2nd SAS, French 3rd and 4th SAS, and Belgian 5th SAS killed in behind-the-lines operations in France.

13. In the open, unarmed and happy. The author *(right)* with Captain Pat Riley in north-west Germany on 6 May 1945, the day after the end of the European War.

14. Disbanded! The 'farewell' parade of the 1st and 2nd SAS Regiments at Hylands House, Chelmsford, October 1945. Brigadier Calvert, CO SAS Brigade, takes the salute. Behind him are Lt. Col Mayne, CO 1st SAS, and Lt. Col Franks, CO 2nd SAS. *(By kind permission of the Special Air Service Regimental Association.)*

15. Germany, 1945. A scene typical of the destruction wrought by the Allies.

16. The memorial to Colonel Sir David Stirling, DSO, OBE, founder of the Special Air Service Regiment, at Keir near Dunblane, Stirling, Scotland.

I looked across at Ken's face. 'God, Ken. You look terrible. It puts me off, looking at you.'

'Well,' he replied, 'it puts me off looking at you,' just as the dispatcher shouted 'Go!' and out he went and I had to follow immediately. He never did 'jib' and later he, together with others of us, volunteered for the SAS. There, too, he was always slow on cross-country training; he was someone we always had to help. Yet between cursing him as a burden, I couldn't help admiring his determination. Unfortunately, during one of the SAS training exercises he broke his arm and never returned to us from hospital. I suspect he might have felt badly about missing out on something he clearly wanted to do, but on the other hand for the rest of us it may have been a blessing in disguise.

Apart from one episode in the Mess between jumps the rest of our training passed off without incident. It concerned Ed Mycock, with whom I became very friendly; we joined the SAS together and we remain regularly in touch to this day. It occurred after a morning jump when we were, as usual, boasting about our perfect exits and side rights when a loud-voiced colleague shouted, 'I say, did any of you see Mycock caught up in the rigging?' A fair question because Ed had made a rather messy exit, but that was not how it sounded to everyone around, including the charming WAAF who nearly dropped the meal she was about to serve and rushed out, pink and laughing.

In case I have given the impression that by this time I was a competent parachutist who took jumping as a matter-of-fact activity, let me record that during the 'plane jumps I did two appalling night jumps that hurt my calf muscles and seemed to jerk my insides into a different position. And I still regard the practice of hurling yourself into space from a balloon or aircraft 800 feet or so up in the air, much higher these days for those who think it's fun to delay opening the 'chute until the last safe moment, relying only on an area of silk rolled up by someone you don't know, as quite ridiculously stupid.

Nonetheless, we completed the course and all the training and felt really proud when we were presented ceremoniously with our Parachute Regiment Wings and hurried away afterwards to sew them onto the shoulder of our tunics. That evening in Manchester, in uniform with the wings prominent, walking almost sideways, shoulder well forward, there was much partying with the tolerant and understanding citizens of that city. I'm sure that at some stage or other each of us gave thanks to the drill sergeants, the instructors, for battle training and parachute training, and to the understanding dispatchers for getting us there. With their help we had crossed a threshold in self-discipline, pride, military confidence and aggression.

Our next destination was to the Parachute Regiment Holding Company, to await a posting to one of the Battalions. Which?

7

Training with the SAS

During our para training Ed and Tom Bryce, who, far from being a dour Scot, had, we discovered, a delightful, dry sense of humour, and I formed a kind of friendly triumvirate. For a couple of days at the Holding Company there was little to do but a few formal parades in between which we speculated about which battalion we would be posted to and what role we might be given. Then there appeared on the notice board a statement that the Special Air Service Regiment was expanding in preparation for the forthcoming invasion of Europe and was seeking volunteers. Major Harry Poat, DSO, MC, second-in-command of the 1st SAS Regiment, would come to the company the following day to talk about the work of the SAS and meet any volunteers. There had already been a lot of publicity about the raids led by Colonel David Stirling and then by Colonel Blair 'Paddy' Mayne and their exploits operating behind enemy lines in the Western Desert. The three of us talked about it and decided to go and hear more.

There were a score or more waiting in the Canteen to listen to what the second-in-command had to say about the Regiment's future role in the liberation of Europe. The Major Poat we met that morning was a very smart soldier with an impressive bearing. Yet it was in easy and relaxed terms and with much quiet humour that he described the development of the SAS from the original 'L Detachment', drawn mainly from the Commandos, working with the Long Range Desert Group in the Western Desert, to its Regimental status. He spoke of the highly successful raids on enemy airfields and installations by small groups penetrating deep into enemy territory, commanded by David Stirling, until he was captured on a raid at the far western end of Libya close to the Mareth Line, which barred the Eighth Army's way into Tunisia, to join up with the First Army, then by Paddy Mayne who had already won two DSOs. He went on to explain the need to expand to Brigade strength comprising the two British regiments and the French and Belgian battalions as regiments in order to continue its role in the forthcoming invasion. There was no flamboyance or bravado in his talk. His descriptions of actions they had fought were quite matter-of-fact. After answering a few questions, he simply said that anyone who might want to volunteer should turn up the following day to be interviewed by the CO, Colonel Mayne.

Harry Poat, as we knew him later, is one of the unsung heroes of the SAS. At that time of expansion, the 'originals', experienced in the unusual, self-disciplined environment of raiding operations in the war in the Western Desert, had to adapt to the acceptance of 'newcomers' and learn to be part of a larger and more formal military formation, Harry Poat's quiet attention to regimental detail in support of the temperamentally different Paddy Mayne was crucial. Yet he was also a brave and resourceful SAS soldier, as his decorations showed. Similarly, though in a much more important context, Paddy Mayne's legendary successes in the Western Desert after David Stirling's capture ensured the acceptance by the British Army, for the time being, of the value of that type of warfare and ultimately, after a thoughtless break, the continuation of the SAS Regiment. But I am getting ahead of myself.

That evening over a drink or two the three of us, Ed Mycock, Tom Bryce and myself, discussed whether or not we wished to volunteer. I think what we had heard made us even more incredulous of what the Regiment, small in numbers, had already done. But at the same time we were impressed by Harry Poat's level-headed account of those achievements in Sicily and Italy as well as in the Western Desert as part of an important strategy. He clearly believed that the role allocated to the Regiment in the invasion of Europe would provide opportunities for a more extensive use of small-group raids to disrupt enemy lines of communication and installations.

We were definitely interested, but told ourselves (unnecessarily, I think) that we needed to think more about how it might work in a European countryside – the need for good cover, the degree of mobility needed, the types of targets, the likely strength of the enemy, and so on. It was on our way back to the Mess that the questions were answered. We were walking along a lane with fields on either side. Beyond the fields were woods. I said, 'How do we know whether there are enemy parachutists hidden there? Unlikely so near a military depot, but even so. And if there was such a fear how long would it take to scour both woods?' 'And,' said Ed, 'if the garrison were even farther away, the chances of being caught would be much less.' The die was cast.

But for me – I don't know about the others – the die had been cast much earlier. The appeal of the excitement, and belief in the effectiveness of guerrilla warfare in support of a main strategy, born from my reading of the Boer War and the Spanish conflict (the lessons from which were ignored by our High Command, just as they seemed to take little notice of the use by Germany and Italy of that insurgence as a dress rehearsal for their invasion of the low countries and France) and my reading of *For Whom The Bell Tolls*, meant that the SAS was my, perhaps romantic, answer to worries about doing too little while others were fighting. It had been an unforeseen but probably fated route from Algeria and a visit to the Parachute Regiment in the Atlas Mountains to the Special Air Service Regiment.

Next morning the three of us returned to the canteen to meet the legendary Paddy Mayne, DSO and bar. There was no recruiting talk. He simply wanted to interview personally those who had decided to volunteer. As Ed, Tom and I had decided we would like to serve together in this, to us, new role, I was deputed to be last to be interviewed and to tell Mayne that if he was not prepared to accept us all, none of us would wish to serve!

I went in and saluted smartly as befitted a 'qualified' Paratroop officer. This huge man was seated awkwardly behind a table. 'Good morning. Sit down, Mr Close,' he said softly in his Ulster brogue. He asked questions about my background in the war, especially about how I felt on the road to Dunkirk and on the beaches. And then came the inevitable 'Why the SAS?' I murmured something about the strategic value of guerrilla war, the lessons of Spain and the proven value of the SAS's small-group raids. Rightly, he was quite unmoved by this prepared response but did not challenge it. It was then that I put our request. We would all hope to be accepted, or none of us. I think he smiled a little, then said (I remember it well), 'So, it's giving the Commanding Officer an ultimatum already, is it?' I stuttered something about not meaning it like that, just that we were friends. 'Very well' he said, 'I'll bear it in mind.' I saluted and went out feeling very embarrassed.

Outside Ed and Tom were waiting rather anxiously. 'We've blown it,' I said and described Mayne's reaction to our request. After a brief discussion we concluded that we were individually keen to join and that it had been a mistake to ask for 'three or none'. It was now likely to prejudice the chances of each of us individually. I was deputed to ask to go back in and apologize and say we would each take our chances. When I was admitted the second time, giving an even smarter salute, Paddy Mayne said, 'Another ultimatum?' I tried to explain, with apologies, our change of mind as showing individual keenness to join. 'Thank you,' he said. 'I'll bear that in mind also.'

We left feeling very depressed and rather ashamed that we had made such a stupid error. So, it was with surprise that a few days' later we saw on the notice board in the Depot that we had all three been accepted. We were entitled to a week's leave before reporting to Darvel in Ayrshire where the Regiment was re-grouping and training for its role in the invasion of Europe. To this day I do not know whether it was because we had the nerve to ask him for an 'all or none' decision or because we had the courtesy to apologize that Paddy Mayne agreed to take us all. Whichever it was, we were grateful and encouraged.

I'm sure I enjoyed my week's leave, but I remember nothing about it. I do remember being keen to get to Scotland to join my new Regiment. Perhaps too keen, because, coming straight from my Parachute Regiment training, I think when I got there I reeked a bit too much of 'bullshit' for the relaxed yet quietly understood discipline of the SAS. It was early evening when I arrived at Kilmarnock station dressed in a smart, freshly pressed battledress with tie and perfectly blancoed gaiters and belt with gleaming polished brass. A truck was waiting for me. I was surprised to see that the driver was a fellow subaltern, who greeted me with a friendly smile and a quizzical glance at my smart turnout. He asked if I had had a comfortable journey, which I hadn't but did not say so, and suggested dropping me at the Orderly Office so that I could report to the Adjutant.

Darvel is a village in the Irvine valley in Ayrshire, surrounded by Scottish hills not far from Kilmarnock and Irvine. It had one main street and little else. The area had been chosen for the re-formation of the Regiment and its expansion to Brigade strength, and for training opportunities in the rolling hills. The original formation became the 1st SAS Regiment under the command of 'Paddy' Mayne. A second formation, also fresh from North Africa, which became the 2nd SAS Regiment, commanded, first by Lieut. Col. 'Bill' Stirling and later Lieut. Col. Brian Franks, was located near by. A regiment comprised three or four squadrons, commanded by majors, each of two troops, commanded by captains, each comprising two or three sections commanded by subalterns. These, together with a Belgian Squadron, which became the Belgian SAS Regiment, two French regiments, and a squadron of 'Phantoms' (GHQ Reconnaissance Regiment) who took care of our signals requirements, formed the new SAS Brigade. It was charged with the familiar task of carrying out raids behind enemy lines in occupied Europe, in very different territory and conditions from those familiar to 'originals' and 'newcomers' alike. The first CO of the Brigade was Brigadier R.W. McLeod, (later General Sir Roderick McLeod). Our training was to be carried out over the hills, across the moors and around the towns of this part of Scotland.

The decision to expand the Regiment in this way was a tribute to the Regiment's successes in the Western Desert, Sicily and Italy. High Command's acceptance at that time of these SAS types of operation was epitomized by a striking commendation from General Dempsey, CO of 13 Corps in the Middle East, after the operations in Sicily. He said, as has been reported in other accounts of the Regiment's exploits: 'You were originally lent to me for the first operation, that of Capo Murro di Porco. That was a brilliant operation, brilliantly planned and brilliantly carried out. Your orders were to capture and destroy a coastal battery, but you did more . . . You went on to capture two more batteries and a very large number of prisoners. Then came Bagnara and finally Termoli . . . In all my military career, and in my time I have commanded many units, I have never met a unit in which I had such confidence as I have in yours.'

He included in other comments at that time his reasons for the SAS success:

'First, you take your training seriously . . . which has always impressed me.

Secondly, you are well disciplined . . . you maintain a standard of discipline and cleanliness which is good to see.

Thirdly, you are physically fit.

Fourthly, you are completely confident in your own abilities.
Fifthly, despite that confidence, you plan carefully.
Last of all you have the right spirit, which I hope you will pass on to those who may join you in the future.'

This was the regiment I was joining; my comrades would be, for the most part, people who had performed such deeds. How would they react to newcomers?

When I was taken to the Regimental Headquarters in a large Victorian house at the end of a long drive the Adjutant checked my papers and suggested I report to the Colonel right away; he would be in the bar having a pre-dinner drink, then added, 'See the Quatermaster tomorrow and get a Regimental beret and cap badge.' So it was 'goodbye red beret, hello beige ditto; farewell Parachute Regiment, hello SAS.' But the Parachute wings stayed on the shoulder of my uniform, at least until I could earn my SAS wings by completing a successful operation, which could then be proudly worn on the left breast.

It was not difficult to find the bar in the Mess. I just had to walk into the hotel. I would have found it by the direction of chattering voices and laughter emerging from an open door along the hall. I went in. In the half-light I could see a crowd of officers with glasses in their hands, talking and drinking. Several looked round; one broke away and came over. It was the one who had met me.

'Ah, you've made it. Come and meet the Colonel.' He led me over to a corner of the bar where this huge man was leaning on it with one elbow, surveying the scene. He was dressed in battledress with tie, but my eyes focused for a moment on the medal and decoration ribbons across his left breast. He had already won a bar to his DSO.

'Paddy this is . . . er . . . Lieut . . . er . . . er . . .' I volunteered my name to help him out.

He looked at me silently for a moment, then, 'Ah yes, the sassenach who gave the CO an ultimatum about whom he should recruit.' His memory was embarrassingly good, 'Welcome to the Regiment.'

'Thank you, sir. I'm sorry that . . .'

He ignored my attempted apology. 'Have a drink.'

'A beer please, Sir.'

He gave me what I thought was a pitying look.

'A sassenach drink,' he muttered. Then over his shoulder to the steward, 'A pint please, Corporal.'

I raised the tankard to my lips. 'Thank you, sir. Cheers.' I took a mouthful and went to put it back on the counter. 'Come on man knock it back. Cheers,' and he swallowed his whisky in one.

I could see I was being tested. I drew on all my limited experience of beer-drinking, opened my throat and poured it down.

'Another pint, Corporal,' I heard him say in his soft brogue. I was conscious that the conversation among the other officers had become notably quieter and many faces were turned in our direction. The pint appeared, together with another glass of whisky. This was it. I drew more deeply on past binges, drew a deep breath, gulped it down without a pause and banged the tankard down on the counter (not in defiance, but because I wasn't sure where it was). I then tried to concentrate all my muscles on ensuring my stomach would not throw it all back.

'Good man,' the Colonel said, smiling. 'You drink well. Are you a strong man?' I was bit nonplussed. 'I . . . I . . . er . . . think so, Sir.'

'Good. Try this.'

He picked up one of the crinkled metal tops of a tonic bottle from the counter. He held it between the thumb and first finger of his large right hand and squashed it! Another test and I knew I was on a loser. I picked up another bottle top and put it between the fingers of one hand, brought another hand in to help, in fact tried everything except stamping on it to flatten the disk No use. I looked up at him shamefully and was relieved to see a kindly, amused look in his eyes.

'It doesn't matter. I expect your fighting is better than your strength. Come in and join me at dinner.'

We had a quiet, unchallenging discussion. He had such a soft voice. I remember he asked me what I thought of my parachute training – exhausting, exciting – and about the 1940 breakthrough and Dunkirk – outgunned, disastrous. 'It'll be different this time,' he said before turning to talk to others. From that moment we had an appropriate CO-subaltern relationship. As with his other officers, and his Warrant Officers and NCOs, it was unstrained. In a curious way we were like a self-disciplined family of which he was the head. My lasting respect for Paddy Mayne began at that moment.

Of course it was there that I, and other 'newcomers', met as colleagues the officers and men who had already performed great deeds in the operations in the Middle East campaigns; Major Bill Fraser, MC and bar; Major Tony Marsh, who won a DSO at Termoli, aged 21, and was Mentioned in Dispatches, who became my

Squadron Commander. He was a very youthful, fair-haired, good-looking man who had a relaxed, friendly manner of command, which was much respected by all who served with him. For me it was rather like working with a friend. He survived the war but sadly suffered a fatal heart attack in the fifties, dying far too young.

There were also the remarkable Captain Johnny Cooper, MC, DCM, who served with the Regiment after the war, Captain Pat Riley, DCM, who as an NCO brought a group of men safely back to base across the desert in North Africa and was commissioned in the field, Captain Derek Harrison, who was to win an MC in France and who became my Troop Commander, Major Mike Sadler, MC, MM, who joined the Regiment from the Long Range Desert Group and was David Stirling's and Paddy Mayne's star navigator in the Western Desert, CSM Jim (Gentleman Jim) Almonds, MM and bar (later commissioned in the field), CSM Reg Seekings, DCM, MM, CSM Bob Lilley, MM, BEM, and the legendary Sergeant–Major Bob Bennett, MM, BEM, Greek War Cross. Many of them had served in 'L' Detachment with David Stirling in the Middle East. They, together with the many NCOs and men who wore ribbons on their tunics, were as noble a group of men you could meet anywhere. One could not fail to be impressed by them and admire their quiet (except at Mess parties) dignity, and with them in the environment of shared action one could not fail to form friendships that lasted well into the post-war years.

And of course, there was the highly decorated Commanding Officer himself. Paddy won his first DSO when he was a Lieutenant in the original 'L' Detachment, SAS, in 1942; his second was won in Sicily in 1943 for his part in the raid at Capo Murro di Porco in Sicily and in the capture of Augusta. The second bar was to come later for his work with the Regiment in France, crossing into enemy territory many times and for which he was also awarded the Legion d' Honneur and Croix de Guerre. The third bar to his DSO was won in Germany, as I was to see for myself. Much has been written about Paddy Mayne, some of it good, some nonsense.* But to those who served with him he was a brave and tireless leader with a quick, clear tactical brain, loved and admired by the men whose safety was his great concern.

---

* The best biography, in my opinion, is *Paddy Mayne: Lt. Col. Blair 'Paddy' Mayne, 1 SAS Regiment* by Hamish Ross, Sutton Publishing.

It was obvious that, with such a wealth of battle-hardened experience, there could have been a gulf between the 'originals' and the 'newcomers' which would have been disastrous. One of the key tasks at Darvel was to turn this larger, reinforced unity into an integrated regiment, the members of which respected each other and shared the very special SAS *esprit de corps*. For those of the 'newcomers' who had seen action there was no feeling of embarrassment; we admired what the 'originals' had done and at the same time we could share our own different experiences. (It was interesting that I met there a former Guardsman, Sergeant-Major Feebry, DCM, who was in the trenches defending the perimeter of Dunkirk when I and colleagues had passed through, handing them our guns and ammunition.)

For those who had not seen action, but were anxious to do so, it might have been more difficult. But it was not. The 'originals' had been alerted to the dangers of a divided regiment and were as keen as the 'newcomers' to integrate. It worked. We integrated and shared a good-humoured camaraderie, a great contribution to which was the 'newcomers' recognition that past successes had been based on determination, initiative and flexibility, and that the Regiment's relaxed but strict code of discipline was based on mutual respect and confidence. There was no great show of rank or authority, but once the unit structure had been established and individual roles assigned, the necessary disciplines followed naturally. Once everyone was engaged in the tough SAS training schedules, famously developed and extended to greater limits of endurance by the Regiment today across the hills and moors of Scotland, the words 'original' and 'newcomer' disappeared from our vocabulary.

That training was, of course, another key task of our stay at Darvel. It was aimed at teaching us to find our way over long distances across strange country unobserved by day and night, carrying heavy rucksacks on our backs, without leaving obvious trails, to do that using only map and compass when we had no knowledge of our starting point, to lie up concealed over a long period observing a target and withdrawing under cover, to practice jumping by day and night with containers of equipment, following 'dropping zone' procedures to ensure rapid and stealthy clearance of the zone. We had been allocated the men with whom we would be operating, sections of nine men, so necessarily we carried out the training as teams.

The 'drill' for the cross-country 'orienteering' was that early in the morning we were driven in the back of a sealed three-ton truck to an unidentified destination (a long way from Darvel to judge by the time spent in the truck) in the midst of a vast area of moorland. We were told that we had to get to a certain map reference by 1800 hrs without being 'caught' by the enemy, in this case other colleagues whose task was to capture as many groups as possible. We had heavy packs, a few rations, a map and a compass. Obviously the problem was that we didn't know where we were starting from. Consequently we had to spend valuable time trying to recognize nearby features on the map. Once done, the next problem was to plan a route that could afford us maximum cover, even though it may have been longer. Apart from the test of map-reading and concealed approach to a target, if a secondary test was to take us to the edge of our stamina it succeeded!

Night exercises were similarly conducted, with the added complication that once dropped we had to 'orientate' ourselves and check our position *en route* by shielded torchlight. In three of these exercises my section was 'caught' twice, but only when we were almost 'home'. Naturally I protested about the unenterprising tactics of 'defenders' sitting waiting near the target! My protest was met with a smile, a shrug and 'Perhaps the enemy will do that. Bear it in mind. But you did quite well.'

I remain embarrassed about my incompetence on one exercise when we were transported to a very distant point on the moors and given a target, but we were also required to experiment with a method of improving the way we could 'live off the land' by having a decent roast meal! We were given a small cube of (reconstituted?) meat, a small potato, to which we were meant to add nettle leaves, dandelion leaves, as green vegetables, and cook them as a roast Sunday lunch. How? By finding a grass-covered bank, of which there were many in the moorland north of Darvel, and cutting a circle of turf from the side, scraping out a small cavity, being careful to distribute the soil so that it would not be seen, light a fire inside, being careful to ensure no smoke became visible, place the mess tin inside and replace the circular sod so that a casual walker would not be alerted. We could then go about our observations and return to a hearty meal. But I had a problem. I could not find the green bank in which my dinner was cooking. Full marks for concealment perhaps, but none for orienteering and none for ability to organize an up-market meal while living off the land. That mess tin containing

100

a roast dinner is still there somewhere in those Scottish moors waiting for a hungry traveller.

Training also included parachute exercises and practicing dropping zone procedures. Apart from keeping 'our hand in' with jumping, so to speak, we experimented with new ideas of jumping with the weapons and equipment we would immediately need, rather having them dropped in separate containers and then spending valuable time searching for them and unloading them on a DZ in occupied territory.

This new idea was to pack the weapons, etc, in kind of 'kit-bag' which would be attached to our belts by a long cord and then strapped to one of our legs. Once out of the aircraft and floating safely under the silk canopy, we would release the bag from our legs and bale them out to the extent of the attaching cord, about twenty feet. It was an interesting experience: parachute above, heavy weapons bag below and us in the middle. We immediately recognized two advantages: the bag stabilized the descending oscillation and, as it hit the ground, telling us where we were, it reduced the weight of the descent causing the 'chute to 'breathe' and slow the final few feet. We were jumping from Albemarles which were short of space inside the fuselage, but at least we could stand up and hobble along to the larger exit with the 'kit-bag' strapped to one leg. On the whole those exercises were successful; we not only liked the idea of having our equipment with us when we jumped, but also got used to managing the descent.

The exercises were designed to train us in appropriate dropping-zone drill, bearing in mind we would be dropping into occupied territory at night onto a DZ marked out by members of the Maquis who would be as anxious as we would be to act quietly and quickly, clearing the DZ of any signs of activity and move off even more quickly. On one of these exercises, carried out in daylight but simulating a night-time 'drop', the difference between a Parachute Regiment landing and an SAS landing was starkly illustrated. Our descent and landing on the specified DZ was being observed not only by our own 'top brass' but also by other senior officers and officials. When my stick, and another, landed exactly where designated, our equipment kit-bags within reach, we quietly slipped out of our parachute harnesses and began to roll up our parachutes and take them with our kit-bags into nearby trees.

However, a senior Parachute Regiment officer observing the exercise clearly had not been properly briefed. He ran towards us shouting, 'What are you waiting for? At the double. Get your weapons and deploy your men in all-round defence formation. Indicate the direction of the enemy – enemy 12 o'clock or enemy 3 o'clock.' We heard him and looked at him, rather sadly I think, and carried on quietly folding up our 'chutes. I saw one of our senior officers take the man by the arm and lead him a little way off and whisper in his ear. Nothing more was said and the only reaction came from one of my men who asked pointedly but with little tact, 'Who was that twit?'

On other occasions we were taken to a power station to be shown where to place the explosives for maximum damage and to a railway siding to see how to do maximum damage to sets of points; we also learned how to drive a steam train, should we need to capture one.

Then there were more 'official' exercises that involved the Home Guard, training battalions in the locality, police and Fire Brigades. In these exercises we had to penetrate all defence formations in order to reach and destroy a specific target within a time limit, all of which had to be carried out according to 'exercise rules' and under the supervision of military referees.

I remember vividly the one set for my section. Our objective was the Police Station in the centre of Kilmarnock which, for the purpose of the exercise, was an enemy-occupied town with a radio transmitter in the Police Station that had to be put out of action. The rules of the exercise allowed for the killing of protagonists on either side by pointing a weapon (unloaded, of course) and saying something like (I forget the exact mantra) 'exercise blankety blank; you're dead.' As usual we were taken out early in the morning in covered trucks and dropped we knew not where, with maps and compass. We had to attack our target that night, so we needed plenty of time to 'recce' our route into the town.Fortunately it did not take long to discover where we were. Having taken a good look at the topography to assure ourselves that our approach, if we were careful, would be concealed from the 'enemy', we set off.

It took several hours of cautious approach work before we found in the late afternoon a spot from which we could observe the entries to the town and the coming and goings. From my point of view there was a downside: the midges. I was, and still am, very suscep-tible to insect bites. By the time nightfall came all exposed parts were their feeding ground. The irritation was maddening. As we got ready to move in, having identified a road that would lead to the Police Station, but which we could access by a roundabout route, my Sergeant looked at me and exclaimed, 'My god, Sir. Your face is awful!'

'I think I could put you on a fizzer for that Sergeant,' I replied, trying to smile.

'Yes, Sir.' he replied, grinning.

Moving slowly and quietly, we went down from our position and entered the town as it got dark. We took a circuitous route of back streets that we knew from our observations would take us close to our target. There was no opposition. Perhaps the 'enemy' had not sufficiently studied, if at all, SAS methods. Or they had decided to let us get to the point where we would have to make our final 'attack'. Certainly we knew we would have to get into the main road to force an entry into the Police Station and then we would be vulnerable. But so far all was well and as we approached the main road from the last side street before the Police Station we hid in someone's front garden to see if we could identify where their guards were positioned. Wait and watch is a good maxim. It is very difficult for a guard to keep quite still for a long time. Sooner or later he must scratch his nose, ease a cramp, look round, or something. After several minutes our patience was rewarded. We detected a movement under a hedge in the Police Station's own front area. Was there another? We waited. Yes there was, on one side of the main entrance.

Now we knew how to make our final assault. We would have to rush the building; there was no way we could sneak in. My Sergeant, with two men, would concentrate on 'eliminating' the two guards while I, with the others, carrying parcels of plastic explosive without detonators, would charge through them to the inside office, wherever that would be, and simulate the destruction of the alleged transmitter and anyone else who was around. Simple plans are the best, we thought.

After taking another careful look, as well as we could in the dark, to check where we had seen the hidden guards, I looked round to see if everyone was ready, tapped my Sergeant on the shoulder, crept out of our front garden 'observation post' and moved, crouching, alongside the low wall towards the entrance to the Police Station about twenty yards away. I raised my arm, instantly we stood and rushed the target brandishing our Colt '45s, unloaded of course. I saw my Sergeant and two men make for the guards shouting the exercise 'mantra' proving they were no longer operative. I headed straight into the Station, past a reception desk, disposing in the same way of the officer behind it, and headed down a corridor towards what I guessed would be an inner office. Suddenly, in front of me there loomed a huge figure in Police-blue uniform. I pointed my '45 at him; 'Blankety blank exercise, you're dead'.

'Och no I'm not, laddie. You're for the lock up,' he said and swung a large-fisted right hook in my direction. I managed to turn my head from the blow, but it caught me on the shoulder and bowled me over. As I scrambled to my feet I quickly changed my hold on my '45, held it by the barrel and, lifting my arm, threatened the zealous Sergeant with the butt end as two of my men rushed forward and pinned him against the wall.

'You don't want play by the rules of the exercise? That's OK by us. Now take me to the officer in charge of the station or I'll use this on you. The rest of you go through the building and deal with any one else under the rules.' My own Sergeant, having 'killed' the two guards, arrived by this time and said, 'OK , Sir let me deal with him.' The Police Sergeant looked at him, then at the men holding him and then at my raised automatic. 'All right. This way.'

He led us down the corridor to an office where two of my men were already pointing '45s at the officer behind the desk.

'What's all this?'

'I assume you know the rules of the exercise?' He nodded.

'Your Sergeant ignored them.' I went on to explain what had happened and pointed out that, whereas we would have dealt with his men, planted our 'explosive charge' and begun our withdrawal, now we could not. 'We must ring the Referee and get a ruling. It's important for my men. I have his number and so do you.' After some argument he agreed, picked up the telephone and dialled the number. As the one who had a complaint I insisted on speaking first. I explained the situation from my perspective, then handed the 'phone to the Inspector and heard a few reluctant confirmations. The 'phone came back and the ruling was that our assault on our target had been successful and we should have begun withdrawing without opposition, so we were to be given ten minutes to withdraw before the Police notified the defending forces of our whereabouts.

Given their performance so far, I did not trust the Police, but agreed. We shook hands and I walked out of the Station with my section quite openly and down the road. Bearing in mind that this elaborate exercise was meant to indicate how good we were at our job, I paused to reassure my comrades that the 'cock up' was not their fault. They had done everything required of them skilfully and properly.

'We'll walk to the end of the road, then we have to find a hidden way out. We're supposed to get back to base safely, but after what happened, they'll soon be after us.' I was walking beside one of my corporals. 'Very unfair all that, Sir. Still I hope the Inspector doesn't put his hat on too soon.' I was another few paces on before I realized there could be trouble in what he had said.

'What the hell do you mean?'

'Just a plastic visiting card, Sir.'

It was a moment or two before I realized what he meant. 'Get into a garden and wait,' I said as I turned and ran back to the Station and, passing a couple of policemen, straight into the Inspector's office. Not surprisingly he was and looked astonished. 'What the hell? You're supposed to be on your way.'

'It's just that I've been talking to my troops and, although we were very angry, we want you to know there's no ill feeling. Oh, sorry!' As I stretched forward to offer my hand I knocked his hat onto the floor. Picking it up to replace it, I kept the small ball of plastic explosive, unprimed, in my hand. It would not have hurt him, but he would have had cause for a very serious complaint.

We shook hands and parted, him still surprised, me relieved. I was not pleased with the turn of events and the Corporal soon knew very well that I was not. At first I wondered about his future, but then reflected that we might benefit later from his type of cunning and initiative. I did not regret the second thought. He was a good and reliable Corporal. All in all it was a very satisfactory exercise. By taking a very circuitous route, we returned to 'base' undetected. We had shown endurance. We had worked as a team and we now had confidence in each other, a vital ingredient for our future work behind enemy lines.

There was more useful experience to be absorbed in this well-thought-out training programme. We had elementary lessons in French and German. We learnt about German military structure and their regimental uniforms and insignia. We were taken to a power station to be shown where explosives should be placed to cause the maximum damage. We went to a railway marshalling yard to see how to mix up the destination instructions on the trucks, to see how

105

destroying points in the yard could cripple the marshalling of trucks. And we did lots of firing with our .45 Colts and .300 US carbines on the range.

We had talks from escaped POWs who had used the MI9 escape route and from SOE operatives on the things to be avoided when moving across country in occupied territory. One of the memorable pieces of advice was, when wanting to contact a Frenchman or woman (women were thought to be more sympathetic than men, who were more conscious of the consequences of helping), after a period of concealed observation, wait for the inevitable visit to the wooden loo at the bottom of the garden, but do *not* try to make contact on the outward journey, rather wait for the return when the individual would be more relaxed and have more time.

And we were warned about the orders issued by Adolf Hitler to the German High Command that 'all enemies from so-called Commando operations will be exterminated to the last. All parachutists captured outside the immediate zone of combat are to be killed . . . or in particular cases are to be turned over to S.D. (Sicherheitsdienst).'

We were not only as well prepared as we could be, we were also well warned.

Of course during this intensive period of preparation there were also moments of relaxation. We were given occasional passes for an evening trip to Glasgow. Parties in the Mess, boisterous and noisy, not only helped to let off steam but also cemented our relationships. Old and new, irrespective of rank, became comfortable with each other, confident that we had all accepted the hidden disciplines that were part of the unique regimental spirit. As the beer flowed the songs got louder while our Church of Scotland Padre, the Reverend J. Fraser Mclusky, serenely played the piano, occasionally wiping spilled beer from the keys with his handkerchief. It was a bit of a shock to the 'newcomers' to discover that the Regiment's favourite song was *Lili Marlene*, so loved by the Germans, but now 'legitimized' with the Regiment's own words. When loud songs turned to lewd songs, the Padre would just stand up from the piano and turn to the Colonel: 'Permission to withdraw sir?' To which the answer was always, 'Certainly, Padre. Good night.' And to a resounding chorus of 'Goodnight Padre' from momentarily sobered members of the Mess he went up to his bed.

Fraser Mclusky was simply the best Padre the 1st SAS could have had at that time. He was, is, admired and loved by all who served with him or who have known him since. He is a big impressive man, quiet and kindly in manner, with a wonderful sense of humour, who understood and listened to his disparate flock of warriors, never forgetting the name of a spouse or child. When he parachuted, unarmed, into France he carried a wooden cross, now displayed in the Regimental Chapel at Hereford, and an altar cloth in a suitcase and, avoiding discovery, made the rounds of our operational groups to hold services, attended always by everyone, in the various wooded locations. Often he avoided trouble by a hair's breadth; he visited our wounded wherever they were being secretly cared for. In thus devotedly discharging his pastoral duties in enemy territory he was also a wonderful source of information. For all this he was rightly awarded a Military Cross and Croix de Guerre. After the war he wrote two inspiring books, *Parachute Padre* and *The Cloud and the Fire*, describing his adventurous time with the Regiment and the fervent belief in God that guided his life as a Padre and Minister.

In *Parachute Padre* he speaks of the services he conducted with us behind the lines. 'Certainly our common danger was one of the bonds that united us in worship. Fear is not to be despised as an incentive to worship . . . We did not worship together in France solely because we were afraid. We lived continually "at the ready", but we did not live in constant fear. Worship had meaning and reality for us because we lived together. We were at one in worship partly, at least, because we were at one in work. We shared life together; we ate and lived together; we shared the same night vigils, the same expeditions, the same chances, the same hopes, the same fears. What more natural, then, that if we worshipped at all, we worshipped together? . . . The ground on which we cooked and ate and slept, the ground on which at any moment we might find ourselves defending our possessions and our lives, was the ground on which we worshipped. Common ground was sacred ground.'

Fifty-nine years later when the SAS's Roll of Honour – two beautifully bound books, one containing the names of the 250 odd who fell in WW11 operations, the other containing those who fell in post-war operations – were dedicated in St Columba's Church in Pont Street, London, Padre Fraser Mcluskey's old Church, in the presence of 'veteran' members of the Regiment, serving members and many next of kin, Fraser, ailing but as alert and forceful as ever, sent by video link from Edinburgh the following message:

107

'My friends, the men with whom I was privileged to serve in the 1st SAS were men of faith.

They had the necessary faith in their own ability to tackle their tasks.

They had faith in their comrades.

They had faith in the cause they were defending.

In a deep instinctive fashion, they had faith in God. They wanted to have a Padre to lead them in worship and prayer.

They have never ceased to be with me in thought and prayer. I look forward to seeing them all in the greater life beyond the grave.

They will pull my leg as they always did.

"Padre," they will say, "fancy seeing you here."

We shall all be together again; this time for keeps.'

I and my family have an extra special regard for Fraser. After the war he married both my wife and I and our eldest son and his wife, and is godfather to that son.

8

Into Enemy – Occupied Territory

But with it all, the training and the high tension fun, we were increasingly conscious that the long-anticipated invasion of occupied Europe was very close. There were sudden journeys to London by the Colonel and other senior officers. In retrospect it must have been a time when the role of the SAS Brigade in support of the invasion strategy was being thrashed out and lines of liaison with the Special Operations Executive (SOE) and the Free French Forces under General de Gaulle established, with some difficulty, it was said. The role allocated to the SAS by 21 Army Group was to dislocate, in cooperation with local Maquis groups, German communications, road and rail, in areas many miles in advance of the invasion forces, an area close to Orléans and Chartres, and another south of Orléans and east of the Loire around Avallon, Auxerre, Château-Chinon, the Morvan region, where a network of road and rail could be used to reinforce the German Army in Normandy.

At the beginning of June Lieutenant 'Puddle' Poole, with whom I was billeted, came into our room late in the evening from a briefing. 'I've got a job. I'm off tomorrow with 'Chick' (Lieutenant Fowles) and a few men. We're going down to "the cage"', the tight security area close by Fairford airfield in Gloucestershire from which all our operations were launched and where final briefings and training in the use of our codes took place. As we had been told that, to lessen the indications that the invasion was imminent, none of us would be dropped into France before the event, the move of 'Puddle' and 'Chick' with their men was a clear indication to us that the invasion was near. As we watched them go off next morning there was a distinct atmosphere of excitement and anticipation. Who would be next?

It was not until after we had ceased our operations in France with the clearance of the enemy from that territory, as well as Belgium and the Netherlands, that we learnt of the extremely important and hazardous task 'Puddle' and 'Chick' and their men had been required to undertake. Nor, perhaps fortunately, did we know how badly it had turned out. Their role had been to parachute into Normandy, away from the designated beaches, on D-minus-one, together with dummy parachutists and equipped with bombs and simulators to start a diversion to give the impression that an airborne landing was about to be made. Unfortunately they became separated on landing: 'Puddle' was knocked unconscious on his drop; the others could not find the containers holding their equipment. Thus the diversion was somewhat limited. They carried out various patrols and raids until several men, and 'Chick', were wounded, and all were captured. They were released by our forces in August, but sadly the French member of the Resistance who had helped them from time to time was captured and executed.

Just as 'Puddle' Poole and 'Chick' Fowles had been called down to our 'cage', some others left in the same way. One group, we learned later, were dropped not far from Orléans where they set up a base in the forest of Orléans from which they attacked the railway line from Orléans to Paris. But their ability to inflict the damage that local opportunities provided was limited by lack of mobility. The enemy could not be everywhere and roads were often free of traffic, but there was always the chance that round the corner of an apparently empty road was an advancing enemy patrol. Many roads were empty, but none were safe because the Germans, fearing attack by aircraft and by the Maquis, often switched their convoys to minor roads to reach their destinations.

Nonetheless it was clear that our operational groups needed the well-armed Jeeps similar to those used so successfully in the Western Desert. So, mounted on 'trays' with four parachutes meeting in the centre, these and the twin Vickers 'K' machine guns to be mounted front and rear were dropped to the waiting parties. The difficulty was ensuring that the Jeeps landed safely on the small, narrow DZs at night; there was no one on board to pull on the rigging to adjust the drift! Some landed in trees, some were damaged; on operations in another area, one landed in the lake at Les Settons. But while they greatly increased the range and choice of targets of the operational groups, they also increased the risk as they raced along the roads in occupied territory. Sadly it was in one such surprise encounter that the commander of one group was killed with ten of his men.

Soon we were all called down to the 'cage' where we expected to be briefed for our mission, given our codes, printed on silk scarves which we would wear round our necks, and become familiar with the radios we would have to use both to receive coded messages from the BBC and to send reports and requests. All groups in these operations were invaluably helped by having 'Phantom'* officers and men attached to them, all experts in communications and intelligence gathering.

But our expectations were disappointed. There was a delay and we began to feel somewhat resentful that none of us had been given a job. Our irritation was not lessened when we began to get news through Brigade H.Q. of some of the early parties' successes. They had blown up the Lyon-Dijon-Paris railway line, while others had destroyed the Limoges-Tours line, inflicting casualties on the Germans. As lines could be repaired they were attacked several times. Information on targets for the RAF were sent back; German convoys of men and armaments were ambushed and destroyed.

Yet with these successes also came bad news. One of the Squadrons had been over-run in their so-called concealed base. The Germans had discovered where they were, whether as a result of local treachery or carelessness was unclear, and walked through the base firing and bayoneting into every bush. Only a few escaped. Those who were captured were executed.

Another party had dropped into a DZ that had been betrayed by a captured Maquisard under torture. Those who were not killed by the waiting Germans were captured and tortured. They were then told they would be exchanged in Switzerland for German prisoners, but the lorries carrying them turned into a field and they were shot. Some ran for it. Two survived and eventually got back to England.

Unfortunately at this time the weather was unreliable. Several times parties took off only to return, sometimes once, sometimes twice, because the clouds obliterated the sight of the DZ. It was unsettling for the parties concerned, not only because of the let-down from high-tension expectation, but also because of the need

* Members of the GHQ Liaison Regiment, founded by Colonel (later Major General) Hopkinson, the SAS unit of which was commanded by Major the Hon. J.J.Astor.

to negotiate in flight the various 'flak alleys' a second or third time, and the increasing risk to Maquis or SOE reception parties in preparing and lighting DZs two or three times.

It was then that I heard of a change of plan caused, we were told, by the rapidly changing situation with our parties already behind the lines. They needed greater mobility in order to hit more targets, not least the German convoys choosing to use different routes to get to their troops in Normandy. They needed more well-armed Jeeps, and they needed more operational groups quickly. The new idea was that we and the Jeeps could be supplied by glider! So we, our Troop, left the cage to be trained in rapidly 'emplaning' and 'deplaning' troops, and in loading, flying in and unloading Jeeps. 'Remember you'll be in occupied territory'! As if we were likely to forget.

I did not enjoy this part of our training. We were training in American Waco gliders which were smaller than the robust Horsa gliders used to fly our Commandos in to key areas ahead of the beachheads on D-Day. They were not only smaller but, it seemed to me, their fuselages were very thin, perhaps too thin to withstand pressure or blows from breakaway equipment. Nor did I enjoy the experience of gliding once we were released from the 'tug' aircraft. The silence and the apparent serenity were at first quite appealing, but I thought we moved much too slowly and were a very vulnerable target, more vulnerable than being under a parachute canopy dropping from 700 feet at night. And where in central France would there be sufficient space secure enough to get a number of the gliders down at one time?

Shortly after returning to the cage we were encouraged to learn that Derek, our Troop commander, and his HQ group had been called to a briefing. So it would be soon for the rest of us. It was usual for those waiting to go to offer to help the lucky ones with their kit or equipment. It was an offer equally often refused with thanks because every soldier preferred to check for himself all the equipment he was going to rely on for his life. But at least we could chat and wish them an under-emphasized 'Good Luck' and watch as they were driven off in a truck to the airfield. Of course they would not say anything about their mission, so it was not until later we learnt that one of Derek's objectives was to answer one of my unspoken worries. He had to reconnoitre a suitable DZ for gliders.

As subsequent events showed, he did not find one, but all we knew at the time was that there had been another change of plan. We were told that in order to get sufficient Jeeps and men into our allotted area of operations our entire Squadron – two Troops of three Sections each, plus a Squadron HQ, about 80 men and some 20 Jeeps – were to fly to a forward airfield and drive in two separate convoys, by different routes, through the enemy's lines to our destination in the Morvan! There we were to relieve groups from a Squadron that had gone earlier and established a base near Montsauche, and then extend the operational area to the north, east and south. I think many of us were somewhat incredulous when we went to the briefing, and not a lot reassured when we were told that 'the front is fairly fluid; you should be able to squeeze your way through'. Yet it was a typically audacious SAS plan and experience had shown that audacity pays off, mostly.

Anyway that is what we did. When we got to the forward airfield and unloaded the Jeeps from the aircraft we had a final briefing from Tony Marsh, our Squadron Commander, who took charge of our convoy. This convoy comprised 12 Jeeps and 34 men. The operational instructions were precise: 'Radio silence between Jeeps; guns cocked and safety catches off but no firing unless under attack.' (Each Jeep had twin Vickers 'K' machine guns mounted front and rear. A Bren gun was clipped to the side at the front. There was an anti-tank bazooka on board and each man had an American .300 carbine and a .45 Colt automatic. We were capable of doing lots of damage if provoked. Each Jeep was also equipped with two additional self-sealing, if hit, petrol tanks, thus increasing our range.) We removed our Regimental berets and, bare-headed but wearing camouflage jackets, set off southwards towards Orléans.

We knew we had left our lines when we realized that for a mile or two we had not seen any American trucks or tanks. There was an uncanny emptiness about that stretch of country. The few houses we passed were obviously empty. No one wanted to be there. We were for a while in a veritable 'no-man's-land' and it sharpened our senses and made us very alert. My hands were firmly on the handles of my twin Vickers. Then, as we approached some buildings at the beginning of a village, my driver said quietly as if his English words could give us away, 'Look ahead, Sir.' I looked and saw a group of German trucks headed by a tracked armoured car, obviously headed north, but halted alongside a café. Most of the Germans had dismounted and were talking in groups, smoking and drinking what I took to be coffee. None were near their weapons, which I was glad to see, but

113

on reflection thought it was bloody stupid of them, being so near the lines. But we could not see if anyone was in the armoured car.

As they heard our convoy approaching some stopped talking and turned to look. Clearly they were puzzled. Then someone in our column had a bright idea. They shouted something which I think was 'Hello comrade' in German and waved. So we all waved as we went past and were relieved to see them wave back. The rear gunners in our Jeeps watched carefully as they too waved, and my gunner said they watched us all the way down the road until a welcome bend took us out of their view. That was a tactic we employed surprisingly successfully as we made our way down through the lines. There was quite a lot of military traffic on our route and, while we never took our hands off the Vickers' handles, it became a bit of a game waving to them as we went past.

The moment that caused us some concern was when we saw a long column of trucks with soldiers standing up in the passenger seats holding their weapons at the ready, headed by an armoured car coming up the road. By this time we were south of Orléans and I suppose, being that far into 'their' territory, they would not have thought that an organized column of armed vehicles driven by troops in camouflage smocks could be anything but one of their own units, however unusual. Certainly we were conscious of some curious glances as we drove past, but the friendly wave did the trick.

And it did the trick again when I unexpectedly heard Tim, who was in charge of the rear section, on the radio to Tony at the head of the column who was hissing, 'Radio silence, radio silence,' only to hear Tim say, 'We have four more vehicles in convoy!' A small German group had joined us! Fortunately it was shortly before we pulled off that road to head south-east into the Morvan, down past Auxerre and Avallon. As we turned off, the German vehicles drove straight on and we all waved to each other. I think it was on that journey that I felt most friendly towards the enemy, probably for the one and only time during the war. We learned later that the other column of our Jeeps had not been so free of trouble. They had had a brush with a small German column, killing or wounding some, and then taking some prisoners, without losses to themselves.

Our destination was an SAS base in a thickly wooded area on rising ground west of Saulieu, not far from Montsauche-les-Settons. We were nearing the location when we were met by two of Derek's Jeeps sent out to attack what they had been told was a German motorised unit – us. They led us to a track running up into the thickly wooded base on rising ground. There followed a happy reunion with comrades we had not seen since watching them being driven out to the airfield at Fairford. But it was when we met Derek with his hands and arm covered in bandages that we heard how the previous day he and his section had got into a hell of a scrap in which they aquitted themselves magnificently.*

They were out on patrol when they saw black smoke rising from a village. A fleeing woman told them that a large force of SS were burning the houses and had lined up the village men for execution. Derek and his section, six of them in two of our well-armed Jeeps, immediately drove into the village to engage the enemy. There were SS soldiers all around, in the square and the adjacent fields. Two villagers had already been shot, but the others escaped in the fight that followed. Unfortunately, with a jammed gun, one of the drivers was killed and a Jeep disabled. Derek had to rescue the dead man's body and run for the other Jeep in order to make their getaway, leaving a wrecked German truck and staff car and over fifty Germans dead or wounded. That night, having heard that the remaining SS had withdrawn taking their dead and wounded with them, Derek sent in a patrol to retrieve the stranded Jeep. By all the accounts they had been very lucky to get out of the fight as well as they did. But the damage done to the enemy was amazing.

When we had arrived at the Chalaux base I was surprised how well organized it was. It was well inside the wooded area. The track into it had hidden defensive positions including a 6-pounder artillery piece which had arrived by parachute. It was with the foresight that characterized our training back at Darvel that we spent time learning to manoeuvre, fire and maintain these guns. Parachutes were made into tents and there was a reasonable stock of food, petrol and ammunition supplied from the air. Throughout our operations in France the delivery of supplies, though subject to the uncertainty of weather and the occasional need, for security reasons, to seek new DZs, was a well-organized lifeline. On the whole communications to and from our HQ in England also worked well, largely thanks to our Phantom colleagues, though later when out on our patrols there were difficulties caused by the failure of the radio sets we had been given.

* See *These Men Are Dangerous; the SAS at War*, D.I. Harrison, Cassell Military Classics.

The Squadron that had arrived ahead of us in this area of operations had worked with two Maquis groups – Maquis Bernard and Maquis Camille. One was of a left-wing origin, the other more right-wing. (It should be remembered that the French Communists were first in the field of Resistance, mainly because, as a banned political organization, they were already experienced in clandestine activity.) Nonetheless they worked well together and with us, not only in finding and marking DZs but also in finding targets and attacking them. However, the relationship between them, though correct and cooperative, was never wholly warm. That separateness has continued to this day in their post-war 'Amicales' (veteran associations). Having said that, we, the older members of our Regimental Association, continue to have very friendly relations with both and we meet regularly on visits to their region.

The arrival of our Squadron made the base at Chalaux too congested and too many of our troops were concentrated in that one area. So the next day we moved out and set up a new base not far from Brassy. Our task was to take over from the existing Squadron and extend the area of operations east, west and south. Sections were sent out on seven-to-ten-day patrols to seek targets and destroy.

I was asked to take my Section south-west towards Nevers. This took us outside the main areas in which the two Maquis groups were operating, so we had to fend for ourselves. There was a main road running from Bourges eastwards to Nevers, Château-Chinon and Autun, and roads running northwards to Clamecy and Auxerre. German convoys and patrols had been reported in the area.

I was to proceed in the first instance to a small town, St Saulge, close to which at a given map reference point I would meet our Padre returning from one of his many heroic visits to our scattered groups to conduct religious services in their hidden camps. He might have up-to-date information about German convoys and patrols. Then I was to go further south, have a look at the Nevers-Autun road and the area round about, seeking targets. I set off with my Section, four Jeeps, eight men (Sergeant Dick Higham, Corporal 'Smudger' Smith, Lance Corporal Joe Craig, Chris Tilling my driver, Alec 'Boy' Borrie, Lance Corporal Johnny Barongelle, 'Woody' Woodward, and myself, before it was discovered that a strong force of Germans had moved into Brassy, which was too close to our new base for comfort: we had to move.

116

We followed an indirect route to St Saulge in order to avoid small towns like Corbigny that might be of interest to German patrols and so were a little late in reaching our rendezvous. (Many of the smaller roads that cross the region were then nothing more than unsurfaced rather superior cart tracks.) When we got there we saw two armed Jeeps by the crossroads and beside some bushes was Fraser Mclusky, the Padre, calmly sitting in his Jeep, while his driver, the huge, muscular Harry Wilson, an ex-Scots Guardsman, as much a body-guard as a driver, kept watch. Padre Mclusky refused to carry arms, saying the troops would not expect a Padre to be armed. But Harry, who would have defended Fraser to the death, insisted on being fully armed and saw to it that his Jeep was fully equipped with the 'regu-lation' twin Vickers machine guns, a Bren and a haversack full of grenades!

'Roy!' Fraser called, 'how nice to see you. How are you? And all your men?' It was the cheerful sort of greeting one might get when meeting someone on a picnic. I posted my other two Jeeps and went to meet him. He said he was glad I wasn't any later because he had been told that a German column was on its way to St Saulge. We decided we should go and find a more sheltered place to have a consultation. Down the road south of St Saulge we found a wood where we could brew up and decide on the next move. While we were enjoying the tea and a chat, during which I informed Fraser of the area I had been told to patrol, we had another, puzzling message that a German infantryman on a bicycle had been seen going towards St Saulge. We doubted the information, but in view of the earlier news it seemed that there might be enemy activity along those roads. I decided that the best thing was to proceed as quickly as possible to the area I was to patrol.

'I agree,' said Fraser. 'I think we should go our respective ways. Good luck to you and your men.' We waved to each other as I went to my Jeep and led my patrol out of that small wood. I did not see Fraser again until much later in England. He was, and is, a most remarkable man. When he had parachuted into occupied territory he refused to carry any weapon, but was persuaded he needed a 'commando knife' to open cans of food, which, in the event, was more useful than he expected. When he jumped he landed in trees and used the knife to cut himself free from the rigging. Unfortunately he forgot to leave the ones that would swing him upright and fell on his head! Obviously in his profession he can rely on special assistance, for when he woke up some time later, apart from being terribly sick, he was unhurt. He was found, happily by one of our patrols, next morning.

Dick, my Sergeant, and I had taken a quick look at our maps and agreed we should try to cross the Névers-Autun road near Châtillon-en-Bazois and find a camp between there and Luzy. We moved cautiously, wanting if possible to avoid trouble at the beginning of our patrol before reconnoitrering the area. When we reached the main road at Châtillon we laid up and watched it for about five minutes. We had good view in the direction of Névers and it seemed clear, but we could not see enough road towards Châtillon, so we sent one of the men across to get a better view. He soon gave us the 'all clear' and we went down and drove along the road as far as the turn to Luzy. We had not gone far down that road before we saw thick woods to our left with a track leading in. I sent one of the Jeeps farther on to see if there was another entry/exit track at the far end. ('Always recce a line of withdrawal.') There was. It was just what we wanted.

9

Action in Maquis Country

That wood became our base camp for most of our patrol. After entering, it was easy to wipe out our tyre marks from the dust of the track. Well inside, we spread our three Jeeps among the trees, one pointing to the entry track, one pointing to the exit, the third at an angle farther back. I think we all had at the back of our minds the fate of our colleague squadron which was virtually wiped out by a surprise night attack on their base. Thirty-four of our comrades were either killed on the spot or taken away for questioning and executed. We dispersed ourselves under bushes close to our vehicles and dug shallow trenches, camouflaged, to sleep in. We worked out a 'sentry' roster for both accesses and then gave ourselves a meal from the fairly ample rations we had brought with us. No fires, of course, but mess tins poised over small tablets of solidified paraffin – smokeless – could give us a hot meal and, more importantly, hot tea.

Over the 'meal' Dick and I consulted our maps to work out a reconnaissance patrol for the next day. We agreed to explore south towards Cercy and Luzy, then swing round towards Autun, and get a mental pattern of the roads, the woods and their tracks. (The whole of our area turned out to be heavily wooded and many of the roads were then unsurfaced and pitted.) We would take the the full section. Better to be at full strength all the time in case of trouble. Then all weapons and grenades were checked, a daily routine, before crawling into our sleeping bags for the night. I do not think I had one night's good sleep while on patrol. Even if we had not been aware of the Bullbasket tragedy, the fear of discovery was natural and real.* One lay awake

* *Operation Bullbasket* by Paul McCue.

119

thinking, 'Had we been careless and left a clue somewhere?' And in the dead of night, senses alert, the rustle of every scurrying creature, or falling twig could be the stealthy footfall of the enemy.

When we reached Luzy next day I decided to ask Johnny, my French Corporal who had escaped from occupied France in 1940 to join the British army, to put on his 'civvies', blue trousers, shirt, beret, not forgetting the shoes, important not to wear give-away army boots, and go into Luzy to find out if the road to Autun was used by the Germans. He was told it was, but not recently, which was disappointing because we had found an ideal ambush position in an overgrown gulley alongside the road. We decided to wait there all night in the hope that the information was unreliable. We slept beside our vehicles, with our sentries concealed close to the road at either end of the gulley in case there was any night-time activity. There was none. In the morning we waited and watched, but saw only two farm carts, one car and two cyclists, all unaware of our concealed position. So we patrolled the road towards St Leger, but again drew a blank.

We patrolled for two more days making a circuit south and west towards Bourbon-Lancy and up towards Decize, but to no avail. People we asked for information were either too unsure of who we were and did not want to say anything or were those who, though prepared to talk, said there had been no German activity there for many days. We became increasingly depressed. We had heard on our radios that the main battles in Normandy were moving east. Were we too late to catch any reinforcement or supply columns going north? So we turned round and headed back to our base. On the way we stopped to question a farmer working in a field. He was nervous and suspicious until Johnny, in a long and obviously persuasive conversation, won his trust. He told us that German convoys had recently been using the Nevers-Autun road. Johnny was confident this was good information. So it proved to be.

Back in our woods, which we did not enter until we had watched, hidden, for some time to ensure everything was 'normal', we picked up on our radio the sad news that a colleague officer, 'Monty' Goddard, had been killed when he ran into a German column on his way back to the Squadron's Brassy base. (Without precise information it was impossible to tell where or when columns or patrols would appear.) He had single-handedly wiped out a 36mm quick-firer and its crew before being hit by fire from a second gun. We also heard that Ian Fenwick, a well-known cartoonist before the war, who commanded another squadron, had been killed in a brave attempt to stop the execution of French civilians. This was far from encouraging, but none of us commented. Listening later to several messages from the BBC under our call-sign 'Sur le pont d'Avignon', though none were for us, lifted us from earlier thoughts, giving us the feeling we were in touch with 'home', however distantly.

Next morning we agreed that we should follow up the previous day's information and have a look at the Nevers-Autun road. On the way we sent Johnny into Châtillon-en-Bazois to see if there was anything new. He was away some time, which made us a bit twitchy. Had he been picked up, betrayed by someone he was trying to contact? Was he being questioned? How long before the Germans started a search? How long should we wait? Should we make a sortie into the town on a rescue mission?

Dick and I were eyeing each other with the same unspoken questions in mind when Johnny reappeared, walking quickly towards us, smiling broadly. He had made a good contact with one of the tradesmen in the town who, he was sure, could be trusted. This informant had heard that a German column had arrived in Névers the night before. They had parked overnight but were preparing to move, possibly to Autun rather than Orléans because they had parked near the Autun road. It sounded like a target opportunity at last. The information was over an hour old so if they were to take the Autun road we had a little time, but not much.

We quickly checked that all weapons were armed and grenades primed and set off, emerging onto the road to the east of Châtillon. Between there and Château-Chinon were several bends and good cover. We picked our spot for the ambush on a stretch of road between two bends where there was cover on one side, though more sparse on the other beyond a ditch. We chose the woods on the north side so that we could withdraw along a track away from the direction of our base. I placed my Jeep inside the trees just in front of one of the bends facing the direction the convoy would be coming from so that I could stop the leading vehicles. The others follwed me in and deployed to the other corner to take care of any vehicles that might be approaching that bend where we stopped the main part of the column. Dick positioned himself halfway between to do maximum damage when the convoy stopped.

We were almost caught off guard. As Chris, my driver, was

reversing under the trees we heard the sound of approaching traffic and round the far corner came a motor cycle outrider with a Schmeisser machine pistol across his chest, followed by a staff car. They came slowly forward, followed by a truck containing armed Wehrmacht infantrymen, then a covered truck, then another, another and another. I did not count how many because I was watching the front of the convoy to judge the latest moment I could open fire so that as many trucks as possible would be caught in the ambush.

They were very near our corner of the road when I told Chris to ease forward. We were in the open when I pressed the triggers of the twin Vickers guns. Chris stopped, grabbed his carbine and opened fire also. The formidable fire-power of the Vickers quickly got rid of the outrider, whose bike slithered into the ditch opposite, and the staff car, its occupants slumped forward, though the machine-gunner got off a few rounds, which went wide of us, before he fell. I could hear my far Jeep engaging those trucks that had not come round the furthest bend, and from the corner of my eye saw Dick's guns in action. The infantrymen reacted quickly, jumping from their truck and taking positions under the wrecked staff car and the trucks behind them to engage us and Dick's Jeep.

One or two of them got caught in our fire as they jumped and I turned my attention to the truck behind them. Men in that and following trucks leapt out and made for the insufficient cover on the other side of the road. I saw someone from Dick's Jeep lob a grenade over a truck in their direction. The response from troops lying under trucks and firing from behind the wheels was becoming worrying; they had identified our positions. I shouted to Chris to concentrate on them with his carbine.

It was then that the unexpected occurred. A large truck had, in coming to a halt, slewed towards our side of the road and its canvas cover had fallen away to reveal two tripod-mounted heavy machine guns, probably Spandaus, one towards the front, one to the rear. Although at short range, their first bursts were aimed generally towards the woods; fortunately they had not immediately located us. The next bursts were too close for comfort, but in the split second it took them to get our range I had been able to swing the Vickers up to take on the front gun. I was conscious that Dick was engaging the second. We came under sustained fire for a few minutes, but between us we took them out. By this time four or five trucks were wrecked, some on fire and others badly damaged.

122

On the road, under the vehicles and in the far ditch there were more than a dozen prone figures of dead or groaning wounded. In spite of the din, I suddenly heard vehicles approaching from the other direction, coming towards the corner behind me – more likely to be a patrol attracted by the firing than French civilians. I judged we had done enough and gave the signal to break off. I saw the other two Jeeps swing round on to a track in the woods. Unfortunately a late burst from the enemy hit Dick's Jeep, wounding the driver, Joe, in the hand, causing him to crash into a ditch. Dick managed to get out and Alec 'Boy' Borrie, the youngest member of the patrol, coolly reversed alongside the ditched vehicle and helped Joe on board. Meanwhile Chris had reversed into the trees and swung round in a clearing; as he did so I saw that two of the Wehrmacht had climbed up into the 'Q' truck* to man their guns again. As we joined the main track out of the woods we heard the bullets zipping past and smacking into the trees around us, but they were unable to get a clear shot through the woods anymore than my rear gunner could at them. Soon the firing stopped and the only sound was from our engines and the fading shouts of alarm and pain behind us.

The taut feeling of excitement began to slip away, but there was no time to relax; we had to be sure we were not being pursued and that no widespread search was in train. We decided against trying to return to our base that night as we would have to cross the road on which we had carried out the ambush. At the same time we had to avoid villages and towns, not least because we did not want to compromise any of these communities when the Germans would certainly be on high alert. We converged on the road to Aunay-en-Bazois, but we skirted the village and found good wooded cover between there and Montreuillon where we rested for the night. We had neglected to bring much food with us, so it was over hot tea and biscuits that we exchanged impressions of what happened. As a Section it was our first meaningful action, and for four of them it was their first experience of facing the enemy under fire. I was pleased with the way we had performed. We checked our weapons and ammo, and bedded down.

Next morning, after a somewhat restless night, none of us believing that we were not being sought by the enemy, we agreed we

---

* A reference to WW1 'Q ships', harmless looking merchantmen with concealed guns.

should try to get back to our base where we had hidden, among other things, provisions for which we now felt a considerable need. From our position the most direct route was through Châtillon-en-Bazois. Since we had heard no enemy activity during the night – no spotter aircraft, no road activity – we decided, perhaps unwisely, to go that way, fortunately with no adverse consequences. Certainly no adverse consequences, but some embarrassing ones.

We emerged on to the Château-Chinon road cautiously and, finding it clear, turned towards the small attractive town. We intended to drive through as fast as we could, so that any attention we attracted would only be momentary, and we would have to trust to luck that the road the other side would be clear. But as we approached we could see ahead of us more than usual activity in the main street and, getting nearer, we could see banners spread across the road. Small *tricolores* were flying from some houses. I was puzzled. Was it a wedding, a religious festival? Whatever it was, dashing through at high speed was out of the question. I drove on slowly and, I thought, quietly towards the first houses. But a group of people in the road turned and, as they saw us, rushed forward, some clapping their hands, some carrying bunches of flowers which they threw onto our Jeeps, and as we drove very slowly on more people came towards us clapping and cheering. It was neither a wedding nor a festival.

Then the bizarre thought struck me that the people of Châtillon-en-Bazois believed they were being liberated from occupation! This was not only embarrassing, but also as dangerous for them as for us. The Germans could well have patrols out, perhaps not far away. We moved slowly towards the centre through groups of people who were gathering round our vehicles, throwing flowers and reaching out to shake our hands. When we reached the church people stretched across the road blocked our way forward. A table laden with bottles of wine and glasses was set in front of the church. Behind the table were the recognizable, smiling figures of the local Curé and one we took, correctly, to be the Mayor, who beckoned us forward. I was reluctant to leave my Jeep but realized that we would have to explain the true situation. We gathered round the table and listened to the Mayor thank us for liberating them and this part of France from occupation by the enemy. The Curé then offered a prayer for the town's deliverance. Then the Mayor explained that the town had concealed bottles of champagne which were to be opened only when they were free again and it was an honour to share it with their allies.

The champagne was poured. Citizens gathered round for their share, and there was much embracing and toasting of the Allies and the spirit of resistance.

It was my turn to respond. I was apprehensive because I knew I could not do it adequately, but, in a whispered conversation with Johnny, we agreed that the explanation should be made more tactfully by him. I thanked them for their welcome and said what an honour it was to be involved with France in the battle against the common enemy. I then said that as I had a true Frenchman with me I would ask him to say something. I did not understand every word he said, but Johnny was magnificent. He made many patriotic comments which brought applause and cheers from the citizens, but I did understand when he said that, while we carried out our task as part of the liberating armies, we were only an advance unit and the main force would follow some time later, and as the enemy had not been totally driven away, and might still have active patrols, we had to move on and it would be wise to take down the decorations and clear away the wine and flowers in case a patrol came along.

The change in mood was remarkable. People turned immediately and began dismantling the flags and bunting, hustled away the wine table and, waving briefly, started back to their homes. After brief words with the Mayor and the Curé, which mainly comprised 'Nous comprenons; nous comprenons', we drove off towards our base, relieved but hoping desperately that we had not compromised the citizens of this charming town.

Later we learnt that shortly after we left a German patrol had come through the town on the outskirts of which they had stopped the Curé on his bicycle, who had been busy picking up scattered flowers, and asked him why he had so many flowers in his basket. He replied that he was going to visit a sick parishioner and got away with it. Interestingly, as we prepared to leave the Mayor told Johnny that after the ambush the Germans had brought their dead and wounded into the town before evacuating them and towing off their transport. Five lorries, a staff car and a motorcycle had been destroyed, some others damaged by our fire, while fifteen Germans were killed or seriously wounded. It confirmed our own estimate of the damage we had done. Thankfully there were no reprisals against the town.

Next morning we were rather subdued. The adrenalin had ceased to flow. Dick and I were deliberating whether to get Johnny to return to his contact in the town for more information, bearing in mind that he might feel differently following the 'false' liberation of Châtillon, or whether we should go on a search patrol when something very strange occurred. We heard a voice calling out, in English, 'Are you there? I think you are somewhere there!' The question was repeated and getting nearer. We all quickly went to ground, crawling under our bushes, weapons at the ready. There was a very narrow track running through the woods not far from where we were which we had taken to be no more than a rabbit run. The voice was coming from that direction. Then I saw this strange figure on a bicycle riding along the track, still calling, 'Are you there?' It was a man dressed in tweeds and wearing a deer-stalker hat. He rode straight past our patch. I waited. Then heard him coming back, persisting with his question. He disappeared. We waited several minutes before we emerged, puzzled and apprehensive. To have someone aware that we were somewhere in that wood was bad news.

It was another bizarre situation. Here deep inside enemy territory someone dressed like an English country gentleman was confident or stupid enough to call out to an unknown audience in English. Was he a decoy, trying to bring us out into the open? Dick, Johnny and I held a council. We needed to know fairly quickly what was going on in case we were compromised and needed to move. So Johnny donned his 'civvies' again and went into the town. We waited nervously 'on the alert', putting guards out in concealed positions all round the area of our camp. It was nearly an hour later that we saw him returning along our entry track. He was smiling.

'All right, it's OK, Sir,' he called.

'Well what's going on?'

He told us that the mystery man was the Marquis de Pracontol who lived in the château at the edge of the town with his wife and son. He was well known to Johnny's contact, the boulanger, and had helped the Resistance. They frequently exchanged information. He had heard the ambush and saw the results and was in the crowd at the 'liberation ceremony'. The boulanger said he was 'Anglophile' and wanted to offer us some hospitality!

It was a strange situation. Was the man really genuine?

Dick was doubtful and rightly urged caution. The Marquis knew where we were and if he was not genuine he could already have betrayed us, or was he confirming a suspicion he had about us and wanted to be sure of our location? But if that were the case, why try

126

to get us up to his château? Johnny, on the other hand, was sure we could rely on the boulanger's information that, though he was not a Maquisard, the Marquis was a supporter of the resistance and a friend of Britain.

Clearly much depended on Johnny's trust in the boulanger. From earlier conversations I had had with Johnny – his background and how he came out of France – I had formed the opinion that, if he was not actually a member of the Communist Party in France, he was a young man with very left-wing ideas and I had much sympathy with him, and after making his first confident contact in Châtillon it occurred to me that he might have found a like mind. It seemed to me that it was likely that Johnny was right; the baker was reliable.

I put this to Dick, saying that we needed to make a decision because if we had strong doubts the sooner we cleared off to find a new base the better. Dick agreed that on balance the man was probably genuine, but felt that we should make direct contact before coming to a final decision.

I asked Johnny if his contact could arrange for me to meet the Marquis on my own. He said he could, donned his 'civvies' and set off. It was arranged that we should meet in a couple of hours at the point where the track joined the main road. It was agreed that I would go on foot with Johnny, fully armed, while Dick would stay with the rest of the section, with look-outs posted, but ready to move at short notice if anything went wrong. He would then take charge of the section.

A bit before the appointed hour we went up the track and stood under the trees just short of the main road. We both carried our carbines and had our .45s in the holsters on our hips. The appointed hour passed and then another quarter of an hour and I began to get uneasy. I could see that the optimistic Johnny was also looking worried and I started wondering if I had made a bad, and possibly dangerous, decision.

'I think we should wait a bit longer,' Johnny said, interrupting my doubts. I nodded. It must have been another ten very long minutes later that I saw this figure dressed in a trilby hat, tweed jacket, collar and tie, with breeches tucked into gaiters, turn hurriedly off the main road and stride down the track towards us. As he approached, we stepped out, my carbine under my arm, to meet him. He hesitated a moment, then came forward, hand outstretched. I remember well his greeting, so calm and polite in such unusual circumstances.

'Good afternoon, Lieutenant. I'm sorry to be late,' he said in impeccable English. 'I was busy when the baker telephoned me. I am happy to meet you. My name is Pracontol.'

It was hard to believe that I was deep in enemy territory with a French aristocrat dressed like an English gentleman and speaking fluent English. Yet the situation was to become even more unbelievable. I responded to his greeting with what I hoped was equal politeness. I told him my name, introduced Johnny and said I was in charge of a forward reconnaissance patrol of the Allied armies and I hoped he would treat our meeting with the greatest discretion. He smiled and said I need have no fear on that score.

As I looked at him I realized that I had walked beside him down the main street of the town without knowing who he was, during the celebration of their 'false' liberation. He referred to the occasion and apologised for not making himself known then, but pointed out that the celebration had ended abruptly following our warning. He said that he was a great admirer of the British; he had many friends in Britain whom he had often visited before the war. He knew the British were helping the Resistance in many ways. He too was doing what he could, but had responsibilities alongside the Mayor and the Curé in the community. He congratulated me on the success of our ambush and said that the Germans were very frightened when they brought their dead and wounded into the town and had moved on very quickly.

Then he said, as I remember it, 'I would very much like to invite you and your men to dinner with me and my wife in our home! I think you would all appreciate a nice meal, and for us it would be an honour.'

I was staggered. It was such a courteous encounter, perfectly normal anywhere else, but incongruous in enemy-occupied territory. It took me some seconds to come to terms with the situation. Then I thanked him for his kind invitation, but said it would be difficult to accept as we were on duty and had to be alert and must safeguard our equipment at all times. As I was saying this I was still wrestling with the thought that this could be an elaborate trap.

Yet his manner was quite straightforward. He said he understood my hesitation, but I would find his château very secure. Since the tenth century it has never been taken. There is only one way in. The gates were kept locked and the long drive, overlooked by the battlements, led to a large courtyard inside the walls. All our equipment would be safe. There was even a tunnel from his cellar which went under the main road out to the land by the river. And he had friends in nearby towns who telephoned him or the baker about nearby German movements. He assured me we would be quite safe.

It was so reassuring that it seemed impolite, perhaps insulting, not to take him at his word. But there was more than my life at stake. I could not commit my section to either course simply on the basis of my own gut feeling. So I thanked him for his reassurance and his generous invitation, but said I would like to consult my comrades.

He agreed and said if we decided to accept the invitation we should let the baker know, in which case he would be at the gates of the château at six-thirty to meet us. We bade each other *au revoir* and Johnny and I watched him until he reached the road. Then we turned and, somewhat bemused, walked back along the track into the woods and our camp.

Of course everyone wanted to know what had happened; was he 'safe' or should we move out? So we held a 'council', not of war but of 'trust'. I explained the situation and, as impartially as I could, put the pros and cons of our alternatives, pointing out at the same time the baker's confirmation of the Marquis's Resistance credentials. We all felt that had the Marquis been 'one of them' he could have betrayed us without the need of an excuse to get us into his château.

We agreed that, subject to suitable precautions, we would go. So we sent Johnny off, in his 'civvies' again, to the baker to say we were pleased to accept the invitation. We decided we would leave three men with the Jeeps in the château courtyard, who would be relieved halfway through the meal. I explained this to the Marquis when we arrived. He readily agreed and said he would ensure they all 'got their dinner'. I am still sure that our decision was a reasoned one, unbiased by the thought of food and wine! The instinct for self-preservation is more powerful than hunger and thirst in wartime.

So go we did. I think it was probably the most unwise decision I made in my army career, but in the event it caused no problems, and in a way gave us a better understanding of how the French lived under the German occupation. I felt that we benefited by that understanding, as well as from the hospitality. In both the main towns and in the countryside the anger and shame of occupation was the same. But in the countryside there was movement and uncertainty, for although France was totally defeated and cruelly occupied by the

Germans, that occupation could not be total, in the sense of every town and village being garrisoned by enemy soldiers. Large towns were garrisoned, surrounding countryside patrolled and smaller towns and villages occupied from time to time, with enemy traffic moving freely. Some movement by the French was possible, even necessary for those going to and from their work. This meant that information about the enemy could be passed by a variety of means and people could be forewarned about enemy movements. Enemy installations could be observed and reported on to those with the means – the Maquis, other Resistance groups and us – to damage or destroy them. But enemy patrolling, unpredictable occupation of towns and villages, and occasional ruthless searches and questioning could happen without warning, and therein lay the danger for the French, and for our own patrols.

But there we were, in the centre of occupied France, with our armed Jeeps parked, under guard, in a château courtyard, badly shaven, not wholly clean, in clothes we had not taken off for some days, sitting round a large table under a crystal chandelier in a stone-vaulted dining room surrounded by family oil paintings, with an Anglophile Marquis and his wife and their rather sickly son. Over one of the most welcome dinners imaginable he told me how much he had enjoyed visiting England before the war and had hunted with friends in Lincolnshire and Warwickshire. He mentioned several names of rich and powerful British friends and seemed surprised that I had never met any of them. He spoke of his hopes and fears for post-war France. He hoped that France's deep social divisions could be healed after the war, but had little faith in the French political system. He feared that their defeat and occupation, which had produced both collaborators and resisters among the large numbers who had no choice but to acquiesce, would leave damaging enmities and deep scars that would take years to heal. He pointed out that Châtillon was his summer residence and that he actually lived in another château, at Champlatreux, not far from Paris. He invited me to visit them there after the war.

I did visit the Pracontols at Champlatreux in 1945 when I was stationed in Paris helping to find answers to unresolved questions arising from our SAS operations and to take letters of thanks from our Brigade Commander to those who had helped us in our work. I remember going up a long tree-lined drive to the entrance. Through the huge double doors was a long tiled corridor lined with statues, tapestries and what I took to be Louis X1V furniture. All the statues had been decapitated, the tapestries and furniture slashed. The château had been a German Headquarters during the occupation.

We left the château at Châtillon, well dined and wined (though not excessively so) and graciously entertained. That night I pondered the Marquis's hopes and fears for France. Even today some of his fears can be detected behind the façade of French nationalism.

We were slightly apprehensive about returning straight to our camp. At the back of our minds was still a suspicion that the dinner had been a ruse to get us away from our hiding place in order to get troops in there to 'receive' us on return. It was a very unworthy thought; nevertheless we waited, watched and listened. Then we sent in one man on foot. They found nothing and signalled us in. Safely in, I reflected sadly that our precautions were an unworthy slur on the good faith of our host that evening.

Next morning, as Dick and I discussed where we should look for our next target, I recalled that the Marquis had heard about a large house standing in grounds between the roads from Bourbon-Lancy to Autun and from Gueugnon to Autun, which the Germans used as an occasional headquarters from which they sent out patrols. He had not known the exact location, but we decided to go and look for it. Taking a roundabout route, it was some time before we reached the area. It took longer still to find the house. We spotted a property in its own grounds that seemed to match the Marquis's description. But in case it was the residence of a harmless French family, we decided to get off the road and wait and watch. The drive was short and in the open. Trees were few and far between. It was such a peaceful scene that I thought what we had found was not our target. We waited and watched.

The light was fading fast when patience was rewarded. There was movement at the back of the house. Some shadowy figures in uniform. We could not distinguish who they were nor what was in the house. As it was getting dark and we had a long way to go on the return journey we decided to do a quick 'blind' shoot-up. I took my Jeep into the drive with the others on either side. We concentrated on the side and the back of the house where we saw movement and then raked the building top to bottom, concentrating heavy fire into the windows. There was no further sign of movement. It was almost dark as we moved closer, but all was still and quiet. If, as the Marquis had said, it was used as an occasional headquarters for patrols, that day

131

was not such a one. If anyone had been there they were no more than 'caretakers'. It was now dark and, as there was no more sign of movement, we decided to start on the return journey. It was late before we got 'home'.

It was a fairly futile operation, but later, on a post-liberation visit back to the area, I learned to my surprise that half a dozen Germans had been in the house at the time and had been hit. Whether killed or wounded was not clear, but the house was evacuated and never again used as a temporary base.

Next day we received a signal from London telling us to contact a Maquis group some way outside our area and apparently unconnected with the two groups, Bernard and Camille, with which our squadrons cooperated so successfully. We were given a map reference and a password and told to find out, and assess, what arms and other help they needed, the emphasis being on 'needed' rather than 'wanted'. We studied the map and decided we would work our way across by minor roads and tracks.

Our 'safe' route was also a long route and it was late afternoon when, driving down a track just inside a large wooded area, I judged we were just about on the given co-ordinates. So it proved to be, for suddenly there appeared from the trees on either side of the track half a dozen unfriendly-looking men in dungarees, wearing blue berets, brandishing rifles and Sten guns. Two stood in front of my jeep aiming their weapons, while the others covered the jeeps behind me. Of course we outgunned them and one nervous shot would have caused havoc.

Realizing we had reached our destination, I quickly stood up and shouted, 'Ne tirez pas. Ne tirez pas. Nous sommes soldats Anglais.'

The reply was hilarious. A voice with a marked cockney accent yelled, 'Oh for Gawd's sake talk English. I've 'ad nothing but this foreign stuff for months!'

It came from one of the group holding a shotgun. As we climbed out of our Jeeps, somewhat relieved, the figure came forward pulling his beret off. 'Flight Sergeant Tom Smith,' (I have forgotten his real name) he said, ''Ow are you?' We shook hands. All around us there was a general shaking of hands and warm embraces and, in answer to my unasked question, Flight Sergeant Smith told us that he had been shot down almost a year ago. His colleagues were killed. He baled out and wandered around at nights for about a week not knowing where he was, until a kindly farmer pointed him towards the Maquis. He said they were expecting someone, but did not know when. He invited us to follow him into their camp where he would introduce me to the Commandant. As we remounted he called out, 'What made you choose that track to reach us?'

I said we wanted to avoid the main roads.

'You were quite lucky.' he said. 'We mined that track last week!'

'Didn't do a very good job, did you?' I replied.

'No,' he said as he walked towards a track into the woods and we followed. Farther down the track we turned on to a narrower track, densely wooded on either side. I saw two guards behind trees. Some way along it swung right and I noticed two more armed men fairly well hidden in the bushes just short of what seemed to be the entrance to something of a clearing. They had been careful to choose a place where there was no large gap in the tree coverage which would have been visible from the air; the trees remained but the undergrowth had been cleared and, as we had seen in the squadron camp at Chalaux, parachutes hung as tents from the trees. I also saw that many of the Maquisards, who stopped what they were doing as we entered and came forward smiling to greet us, wore shirts made of parachute silk. Clearly they had already been supplied by an 'air drop', perhaps not too long ago.

'Wait here,' shouted the Flight Sergeant. He ran forward as I got out of my Jeep and walked back to the others. I told Dick it might be a good idea to dismount and start making friends while keeping a sharp eye on our weapons. As I walked back to my Jeep Smith was coming towards me, trying to keep pace with a middle-aged man of medium height and trim build who was dressed in dark blue trousers and a blue shirt, on which were pinned two badges which I did not recognize, and the inevitable blue beret. He stopped in front of me and saluted. 'Capitaine Pierre.' (Again I forget the name he gave me.) 'Happy to meet you.' I returned the compliment and gave him my name. As we shook hands I told him I had been asked to make contact to see if we could be any help. I was uneasy. The atmosphere was too relaxed. I thought it best to show a correct but cool friend-liness until we knew more.

He thanked me and invited me to accompany him to the Mess, which he said was a shared Mess and that Sergeant Smith would bring my comrades along. I had guessed by this time that the Captain had been an officer in the French Army. I told him that I would want to put our own guards on our Jeeps. I feared he might be offended by this apparent lack of trust in him and his men, but he agreed quite readily. As we walked through the clearing to the Mess I noticed a half-naked man tied to a tree. His body was scarred and there were dark shadows round his eyes. I stopped.

'Who is that?'

'A collaborator whose betrayals caused the death of some of my men and some local civilian resisters.' I asked why he was being treated like that. Was he not a prisoner of war? 'No,' said the Captain. 'He was a traitor, well known in the locality.' I asked what would happen to him. He said they would put him on trial here. The witnesses would be the relatives of those who were tortured and shot because of him. There was no doubt he was guilty, he said, but he would have his say and then he would be shot. He saw by my expression that I disapproved.

'You do not like that, Lieutenant?' he asked.

I said I did not, that he should be kept prisoner and handed to the authorities after the liberation. I remember the rather pitying look he gave me as he told me I did not understand, that in England we had been spared the shame of an occupation that divides the people, divides families, brings torture and death. 'This is not for you, Lieutenant. Leave it alone. In any case who will be the authority after liberation, the right or the left? Both are dangerous.' This was another lesson for me into the realities of defeat and occupation. We walked on to the Mess.

The Mess was an area covered by about three suspended and spread parachutes under which were a variety of chairs, benches and a few tables. Certainly more 'luxurious', if that is the word, than I had seen briefly in the camps of Maquis Bernard and Camille before we came out on patrol. The lunch we were served proved the point. We had cold meat, salad and plenty of wine. The atmosphere was jolly, though I could not dismiss my feeling of unease about both the prisoner and the general set up. We were told that the high standard of food and drink we were enjoying was by courtesy of Flight Sergeant Smith. When he joined the Maquis group he had been made responsible for keeping the Mess well supplied by ambushing any German convoy that could be carrying supplies.

'You've obviously been successful,' I said to him.

He agreed, but then asked me, surprisingly, on which side of the tree you put the explosive to get the tree to fall across the road. I told him that you put the charge on the side you want the tree to fall as it blows the base in the other direction. He laughed and thanked me. 'I don't always get it right. I have to have a horse handy to drag it round if I get it wrong!'

There was much hilarity, especially when Captain Pierre accused Smith of having had the opportunity to end the war in France, but failed. The story was that recently, when he was preparing to ambush a convoy they had received information about, he was surprised by a convoy of limousines preceded by S.S. outriders on motorcycles, with a similar group bringing up the rear. It was Marshal Pétain heading for Belfort, the gateway to the remaining escape route into Germany. We had already heard on our radio link of the success of the British army in breaking out of the Normandy bocage and of General Patton's 'right hook' south of Normandy which was causing the German occupation forces in France to make for that escape 'hatch', which accounted for our difficulty in finding more suitable targets. There was obviously much fun in the way Captain Pierre's men teased Sergeant Smith, but he took it in good part and responded memorably with the unforgettable excuse: '*Qui, moi, avec douze SS en avant et douze en arrière? Jamais dans votre vie!*'

The company was convivial as we talked about the war and I asked about local targets Then I asked if I could walk round the camp. I wanted to get an impression of the state of their armaments. I concluded that they were quite well supplied and faced no great threat in the area. I was aware that we should not provide arms that might be used in some period of post-liberation unrest, so when it was time for us to return to our own base I pointed out to Captain Pierre that, as they were well armed, not in immediate danger and the Germans were now pulling out of France, calling up arms that our forces could use elsewhere could not be justified. He protested, but I had the impression he did not really expect any other response. He seemed to be happy living the way he did.

Before leaving, I said to Flight Sergeant Smith that, although I could not help the Maquis, I could take him out and arrange for him to be picked up and taken home. His response was both unexpected and revealing. 'Oh no,' he said. 'The RAF know I'm alive, so my pay is piling up at home and I'm here living well on French food and wine. I'll wait a bit longer.' As we left I contrasted that 'Maquis' with the determined attitude of Maquis Bernard and Maquis Camille with whom we had collaborated so successfully, the friendship of whose remaining members we still value today.

The following few days showed that the campaign to liberate France was almost ended. Our search for more targets was somewhat restricted because we were getting short of fuel. It appeared that supply drops expected at Chalaux had been cancelled because of bad weather. Other patrols were also running out of targets, though one patrol to our north-east had negotiated the surrender of a garrison of German troops and an enemy convoy heading north was ambushed, destroying several trucks before fire from another 'Q' truck ended the engagement. We found only two more targets. One was a German troop transport parked outside a café on which we placed time bombs. The troops were inside but so were French civilians, so we could not attack them. The other was a lonely motorcycle patrol, perhaps left behind for some reason and trying to catch up with his unit. He didn't make it. It was September 1944 and the Germans were fleeing from France.

It was a couple of days later that I received a message from Derek, my Troop Commander. He had been instructed to make contact with General de Lattre de Tassigny who commanded a French army pushing up from the south, to establish his position and his intentions, and possibly work with him. Derek wanted another patrol to accompany him. Could I oblige? The fuel situation was tricky, but we thought we had enough for a reasonable mileage. But where were the General and his army? No one seemed to know for certain. When we met Derek we agreed that it was reasonable to assume he would be coming up the Rhône valley, perhaps at Lyon, perhaps Mâcon. So we set off across France looking for an Allied army. We decided to try Mâcon first.

We were fairly sure that the Germans had left our area of operations and so we travelled quite openly, no longer seeking the side tracks nor trying to ensure we were always near the safety of a forest. We asked questions on the way, knowing that news of a French army under an heroic and legendary General would travel fast. But so would the rumours. One informant said that the General was in Autun, which we had left behind. So we ignored that. Near Mâcon we heard that he had been through the town heading for Dijon, so we turned and headed north. It was in Dijon that we found him. There we were directed to an hotel where the General had set up his headquarters.

Derek decided to take me and Johnny, for his fluent French, into the HQ, while curious citizens of Dijon gathered round our Jeeps admiring the weapons and trying their English on our colleagues. We were dressed in the clothes we had lived in for many days – parachute smocks, battledress trousers, gaiters and boots, dirty, not very well shaved, if at all. We climbed the steps of the HQ hotel where two smartly dressed French guards saluted as we walked through the door. In the entrance lobby of the hotel we found an officer and told him, through Johnny, that we were English officers who had been in France for some time and had received a radio message from London to contact the General, ascertain his intentions and see if we could be of any assistance. He asked us to wait. He went into a room at the back of the lobby. While we waited junior officers and NCOs went to and fro around us, passing puzzled glances without delaying their purposeful progress.

When the officer returned, with a colleague, he said that the General was in conference and could not break off at present, but the Intelligence Officer, to whom we were then introduced, would be able to answer our questions. The Intelligence Officer conducted us to another room festooned with maps marked with arrows, squares and circles. He proceeded to give us his assessment of the position of the British and American troops to the north and the route the German forces were taking in their flight through the Belfort Gap into Germany. The General's Army was also heading for the Belfort Gap to attack the fleeing Germans. Perhaps we could go there and help stop them!

We took all this in and then Derek asked, 'Do you know who we are?'

'Yes. British officers.'

'How do you know?'

'You said so and you are in British uniform.'

'Have you not heard of how the Germans dressed in Allied uniforms in the invasion of France? No one has asked for our identity. We could be Germans. You have given us some very important information; there are three of us; we could kill you and walk out with that knowledge and your maps. What is more, the idea of our three Jeeps being able to attack thousands of disciplined German troops is quite ridiculous. Tighten your security and give the General our respects. Good day.'

As we left the Dijon HQ Derek said, and I agreed, 'That was a bloody shambles, a disgrace.' He said he would signal London that the General was in Dijon and headed for Belfort, but there was nothing we could do to help.

The day after we had returned to our own camp we received another signal,the one we had been expecting for a couple of days, the one that signalled the end of our mission in occupied France. We were to meet our Squadron Commander, Tony, at Cosne to await orders about our next move. We left our forest camp next morning, pleased but also a little regretful; the shelter from those trees and bushes had kept us safe. By this time we had acquired an old Chrysler Plymouth saloon which we found abandoned on the way back from Dijon. So, with three Jeeps and an old Chrysler, we headed west to Névers and took the road alongside the Loire to Cosne. We travelled quite openly, while keeping wary eyes open, but the news of the German exodus was everywhere visible with people moving freely on the streets and waving as we passed through the villages. Our part in the campaign to liberate France and push the Germans back into their own country was over. We were happy about that and, though we realized that the final assault was yet to come, that was something for the future.

At Cosne we were told we would probably be there a few days until our orders came through. So we had to find another place to camp just outside the town, but on this occasion we had no need to seek cover and concealment. It was like being on holiday and with the willing help of local people we took the opportunity to bath, shave properly and wash our clothes. Derek and his Section were already there and the Squadron's other Troop, under Peter Davies, was camped a short distance away. From him we learned they had shot up a large convoy protected by infantry and anti-tank guns near Nannay. They destroyed many vehicles and inflicted a large number of casualties. But he too suffered from a 'Q' lorry's fire and lost two Jeeps. One of his men was captured, but by landing unsportingly low blows on his captors, escaped.

Tony had set up his headquarters in one of Cosne's hotels where we enjoyed happy hours exchanging experiences over glasses of wine and the occasional omelette. How delicious those French 'liberation' omelettes tasted! We were there for about a couple of weeks; apart from the need to re-fuel, repair and overhaul the Jeeps and check and clean our weapons, they were glorious days of relaxation, sleeping peacefully and becoming fairly civilized, which stay in my memory as a short idyllic episode.

When Paddy Mayne arrived from England with our new orders, Paris had been liberated and the British Army had occupied Brussels.

When the Squadron gathered round Paddy he told us how well we had performed in France. Overall the Regiment had inflicted great losses with small casualties to ourselves. This was especially good news for those of us who had not previously operated with the Regiment, because, with a mission successfully carried out, we would now be entitled to remove our SAS wings from the left shoulder of our tunics and wear them on our left breasts. Within the Regiment this was regarded as an individual battle honour. It had been granted by the Army's High Command following the earlier highly successful exploits in the Western Desert, though not much liked by the RAF who regarded wings worn on the breast as their prerogative.

Paddy went on to tell us that we were to go to Brussels, the British Armies' HQ, to be re-equipped and re-fitted. We would then proceed to Holland for the winter, working with Second Army's Field Security Police patrolling along the line of the Maas to prevent or mop up enemy incursions from the other side of the river. He suggested a route from Cosne to Brussels that would take about two days to complete: we were to avoid Paris which was the American Armies' HQ and out-of-bounds to British troops. He said he would meet us in Brussels in about four days' time!

After the meeting I got together with my Section to consider our own movement timetable with what I thought was a perceptive interpretation of our orders. Johnny had cousins in Paris and he was anxious to find out if they had survived the occupation. He knew a variety of routes into the capital and had a friend with a large lock-up garage where our Jeeps could be left under guard while the rest of us proceeded to Paris. It looked like an opportunity not to be missed, so we set off in the battered old Chrysler for newly liberated Paris, the US Armies' Headquarters.

Approaching the centre along the Porte d'Orléans we stopped at a corner café with tables and chairs set out on the pavement. Johnny had wanted me to accompany him on his search for his cousin on the grounds that if he was stopped by US Military Police I would be able to talk him out of trouble! I agreed and decided to take Dick with us. I told the rest of the Section that they had twenty-four hours to enjoy Paris. I would meet them back at the café mid-morning the next day. And I added that anyone who got into trouble or who was absent next morning I would personally shoot!

Johnny, Dick and I set off for the distant *arrondissement* where his cousins were living when he last heard of them. By avoiding the main streets and boulevards on which there was quite a lot of US military traffic and pedestrians, but no civilian traffic, it took us until the afternoon before we found them. It was far from being a wealthy neighbourhood. The cousin was a middle-aged garage mechanic. His wife, also middle-aged, seemed to me to be plump and placid. Their reunion was happy and emotional, wonderful to see, tearful, embracing, hugging and kissing We were ushered into the small apartment where the cousin happily produced two bottles of wine. Over numerous glasses Johnny and his cousin locked themselves into animated conversation, presumably about their respective experiences since France fell. Meanwhile Dick and I singularly failed to engage Mrs cousin in any conversation whatever, receiving only single-word replies or shrugs in response to our efforts. After a while I noticed by their glances that Johnny was talking about us. Then he explained that, as there was not enough food in the house, we should go out and find a restaurant.

So, with us in uniform, the cousin in his dark suit, collar and tie and the ubiquitous blue beret, and Mrs cousin in her dark blue dress, black top coat and black straw hat decorated with artificial flowers round the crown, we stepped out into the fading daylight. A couple of streets farther on the cousin turned into a doorway which led into a dimly-lit vestibule beyond, all of us following. There we were met by a proprietor-like individual who bowed us into a room, not very large, with armchairs and settees round the walls. I was puzzled because I had not seen any sign outside saying it was a restaurant, but thought Paris might still be under blackout regulations.

The proprietor-type had a few words with Johnny and left the room. For a few minutes we sat in uncomfortable silence. When he reappeared he was accompanied by an attractive girl in a black lace kimono which, though it hid little, she proceeded to discard to reveal all her considerable charms. It was certainly no restaurant we were in. It was a brothel. It seemed that Johnny's cousin had thought, with typical Gallic concern for such things, that in view of our recent bucolic and celibate existence we had a need more urgent than that good meal. Right or wrong, there was no way either Dick or I could show any interest; the atmosphere could not have been more inhibiting. There was the cousin and his wife dressed in their Sunday best, he looking impassively straight ahead while she sat below her flowered straw hat, arms folded across her ample bosom, lips pressed together in a thin straight line. So after we had watched, apparently unmoved, about half a dozen of the ladies of the establishment proving to us they had nothing to hide, we got up and left. The proprietor was distraught and apologetic, probably nursing a severely adverse impression, perhaps shared by the cousin, of Anglo-Saxon virility.

A few streets farther on we found a genuine restaurant and enjoyed a very good meal of soup, omelette and salad with a bottle of wine. After more wine back at the apartment, Dick, Johnny and I slept the sleep of the just on the floor. We never referred to the occasion of our first port of call the previous evening.

We got back to the corner café at almost the exact time we had left it the previous day. It was a relief to find all our comrades cheerfully present. How could I have doubted them? I asked how they had got on. A Lance Corporal, a Liverpudlian with a rich Liverpool dialect that sadly is impossible to convey in writing, described their experiences. It seemed that there were some similarities with our own experience.

As they sat drinking beer after Dick, Johnny and I had left a man sitting at a nearby table had heard them talking and asked in reasonable English if they were American. When they confessed to being English he was delighted and embraced them all, bought drinks and offered to show them round Paris. With him acting as a guide they avoided any difficulty with the Military Police. In the course of the tour he asked if they had heard of 'Fairyland'. They had not, so he took them there. It was, it appears, well known before the war as one of Paris's famous (if that is the right word) brothels. It seemed that their guide had a similar gallant Gallic concern for a soldier's peace of mind and personal comfort as Johnny's cousin.

When they arrived at the place the proprietor welcomed them profusely and showed them into a curtained vestibule, as the first English to honour the house since 1939. After a couple of drinks he clapped his hands and the curtains were opened to show all the ladies of the establishment standing mostly unclothed who began to sing 'God Save the King'!

'What did you do?' I asked.

'We saluted of course, Sir, at attention.'

I decided to ask no more. But a mental picture of that ludicrous encounter remains indelibly in my mind.

As we made our way to Brussels, the enemy expelled from France,

Belgium and the Low Countries, it was good to hear that early in September a special message from Lieutenant General F.A.M. (Boy) Browning had been broadcast by him to SAS troops in France (though we did not hear it at the time) complimenting the Regiment on its achievements. 'Now that the story of your operations and exploits since D-Day is becoming known and confirmed, I am speaking to you this evening in order to tell you what Field Marshal Montgomery and the Commanders in the Field feel about your activities . . . .

'It is considered that the operations you have carried out have had more effect in hastening the disintegration of the German Seventh and Fifteenth Armies than any other single effort in the Army. Considering the numbers involved . . . your job of work has had a most telling effect on the enemy and which no other troops in the world could have done.

'I know the strain has been great because operating as you do entails the most constant vigilance and cunning which no other troops are called upon to display.

'To say you have done your job well is to put it mildly. You have done magnificently.

'You will get Field Marshal Montgomery's message shortly.'

Unexpected but much appreciated comments.

Official records show that 2,000 officers, NCOs and men of the SAS were engaged in operations in France, 330 of whom were casualties. They killed or wounded 7,753 Germans, took 4,764 prisoners. 740 vehicles, 7 trains, 89 railway trucks, 29 engines were captured or destroyed; 33 trains were derailed and 164 railway lines cut.

It was an uneventful run from Paris to Brussels. When we reached our rendezvous we found that a Regimental Mess had been opened in a house in the Avenue de Tervuren near the Cinquantinaire, the monument erected to commemorate the fiftieth year of Belgian independence.

10

Winter Along the Maas

As we reached Brussels we did not realize we were entering a long period of frustration, of idleness with a few 'alarms and excursions'. The stay in Brussels, however, was a pleasantly recuperative one. 'Refit and re-arm,' we were instructed, which we interpreted as a time to be sure we were fit, with some running and some football. And a time to ensure our Jeeps and weapons were in good order. Our experiences in France had shown us some modifications were needed. Some .5 calibre cannon of the type used in Typhoon aircraft would soon be available. These would greatly improve our already considerable fire power, as each section would have one Jeep with a .5 cannon at the front and twin Vickers at the rear with a Bren gun and a bazooka, while each man carried a .300 carbine and a .45 hand gun. The other two Jeeps had twin Vickers front and rear and the men also had carbines and hand guns. The armour-plated shields in front of the driver and mate of each Jeep were to be reinforced with a one-inch bullet-proof (to small-arms fire) glass shield on the driver's side and new self-sealing petrol tanks would be set on either side of the rear gunner. Although there was work to be done later in Holland, we knew we were preparing for the final assault across the Rhine.

Happily there was time also for personal enjoyment. Brussels was coming to life again after years of occupation. The Bruxellois were pleased to have us there. Many cafés undercharged us and their regular customers were happy to go along with it. The barman at *Le Grand Serf* in the Grand Place, a rather high-class club which welcomed us as temporary members, undercharged us on all drinks, saying he would make up the difference by overcharging the regular members. We, and I suspect he, had no bad conscience about this because we knew that, with the Belgians' many years' experience as the 'cockpit of Europe', they knew how to live quietly and sometimes profitably under occupation.

The Brussels night life was also reviving rapidly. With Army HQ and various units in residence in the town it was an obvious opportunity for night club owners to open their welcoming doors. There was the *Boeuf sur le Toit*, the *Kremlin* and many others whose names I have forgotten. The *Kremlin* was the most colourful, with a dance band complete with balalaikas and, dressed as cossacks, Russian singing and dancing, and a fair amount of vodka. There was at the time much admiration of the incredible sacrifices of the Russian people and the heroism of the Russian army in the face of the brutal German invasion. During our stay I and several colleagues preferred the *Kremlin* and it was there one evening that, by an accident of mistaken identity, a lifelong friendship was formed. I was there with a charming young lady who was working at the re-established British Embassy and I saw across the dance floor a British officer sitting with a companion, with his back half towards me. I thought I recognised a man called Watson with whom I had served when first commissioned back in England. I walked over to him, slapped him on the back and said something original like 'Fancy seeing you here!' He turned round with a surprised look on his face and of course it wasn't Watson!

I apologized and went back to my table where I explained my embarrassment to my companion. However, she had been watching and had decided she knew 'Watson's' companion. I was alarmed that we might be making real fools of ourselves, but nevertheless went across again. But my companion was right. They did know each other. So we joined them. It was then I noticed the parachute wings on 'Watson's' uniform and he noticed the SAS wings on mine. We decided we might have something in common after all. Francis Cammaerts had been a very brave and effective SOE agent in France during the occupation, responsible for a large area of operations. In spite of hideous torture, Odette Churchill refused to reveal his identity when she was captured. Later he was captured and sentenced to be shot, but was rescued by the audacity of his radio operator, Christine. Tragically, after the war, she was brutally murdered in London. He was on the Vercors plateau during the ill-fated uprising of the French Resistance. He was a man of considerable intelligence,

144

always thoughtful and perceptive, with a warm personality and strong social conscience. The friendship we struck up that evening lasted throughout our lives.

Another friendship, already established, was strangely re-affirmed during this short stay in Brussels. Bill, whom I had met in TA days and who had been instrumental in keeping our brains working during the pre-Dunkirk period by arranging an economic discussion group, interesting us in gramophone evenings and who had gone off to be commissioned into the Recce Corps, turned up one day. He had been on his way to re-join his Regiment when he saw a soldier wearing the SAS cap badge and asked him if he knew where I was. To his surprise he was told I was in Brussels and was conducted to the Mess in the Avenue de Tervuren. Meeting again after a couple of years called for a celebration, a celebration that required us giving him a bed while I and two or three others took him on a 'sight-seeing' tour of the city's new night clubs. Three days later he left us. Sensing that he was uneasy about reporting a few days later than he should have done, we advised him to claim that he had fallen sick in Brussels, which indeed he had done on one occasion. He appeared not to appreciate our advice and left threatening dire retribution when next we met, which he hoped would not be soon! In fact we met sooner than either of us had thought – that winter in Holland.

Before that, my Section became involved, rather uselessly, in the aftermath of the gallant Operation 'Market Garden' – the Airborne Forces' attempt to capture and hold the bridge at Arnhem. That story is well known. Though the Paras held the bridge for several days against great odds, they had dropped close to a hidden Panzer Division. They were surrounded and cut off, suffering many casualties. Though they were gallantly supplied by air, it became clear that the Guards Armoured Division would be unable to relieve them. The only hope for those still alive was to evacuate them across the river, unavoidably under heavy fire. I was asked to take my Section up to Nijmegen to see if we could help. But by the time we had been able to make our way along the traffic-clogged road to Nijmegen all who could be brought across the river were safe. There was nothing we could do. Though the main objective – to seize and hold the Arnhem bridge to allow our armour across, which could have shortened the war – was not attained, the operation was far from a complete failure. The capture of the Nijmegen bridge was a big advance. We returned to Brussels depressed yet inspired by what had been achieved by the Paras and feeling somewhat guilty about our safe existence in Brussels.

Whether or not it is a fact of life it seems to be a rule of war that enjoyable happy interludes like our 'refit' in Brussels have to end much sooner than originally thought. The port of Antwerp was a vital link in the Allied supply chain for the forces in Europe and a major supply base in the preparations for the final assault on the Fatherland. But it was vulnerable to attack. We, together with other troops from Brussels, were sent there to strengthen the defences. By this time the bombing of London and the south coast by V1s was in full swing. We watched them, impelled to look for them by their staccato pulsating engine with flames spurting behind, as they flew over, headed north-west. Some, however, were aimed at Antwerp. And now also began the deadly fire of the V2 rockets whose swoop through the air was heard only after they had landed and exploded. Whereas you could watch for the motor on the V1 to cut out and quickly estimate where it would land, with the V2 there was no warning. The rule of thumb was that if you heard the sound you were OK.

Some V2s were aimed at Brussels, but at Antwerp the town and port were under attack. There was no defence against these rockets, hence a frantic search by the RAF for their launching sites. Tragically one of them landed one night on a large multi-storey building which was the HQ of the Military Police who, like us, had been sent there to defend the town. There were no survivors. On one occasion a close colleague, Tim, who was later badly wounded in Germany, and I were walking along a road towards the docks when a V2 landed not far away. The blast sent our berets spinning, ripped open our battledress tunics and pulled our trousers out of our gaiters. Then came the noise. 'Glad we were able to hear that one,' said Tim.

With the advance to Nijmegen the British forces were able to clear the Germans from all of Holland up to the Maas except for the town of Venlo which was still held by the enemy. It was impor-tant to the Allied cause that the capture of Eindhoven should be effected with as little damage as possible, particularly the Phillips factory because of all the technological information it contained. With the help of Dutch patriots a fast swoop on the town was organized to help the accompanying scientists to get there quickly. My section was ordered to take up position at Geldrop, just outside Eindhoven, and be prepared to be called in to protect the factory

146

and the 'project team', should the plan go wrong. It didn't. Again we had nothing to do.

By this time we were getting fed up with our post-France lack of action. However, a week or so later we were told we were to work with a Field Security detachment in Holland up on the Maas. Apart from the enclave at Venlo, the enemy were on the other side of the river. With the FS unit we were to watch for any incursion from the other side and any patrol activity from Venlo towards us. If there was any such activity, take prisoners for questioning. I was given a map reference at which I was to meet at midnight a guide from the unit we were to join. We were told they operated from a location between a small village called Boxmeer and Venlo.

We made our way there with great difficulty. It was a black moonless night in November and the flat terrain was covered with snow and ice. It was impossible to identify any landmarks. We could not use our headlights and we had to be careful not to wander off the road because we had been told that the retreating Germans had mined the fields.

Eventually we found the junction we were looking for and our 'guide' came forward from the blackness. He was a sergeant in the unit we were to join, but not too pleased to be kept waiting in the biting cold and dark. After a hurried introduction he led us onto what seemed to be a rough track. We bumped along, then stopped. Ahead of us in the darkness I could just make out the shape of a building. The sergeant told us to park our jeeps alongside the building and arrange guards, then went forward and opened a door. Immediately a bright shaft of light illuminated the darkness, accompanied by loud shouts from inside of 'Lights, bloody lights' before a curtain fell across the aperture to hide the glare.

As we went inside we were hit by a gust of warm air, smokiness, shouting and laughter, and a peculiar odour. We were inside a Dutch farmhouse with a living room at one end of the ground floor while at the other end were cattle surrounded by straw, accounting perhaps for the odour. As my eyes adjusted to the light I saw I was facing a strange assembly. It was a mixed group of six or eight British soldiers and three or four middle-aged Dutch civilians; in one corner one of the soldiers was holding an accordion, which, it seemed, he had just stopped playing; all were holding either mugs or glasses. A tall figure came forward dressed in khaki shirt and battledress trousers and introduced himself as Captain Wildblood. He

147

welcomed us with the comment that he thought we would never get there – I didn't think we were that late – and invited us to get out of our equipment and tunics, grab a mug, get a drink and relax, all of which we were pleased to do. After the bitter cold outside, we were already finding the atmosphere oppressively hot. There was too little ventilation for such a crowd in the small room. After a day or two we got used to it; unhealthy or not, the warmth was the important thing. That winter in Holland when the Maas froze over was the coldest I have ever experienced.

Amid the chatter and the singing to accordion accompaniment, Wildblood told me that they were celebrating with their Dutch hosts one of his lad's birthday. He also explained that living with the Dutch family was a matter of 'mucking in', as he put it. Before he and his men arrived the family had been living on a kind of stew made of potatoes and occasional greens dug with difficulty from the frozen ground. So, by giving them their army rations the farmer's wife cleverly combined the two diets to feed them all. Occasionally there was additional meat, not from the farmer's two or three beasts, his livelihood, which he was trying to keep alive until spring, but from a wandering pig or cow that trod on a mine in one of the adjacent fields and which his men could reach by carefully testing the ground. To judge from the number of untouched carcasses I saw next morning lying in the fields this was certainly not often. It was easy to agree to contribute our own rations to the 'common good'.

The farmer had provided a couple of small rooms for Wildblood and his men. We slept quite comfortably in a hay loft above the cattle. Next morning Wildblood showed me his 'bailiwick'. The farmhouse was quite isolated and surrounded by fields, at the end of the track we came by. There are no warning signs, he told me, but all the fields are mined. The Maas was about two fields away. From behind bales of straw at the end of a footpath that had not been mined we could observe German movements on the other side, as, no doubt, they could watch us. The road we had come by before turning onto the farm track went one way to Boxmeer, the other way to Venray, Horst and Venlo. We patrolled in both directions. There was little enemy activity, probably because the Germans were as cold as we were, but we could not rely on it. Vigilance and regular patrolling was the name of the game. Wildblood understood that an assault would shortly be launched on Venlo by our troops to get rid of the enclave. Meanwhile it was important to be visibly active at all times to give the appearance of strength and, hopefully, deter enemy cross-river patrols. The only activity that we should beware of was an occasional morning shelling.

By and large that describes the life we led for the weeks we were there – patrolling, keeping the other side of the river under observation, looking for footprints in the snow, sitting out an occasional shelling while happy to hear the replies from our artillery in the rear and trying to keep warm. On those patrols we could not help pitying the dire circumstances of the Dutch people in that region as we saw them searching for wood and for food in a barren area in freezing temperatures.

Two events stand out in my memory of that drab sojourn. One day on the road to Boxmeer I saw a Jeep wearing the sign of the Reconnaissance Regiment. I stopped it and asked the driver if he knew where Lieutenant Pearson, my old friend Bill, last seen leaving Brussels in a threatening mood, might be. I was as surprised as he was when finding me in Brussels to hear that he and his unit were stationed on the line of the Maas nearer to Nijmegen. That evening, immediate duties over, I set off to find him. When I reached his unit area I was directed to an old disused brick kiln. He was in the innermost chamber, beautifully warm, sitting writing on an upturned case by the light of a hurricane lamp. He was, of course, as pleased about our unexpected meeting as I was. But I became concerned when I learned that he was writing the kind of letter usually enclosed in an envelope marked 'To be Opened if I do not Return'. The reason was that he had been ordered to take a patrol across the frozen river the following morning to bring back a prisoner or two. I tried to lighten the mood by teasing him a bit about it as we took advantage of his 'booze' ration. When I left him some time later I jokingly said, 'I think we both should pray for a thaw: that would save you.' I do not claim that we had special influence in climatic matters but the ice on the Maas did break up that night.

I did not know this until a few days later when I came across one of Bill's Jeeps again and asked the driver to say 'hello' to Lieutenant Pearson for me. His reply was devastating. He said that Pearson was back 'in Blighty'. He had taken a patrol across by boat and unfortunately trod on a mine and lost his lower left leg. Later I learned more of the circumstances which were an example of one of those small acts of heroism that abound in war but go unrecognized. His patrol had come to a field they needed to cross but which to him and

149

his sergeant seemed likely to be mined. He immediately said he would test it and went forward, with tragic consequences. A mine took his lower leg away. His sergeant managed to haul him back and get him across the river to safety.

Needless to say I very upset by the news. We had been firm friends since TA days. I was told he was in the Queen Elizabeth Hospital in Birmingham. I decided I should go to see him. In consultation with Captain Wildblood, it was agreed I could take forty-eight hours' leave over the weekend on the understanding I would be back for the Monday morning shelling. (For some reason the Germans seldom shelled us on Saturdays and Sundays. Scruples, or their week-end passes?)

I went to a US Airforce base near Eindhoven where planes were bringing in supplies from Croydon airport. I found an officer who was in charge of one of the aircraft, a good old Dakota, and persuaded him to take me out that day, labelled on his manifest as 'additional equipment'. (The Americans were wonderfully accommodating in such circumstances, no question of having to 'go by the book'.) The flight was uneventful until we were near our destination. I was stretched out on the floor between various items of returning equipment. I sensed by the many changes of direction and height that we were not on a smooth approach. I went forward. 'Are we in trouble?' I asked. Looking out over the pilot's head I could see fog covering the ground, though we were above it in clear sky.

'Not trouble,' the pilot replied, 'but we can't see the airport. We might have to go somewhere else.' I peered ahead. I knew the area quite well. Suddenly I spotted the tops of two cooling towers that I knew were just beyond one end of the airport. 'That's where it is,' I said. Unfortunately I couldn't remember at which end of the runway they stood. At that moment two Very lights came up through the fog, some distance apart, which indicated the line of the runway. All this was, of course, before Radar and sophisticated electronic air traffic control systems. However primitive the methods, we swooped below the fog and landed safely. It was early morning. As I thanked the crew, they said they would be returning on Sunday morning and I was welcome to ride with them. This meant I could get back for the Monday shelling.

I hitch-hiked to London without difficulty, caught a train for Birmingham and a taxi to the Q.E. Hospital. I found out at the reception desk which ward Bill was in, but then I got cold feet. What do you say to a dear friend who has lost a leg and will be handicapped for the rest of his life? To see someone wounded in battle is one set of emotions. But to see a friend trying to come to terms with permanent disability is another, for which I wasn't prepared. I worried about it going up in the lift, but I needn't have. As I emerged from the lift somehow he spotted me – I was certainly not expected – and called out 'Roy'. I waved and as I approached his bed he said, 'Don't worry. I know what I'm going to do.' He had sensed my concern and put *me* at ease! He was remarkably organized. He was going to try to go up to Oxford on the returning servicemen scheme, read for a degree and then 'get a decent job'. It was an inspiringly positive attitude.

I stayed with Bill for two or three hours and by a similar combination of trains and taxi managed to call in late that evening to see my parents, who then lived in Surrey, eat a decent meal, miraculously produced by my mother from their rations and with, I suspected, not a little self-sacrifice on her part. After a good night's sleep my father sacrificed some of his petrol ration to take me to Croydon airport.

So far all the makeshift arrangements had worked smoothly. But Lady Luck is a fickle companion. When we were over the Channel the navigator came back to where I was dozing, leaning against a large sack of something or other, and said we had a bit of a problem, a burst oil pipe.

'Is that serious?'

'Not very good.'

Fighting visions of being involved in a plane crash into the Channel while on unofficial leave, travelling in an unauthorized manner – a sure case for a Court Martial if I survived – I went into the cockpit. Oil was splashing on to the windshield as it spurted past. I asked the pilot what he intended to do. He pointed ahead to the Dutch coast and said, 'If we get there, I'll try to land on the beach – if the tide's well out.'

Flying lower and lower, we arrived over a comfortingly flat-looking, wide stretch of sand. The tide was out. Lady Luck had not deserted us. With great skill the pilot took just one run at it and brought the aircraft in for a perfect landing. I asked what they were going to do now. He explained that the radio operator had been busy sending out messages and they would wait until someone came along to secure the aircraft and take them back to base. I said I had to get to my base quickly and would have to leave them to it. I thanked them warmly both for the rides and for the skilful emergency landing and hitch-hiked my way back, just in time for the morning's desultory shelling aimed, it seemed, at no particular target!

After another week or two of uneventful observing and patrolling in freezing weather, we were ordered back to Corps Headquarters not far from Eindhoven to guard, protect and be in reserve. We left the colourful Field Security detachment with some regret. Behind their relaxed, friendly demeanour they were very professional.

It was when I got to Corps HQ that I heard of the sad death of Major Bob Melot, MC. Bob, a Belgian, was a former WW1 pilot who was fluent in Arabic and several other languages. He was living in Egypt and knew the desert well. Our people wanted to make use of this knowledge and in spite of his age, probably in his fifties, recruited him into the Regiment. He was invaluable as a guide and as a linguist. He and Paddy Mayne became firm friends and it was while serving under Paddy on a raid on Benghazi that he was wounded. Legend in the Regiment had it that he refused to be left behind. True or not, he later rejoined the Regiment.

He served in Sicily and Italy where he was wounded again and refused to stay in hospital after he felt he was once more fit for duty. He returned to the UK with the Regiment where an SAS Brigade was being formed for operations in occupied France. He was made Intelligence Officer, organizing some of the drops behind the lines, but took an early opportunity to jump into France himself. Once France was clear of Germans and we concentrated in Brussels he obtained permission to take one of our Jeeps to visit his old mother who lived somewhere outside Brussels. He saw her and on the way back crashed the Jeep and was killed! He was an amazing and colourful character who had done and survived so much that such an end seemed more unjust than most.

Life at Corps HQ was even more uneventful than with the Field Security Police on the Maas, and without the diversion of patrolling. We maintained guns and equipment and even had a football to kick around, all in the freezing winter. These were days of considerable boredom until one morning – it was mid-December – as I was walking along the road towards Corps HQ three Messerschmitts came flying very low up the line of the road and over HQ, their guns chattering and spurting flame. They flew so low I could clearly see the pilots in their cockpits under their canopies. Whoever they were straffing it was not us, which was surprising. Had they known what they were flying over they could have got rid of a number of senior Corps officers!

We wondered about this sudden activity after weeks of quiet stagnation; it was the first indication we had of what we learned later was the German counter-offensive through the Ardennes. This audacious attempt by Field Marshal von Rundstedt to strike into the long line of Allied (American) positions and swing round to take Brussels and Antwerp was accompanied by an even more audacious attempt to cause confusion by infiltrating groups of ruthless Germans in allied uniforms. We were put on alert and told to stand by. Day by day the news was increasingly serious. The enemy had penetrated the Allied lines and were making for Bastogne.

We enjoyed a happy enough Christmas, though worried about the deteriorating situation in the Ardennes and secretly wondered whether there could be a role for us there. Several days later I was ordered to take my section down to the Ardennes to see if we could give any help in seeking out the infiltrators. It was not a long journey down round Liège but a slow one because of the abundance of military traffic and the fluidity of the situation. The American Armoured Cavalry, we were told, were in the process of relieving the besieged troops in Bastogne.

When at last I arrived at the HQ of the Para Battalion I had been told to contact I found to my surprise an old friend from our training days in the Para Holding Company in 1943 now a Company Commander. His Battalion had been sent down to help hold the line which had disintegrated under the force of the shrewd German surprise attack. After Field Marshal Montgomery took command of the sector, not entirely to the liking of the American commanders, the situation had stabilized. My friend had been in action and described the situation his company had faced as 'a bloody shambles'. However, once the line had been restored, with the Germans beginning to pull back as Bastogne was about to be relieved, his Company was taken out and was being held in reserve. He was sorry we would not be able to work together.

We stayed with him and his Paras for two or three more days in case the situation changed, doing a few patrols by day and yarning together in the evenings. But again it was a case of returning with little achieved, this time back to Corps HQ and the idleness of our duties as Corps troops. There followed several weeks of frustration, spent partly with Corps troops at Geldrop. Later we were moved back to Antwerp where the V2s were causing many problems. There were rumours that the Germans were planning an airborne attack on the port. We were sent there in an anti-paratroop role. But even this was inactive; there was little we could do except wait for the attack which never came. Meanwhile there was still no firm information about the role being planned for us in the invasion of Germany. Rumours of being sent on leave circulated from time to time, but nothing came of them. Unemployed, we were all getting very restless.

Official records of the exchanges of signals between our Squadrons 'in the field' and HQ in the UK, and between HQ and 21 Army Group, which I saw after the war, showed clearly the indecision in the High Command about the part we would play in Germany and the methods we would employ. It was clear that SAS HQ persistently sought answers from 21 Army Group, who presumably were waiting on SHAEF (Supreme Headquarters, Allied Expeditionary Force), but none were forthcoming. An example of that indecision while we were in Holland was when Squadron HQ was asked to test the practicality of loading our armoured Jeeps on to DUKW, an amphibian vehicle used in waterborne assault operations, finding out how quickly we could load and unload. Apparently the trial was a great success, but, as was normal at this time, nothing more was heard of the proposal.

Of course it is easy to be critical of 'the powers that be' when in the field, necessarily out of the picture during an intensive planning period, trying to maintain morale during a time when there was no reliable information by which we could satisfactorily answer the inevitable questions. Looking back after the event, one could understand the issues of strategy and coordination between the Allied Armies in the planning of the most critical stage of the war.

Then, in March, the long-hoped-for order came: proceed from Antwerp to Ostend to embark for the UK to report to 1SAS HQ in Chelmsford before proceeding on leave!

11

Advance into Germany

We spent about three fairly carefree weeks in England, partly at our HQ in Hylands House, Chelmsford, where there were rumours of a forthcoming operation in Norway which did not materialize, and partly on leave at home. Only 'fairly' carefree because we all knew the next call to action would be the climax of the years spent in uniform doing what was required of us to rid the world of the Nazi threat. In my memory it seemed I had scarcely begun my leave, relishing the news that Allied forces had taken Coblenz and Darmstadt across the Rhine, when we were called back to Chelmsford. Tony, my Squadron Commander, and Derek, my Troop Commander, were already there, as were many of our troops, when I arrived. We had forty-eight hours to check over our Jeeps, fuel up, check and load our weapons – each section of three Jeeps carried the usual twin Vickers front and rear but one Jeep was now fitted with the promised Browning .5 cannon and the driver's armoured shield was surmounted by a semi-circle of bullet-proof glass – ready to move to Tilbury, where we had arrived only a short time ago.

That forty-eight hours was marked for me by a period of anxiety that later turned to a tragedy that still haunts me. One of my NCOs, Sergeant 'Sandy' Davidson, was late in reporting. He was a fine, experienced soldier who had been awarded the MM for his courage in an operation in the Western Desert. When I realized he was late I had an unofficial word with Derek. We decided we would wait as long as we could, hoping for his return, before reporting to Tony, the Squadron CO. To be AWOL at such a time would probably be a Court Martial offence. We certainly did not want that for such a man. At the last minute he arrived. Relieved, but concerned that he should have caused us so much worry, I asked him why he was so late.

He said simply, 'I don't fancy this one, Sir. I don't want to go.'

I was shocked. 'I'm sorry,' I said, 'but I can't do anything about that.'

'I know,' he said, simply.

Later, in Germany, he was killed.

We crossed to Ostend on the night of 6 April, unloaded the Jeeps and headed off for Holland and Germany in a column made up of B and C Squadrons. *En route* we passed columns of tanks and supply vehicles all heading in the one direction towards Germany. This was to be the killer thrust against an enemy determined to defend the soil of the Fatherland. Our first destination was Meppen on the banks of the River Ems in the Weser-Ems region of north-west Germany, where we were to receive our operational briefing. To get there we had to thread our way through the devastated towns of Cleves and Emmerich, almost totally destroyed.

At Meppen we were met, in a wood just south of the town, by Paddy Mayne, the Regiment's CO. Our task was to protect the flanks of the Canadian 4th Armoured Division whose objective was the town of Oldenburg. Because the terrain was flat and boggy with canals running across our line of advance, the tanks would have difficulty in deploying. We were to travel by a roughly parallel route to give cover and to prod ahead in our lighter vehicles and 'deal with' any opposition when (not if) they ran into trouble. Two Squadrons were to operate elsewhere in Germany, while C, our Squadron, and B were to operate under Paddy's command. Paddy would lead C personally, while B under their new commander, Dick Bond, would take a separate route forward. It was not a typical SAS-type operation of infiltrating behind the enemy's lines. This time we were leading an armoured drive into the enemy's territory; there would not be much room for us to manoeuvre, while the enemy's opportunities to oppose our advance were considerable. However, as the records show, Paddy was anxious to keep the Regiment on active service and prove its flexibility, so agreed to the plan. The Canadians were to cross the bridge over the Ems at first light and we were to follow and then deploy either side of them.

We employed an agreed drill by which each section would take it in turns to lead the column – leading the advance in open Jeeps for very long, however well armed, was a bit of a strain – and within the

Section the lead Jeep would be regularly changed. Setting off at first light we soon ran into trouble. Derek's Section was in the lead and at the first canal we reached the bridge had been blown and the column came under fire from the other side. We moved down the canal to the next bridge, which was also destroyed and covered from the opposite bank. If we spent time taking them on across the canal we still would not be able to cross there.

We went on looking for tracks or minor roads that would take us to a crossing, but each time we came to a bridge it was destroyed. By this time my own Section was up front again. I found another track leading to the canal, but that bridge was also blown. Remembering the defensive fire from concealed positions across the canal on previous occasions, an obvious delaying tactic, I halted the column several yards from the bank, left my Jeep and crawled forward on my stomach in approved training school style to view the situation through my binoculars. While I was scanning the far bank I heard a voice in unmistakable Ulster brogue saying, 'Can you see anything down there, Roy?'

I looked to my right and saw a pair of brown boots beside me. Looking up, following the line of battledress trousers and tunic, I saw Paddy standing there.

'You get a better view from here,' he said quietly.

Feeling somewhat rebuked and very foolish, I stood beside him as we scanned the other bank through our binoculars.

'Well, they're not defending this one, but we still can't cross. Carry on.'

I led the column back to the road and tried another probe with the same negative result. We were getting nowhere. Then we heard from Tony that Dick Bond's Squadron had found a crossing. We were to rendezvous with them and cross together. We crossed the bridge in one column. By now my Section was in mid-column. At first our progress against some resistance from concealed positions on either side of the road, which were easily dealt with, was good. We were taking prisoners, but they were a hindrance, so we disarmed them and told them to walk towards our lines with their hands up. Whether they got there or made a run for it I don't know.

We had passed Lorup and were travelling down an incline in uncomfortably open country, unable to deploy, towards a village and I could see the leading Jeeps, Dick Bond's patrol, moving round a bend when we came to a halt and I could hear intensive fire up

157

front. I stood up to see what was happening when over the intercom came the message that we had run into an ambush and that Major Bond and one of his men were killed and others wounded. I could see that the leading Jeeps were close to some buildings on either side of the road.

As I watched, a Jeep came roaring past heading in the direction for the front of the column. It was Paddy Mayne. I saw him stop near the leading Jeep, then shoot forward at great speed, and I could hear the sound of persistent firing from Vickers Ks, though I could not see the action that was taking place. But, as we learned a short while later, and as is well described in Hamish Ross's book*, it was an act of great heroism, typical of his fearlessness and his concern for his men. It earned him a third bar to his DSO, though the citation, signed by Brigadier 'Mad Mike' Calvert, Commander of the SAS Brigade, Major General Vokes, the Commander of 4th Canadian Armoured Division and others including Field Marshal Montgomery, was for a VC!

When Paddy saw that the resistance was coming from farm buildings on the roadside and from a copse on the other side he went forward alone armed with a Bren gun firing into one of the buildings until the occupants ceased to respond. Then, in his Jeep, with Lieutenant Scott, who as a Sergeant had won an MM, volunteering to go with him, he drove past the point where Bond's Jeep had been attacked so that Scott could rake the enemy positions with fire from the twin Vickers Ks, then turned the Jeep, under fire, and drove back with Scott still firing. However, they and the front stationary Jeeps were still under attack from farther down the road and the wounded in the ditch could not move. He turned again and made another run and when he came to Bond's riddled Jeep he got out and lifted the wounded from the ditch into his Jeep while Scott continued firing. By this time the enemy had had enough and what remained of them withdrew. It was then that the two bodies were recovered.

We pushed on through the village, now clear of defenders, white sheets or towels hanging from windows. There was further resistance in the next village which ceased after a short engagement when a number of Germans surrendered. We were making further progress against well-placed nests of resistance. But, as we feared, the land was too marshy to allow us to deploy from the road, so it was easy for small groups of Germans, the fanatical Hitler Youth,

* *Paddy Mayne* by Hamish Ross.

to conceal in copses and ditches to cause us trouble. As a result, we split the two Squadrons again so that each could push forward on separate routes less vulnerably than in one long column. It was progress, but slow progress. What we did not know then was that, although we could hear heavy firing from the direction of the Canadian armour, their advance was even slower.

Several days into the advance we found the going more and more difficult. The lack of room to manoeuvre meant we were constantly held up on the roads we were forced to take by well-armed groups determined enough to let us get close to their well-concealed positions before opening fire. I remember one brush we had, when my patrol was once more in 'point' position on a straight stretch of road and about half a dozen young Hitler Youth hidden in deep ditches on either side opened up on us at very short range. Of course we outgunned them and after a few minutes two or three lay dead, others made a run for it and one came limping forward with his hands up. He had a wound in his lower back. He was not able to walk far in the direction of our lines and we could not provide the necessary treatment. There was a farm cottage nearby, so we took him there and handed him over to the two women occupants. The man spoke to them at some length as he showed his wound. The younger woman, speaking in halting English, berated us as cowards for shooting him as he was surrendering. I asked how was it if he was surrendering that we had hit him in the back? The older woman, equally indignant, was shouting at us in German and wielding a saucepan. We decided to leave at that point and get on with our mission. Was this, I wondered, retreating in the face of the enemy?

Two days or so later – we spent nights inside laagers formed by our Jeeps – we found ourselves in a more difficult situation. B Squadron were attacking a village along their route but found it strongly held and were bogged down; couldn't go forward; couldn't withdraw to take a better position. They needed support. Tony, our Squadron Commander, spotted a track leading to the side of the village and asked Derek to take our troop down it to attack from the flank. When we got within sight of the village we could hear heavy firing, but we could not tell which part was occupied by B and which by the Germans. Should we make a blind rush at it and hope we weren't going for our own men? Derek decided to consult Tony.

We had been able to position ourselves in line abreast ready for an assault, but there was absolutely no cover. Sitting there in open

Jeeps we were completely exposed. That delay for consultation was nearly fatal. Within minutes we heard the tell-tale crump of mortar fire just before the bombs landed among us. The side of the village we were facing was the German side! Fortunately the first barrage landed in front of the Jeeps and between them. They had our range not only with their mortars but also with machine guns that raked our exposed position. We were 'sitting ducks', so we did the only thing possible, dive for the nearest ditch!

I managed to crawl into a very muddy but rather shallow ditch. I dragged my .45 from my holster and momentarily lay there wondering which way to crawl to find a position from which I could see where our colleagues were and what was going on. I realized I was alone. I could hear bullets and mortar fragments peppering the Jeeps. With no logical or tactical reason, I chose my direction and crawled along. I had to keep very low and the mud almost covered me. The .45 in my hand was also covered with mud, squeezed up into the barrel. Then I was conscious of machine-gun fire from my left just a few yards from where I lay, directed over the ditch at the now empty Jeeps. Someone had got round the back of us. Carefully I raised my head.

On a small mound a yard or two away, just above me, were two Germans with a tripod-mounted machine gun, a Spandau I think. They were talking to each other as they fired. How they didn't see me I shall never know. Moving as carefully as I could I wiped some of the mud off my .45 and examined the barrel stuck with mud. I told myself that the first round would clear it, but suddenly the firing stopped. I looked up again and saw that they had picked up their gun and were making their way quickly towards the side of the village. What seemed to have moved them was the sound of approaching Jeeps.

Two B Squadron Jeeps were attacking the village from the flank to rescue the men who had been pinned down. Later we learned that some had been captured with two of our Jeeps. With this attack the German firing from the village stopped. I stood up. Other temporary occupants of that long muddy ditch were pulling themselves up, including Tony and Derek, and moving towards our Jeeps. Some had been badly damaged by the mortar and machine-gun fire and had to be towed back to where we were to rejoin the other Troops of the Squadron. The village was no longer a target: our men had been rescued and the Germans had withdrawn. As my Section lined up to retrace our tracks I saw movements in the distance beyond the village and to the right. It was long range so I moved forward a few yards and told Chris to loose off a couple of bursts. As he did so a bullet shattered but did not penetrate the semi-circle of bullet-proof glass in front of my face. There was a sniper somewhere. Silently I offered a prayer of thanks to the armourers. There was no more movement in the distance, so we rejoined our colleagues who were delighted to have the proof that the glass on the Jeeps was bullet-proof.

By now we were getting worried about supplies. We were thirty or forty miles into enemy territory and food, petrol and ammunition were running low. As we moved we had tried to set up bases, mainly for our workshops. A number of Jeeps needed repairs, but we also needed places to which supplies could be sent from a DZ. Unfortunately the 'drops' were delayed.

However, we moved on, wiping out the many pockets of resistance as we went, destroying equipment and taking prisoners. By this time we had too many prisoners, over 300. They did not like being dragged along in our wake as we fought and captured more, and they were increasingly a handicap for us. Moreover, they outnumbered us! However, Paddy decided it might be helpful if we ran into real difficulty to keep some of them with us, so we carried with us what he described as the 'best-looking' ninety and sent the rest walking back to our lines!

We moved on, anxious to keep parallel, as we thought, with the Canadian Armour. But in fact we discovered we were well ahead of them. We were out on a limb and it was not long before the enemy realized it. We were resting in a clearing in a pine forest somewhere on the road from Cloppenburg when we discovered we were surrounded by a well-organized formation of Germans, including Paratroops. Again we formed a laager with our Jeeps, manned the perimeter and put our German prisoners in the centre. We were under machine-gun and sniper fire, and the prisoners asked for protection under the Geneva Convention, a request that evoked a short but explicit reply from Paddy. A pine forest with trees close together is not the best place to get a good field of fire, so while the German fire was not very effective, nor our counter-fire, we couldn't move out into more open ground unless we found a route through them or round them. So we organized small patrols to probe through the woods.

One such patrol, comprising two great friends, Tim and Ronnie,

161

and one of their men, went through a part of our perimeter armed with a password for their re-entry. They could not find their way back and, sadly, probably because all pine trees look the same, attempted to re-enter our perimeter at a different point, one where the password meant nothing. They were shot by our own men. Ronnie was not seriously hurt, but Tim was severely wounded. Casualties by 'friendly fire' is not a new experience in war. Paddy could see that Tim needed urgent medical attention, which we could not provide. He immediately arranged for him to be taken out to the German lines in a Jeep under a white flag, accompanied by Neville Edwards, an officer from the Royal Engineers who was with us, and a German prisoner who was instructed to tell the Germans that if Tim was not properly looked after eighty-nine prisoners would not get back home, and he was sworn not to give our exact position away.

All this happened while I was away with my patrol looking for a way out on the other side of the perimeter. When I returned I told my patrol to brew up while I went to report our failure to find a way to penetrate the encirclement. As I was talking to Paddy, Neville returned and went straight to him and told him he was fairly sure he saw the prisoner indicate our position on a map. Paddy's reaction was instantaneous, a fine example of his quick tactical brain. Jumping into his Jeep, he told us to take as many prisoners as we could and follow him out of the clearing. Because of our position in the laager my patrol was last to follow. I doubt we were more than a hundred yards away when mortar and shell fire landed where we had been. Again Paddy's quick thinking saved lives.

We learned later that Tim was properly cared for, within the limits of the facilities then available. He had his leg amputated on a school desk where our 'besiegers' had their HQ and after the operation the wound was dressed with loo paper! He was then taken to a German military hospital from which he was repatriated shortly after the cease-fire. After the war we met each year, at first in London, later in Cumberland. He always spoke well of the German military surgeon who operated on him. He never experienced soreness or numbness in his 'stump', in contrast to the experience of my other close friend, Bill, who lost his leg across the Maas in the winter of '44/'45, as I have already described, and was operated on in one of our Field Hospitals and sent to the Q E hospital in Birmingham! He had problems for much of the rest of his life.

In an unexpected way the betrayal of our position by the German prisoner worked to our advantage. The situation had become more mobile and a patrol sent out from the new clearing in the forest we then occupied managed to contact the Armoured Division and alert them to our predicament. Guided by our patrol, two tanks with armoured carriers in support came crashing along the track we had used and rapidly dispersed the surrounding enemy.

Emerging from the pine forest we resumed our role of guarding the flank of the Canadian armour, taking care not to get too far ahead again. It was difficult because we still had to keep changing route because of the unhelpful terrain. We were losing Jeeps from enemy fire and taking casualties. It was frustrating that we could not deploy and hit back. We were advancing, but we did not have total initiative, the effects of which my Section was soon to feel.

We were 'point' section again and, after leading the column in my own Jeep for about an hour, a slow, probing hour, I handed over the lead to the one commanded by Sergeant Sandy Davidson. We had only been going again for a few minutes when Chris, my driver, pointed to a huge crater in the track, surrounded by what I thought were telltale mounds of earth. Fearing the worst, both Chris and I shouted to Sandy to stop. I can only assume he did not hear. He had only gone a few more yards before he hit a mine. There was a loud bang and a sheet of flame as we saw the Jeep lifted high into the air and Sandy's body with it. Alec and Fred, the two gunners, were thrown out the other side. Both were wounded. I jumped out of my Jeep and ran to where Sandy lay moaning, shouting to the Jeep behind to be prepared to give us cover. We didn't know whether the trap set for us would be manned. Sandy was badly hurt and I put field dressing bandages on him and gave him some morphine to ease the pain. I helped to get him to another Jeep which carried the three casualties back down our line of advance to a Field Dressing Station. They all got to a hospital, but Sandy did not survive. The tragedy of his premonition has haunted me ever since.

It was now more than ever evident that the way we were operating was far from satisfactory and causing unnecessary losses in both men and equipment, so it was decided we should leave our Jeeps at a base created near Lorup and operate as infantry alongside and on the Canadian tanks and armoured cars. Once more we were engaged in a role that was very different from the 'traditional' SAS method. Records show that our commanders were as unhappy about this as they had been about operating vulnerably in a terrain that made it impossible to deploy and manoeuvre. I think that in the field, while we were not enthusiastic about it, many of us felt we were nearing the end of the campaign. Certainly it again proved the Regiment's adaptability.

Progress was desperately slow. Able only to advance along a single road, the armoured column continuously meeting well-sited opposition, mostly Tiger tanks and machine-gun nests, this part of our battle was officially described as a slogging match.

Whether a different strategic deployment could have provided the opportunity for a swifter assault on the objective, Oldenburg, is hard to say. Our job was to leap off the tanks when the column was brought to a halt by opposition, plod through the soft ground and clear any supporting positions.

On one occasion a Tiger tank with its deadly armour-piercing gun was seen in the distance lurking by a farm building. Often they had infantry in support. The column halted and my Section ran into the field on that side of the road and moved forward, ready to engage any accompanying defenders. One of the Canadian tanks came alongside us. Its commander was standing in his open 'hatch'. Focusing our binoculars, we could see the crew of the Tiger jumping into their tank and closing their hatch; rather late, I thought.

'Can you get him?' I called.

'I think so.' He fired one round. It was a brilliant shot. The Tiger burst into flame. Only one of the crew emerged, apparently unhurt; other troops ran from behind the building. They were all quickly dealt with.

But on another occasion, just before dusk, the column was approaching a village we were scheduled to take. To my surprise we halted. I went up to the leading tank to find out what was happening, expecting a plan of attack. Instead I was told we were to wait where we were for the night. I was astonished. We were within sight of the objective, but that was where we sat during the night and listened to the sound of tracked vehicles – tanks? artillery? – entering the village. Although the fight next morning was worse than it need have been, it was soon over, as the enemy force withdrew. The German defenders were pulling back all the time.

Shortly after this episode our Squadrons were withdrawn from this unsatisfactory role – the column was bogged down again – and sent to concentrate at a newly established base nearby. It was early in May. We were glad of the rest, but at the same time wondered what next was in store. There were rumours that the German forces were surrendering, that a cease-fire would be declared and that we would then to return to the UK to prepare for a new operation. For once both rumours were based on fact.

It was 4 May. The cease-fire was to take effect at 6 a.m. on the 5th. We were to hold whatever positions we held, but not to advance. However, to circumvent any moves by 'rogue' enemy groups, we should maintain watchful patrols. My Section was ordered to carry out such a patrol from 4 a.m. to 6 a.m. on the 5th. We did, and it was the most carefully conducted patrol of the campaign. Our fieldcraft was perfect. We had been told that the RAF would also be patrolling the area. While we were out there we looked for them and finally saw the small shapes of aircraft high in the sky. They too were conducting a careful patrol!

It was a strange feeling returning a few minutes to 6 a.m. from what was to be our last warlike patrol of our victorious European war. I had expected to feel elated, a sense of triumph, but I didn't. We returned to the clearing from which we had set out, made sure the safety catches on our weapons were on, looked at our watches, checked with each other that it was 6 a.m., then sat down and lit cigarettes, feeling relieved we had got this far but otherwise rather flat.

We had to wait where we were for further orders. It was a fine sunny day and later I lay on my back on the grass beside a great friend, Pat Riley, who had won a DCM and been commissioned in the field. It was so quiet and still, so very quiet, eerily quiet. We lay with our hands behind our heads staring at the clear sky trying to get used to the silence. Suddenly from across the clearing came a shout, 'I can't stand it. For God's sake someone fire a gun'!

A couple of days later we were told the Germans had indeed surrendered and that 8 May would be declared Victory in Europe Day, a day for celebration. We were ordered back to our temporary base to collect our Jeeps, make for Poperinghe on the Franco-Belgian border to meet our other Squadrons, then proceed to Ostend to embark for Tilbury and on to our HQ at Chelmsford. We left Ostend early in the morning of 9 May. From Tilbury to Chelmsford we stopped at nearly every pub en route. There wasn't a pint of beer left! The celebrations of the previous day had left them dry! 'Sorry mate. You're too late,' 'No, sorry not a drop left,' were the greetings we met. We were rather depressed when we reached HQ and, once parked up and unloaded, made straight for our various messes. There, thanks to thoughtful catering by the Mess steward, there was an adequate supply of refreshment. It turned out to be a long night.

We had scarcely recovered from the effects of that homecoming than we were told we were going to Norway to do 'a quick tidying-up' job, then perhaps to the Far East, where the war against Japan was still raging!

12

Norwegian Round-up:
Parisian Summer

In no real sense of the phrase could our Squadrons' activity in Norway be called a war operation. In truth it was more like a summer holiday. The campaign to liberate occupied Europe and defeat Germany by-passed Norway and there was some feeling among the Norwegians that they had been forgotten. Although a Norwegian traitor was responsible for making Quisling an alternative word for treachery, Norwegian resistance played a remarkable part in crucially delaying Hitler's efforts to create an atomic bomb. Though occupied, they had been true allies. But in by-passing Norway the German surrender left a large number of the German military machine still armed and at large. Our job was to help round them up, disarm them and put them in POW cages, ready for their repatriation to Germany, and try to 'smoke out' SS and Gestapo agents.

About a week after arriving at Chelmsford we flew to Stavanger airport en route for the delightful port of Kristiansand in southern Norway. It was mid-May, the Norwegians were enjoying an early summer and their welcome could not have been sunnier. Their friendly hospitality during the whole of our stay was almost overwhelming. But there was work to do. There were several thousand German troops in and around Kristiansand. We frequently went on patrol to nearby towns where there were German detachments who had no wish to argue about being taken in as POWs. Although I did not experience it myself, I was told that some German officers co-operated in identifying SS and other wanted war criminals.

We had been at Kristiansand for less than two weeks when we were sent to Bergen which became our Squadron's base for several weeks. Here the situation was a little different. In and around Bergen and up the coast there were many thousand Germans, mostly submariners and Luftwaffe personnel. The huge submarine pens that had been carved into the rocky cliffs of the fjords were virtually impregnable and many of the U-boat commanders and the officers and men of the Luftwaffe felt that they had not been defeated in battle. They had been ordered by the German High Command under General Jodl and Admiral Dönitz to lay down their arms. They did not refuse, but, when we went to pull them in to POW cages, they complied with a great show of arrogance and did nothing at first to help us identify the Gestapo and SS among them. However, little by little, and with help from one or two German officers, we managed to catch a fair number. One of our men captured the head of the Gestapo in Norway.

It was impossible to carry out those tasks in that sunny, hot summer, one of the best in years, we were told, in the grandeur of the Norwegian scenery and after the tensions of the frustrating advance in north-west Germany, without devoting a part of the time to 'leisure pursuits'. In fact we were told to keep ourselves fit for a possible later role in the Far East. After the flat marshy territory of Germany the magnificence of Norway's mountains and the humbling length, breadth and depth of the fjords were breathtaking. To sail up a fjord and look up at the towering cliffs, or drive round one on a high narrow road and look down at the fjord far below was to be made aware of the insignificance of our human endeavour compared with the works of nature – of God. That was why it was always a pleasurable adventure and not a strain to go on patrol to the many welcoming communities up the western coast to see if there were any stray detachments or war criminals attempting to hide. The villages of white wooden houses with small wooden churches, some-times with a green pasture close by, nestling beside or at the head of a fjord, were quite unforgettable.

Back in Bergen we had established a satisfactory *modus operandi*. Starting early in the morning we went out to round up and corral the mocking, defeated enemy. In the afternoon, having captured a number of German Stormboats (with powerful outboard engines) and having made what passed as water skis from packing cases, we swam or water-skied (involving much involuntary swimming) round the harbour. And when we returned to our billets we always found a number of invitations to drinks, a meal or a 'party' with a Norwegian family. Our days, and much of those nights of little darkness, were full. Somehow, perhaps because of the purity of the air and the energizing feeling that the worst was over, we did not seem to tire. And in the time we were there we enjoyed joining a family at a traditional mountain picnic on midsummer's night, when the sun did not set.

It was all almost too good to be true, as was brought home to me many weeks later. We received a signal from 1 SAS HQ to say the Regiment was opening an office in Paris from which a group of officers, NCOs and men who had carried out operations in France would revisit operational areas and award those who had helped us with letters of thanks from the Brigadier and the Prime Minister, Winston Churchill, and accompanying SAS emblems. It was also to try to find out what had happened to some of our comrades who had been captured – many of whom were victims of Hitler's infamous order that SAS and Commandos were to be handed to the Gestapo and executed – or who were just 'missing'. Some of this proposed group were selected from the Squadrons at Chelmsford, but HQ also wanted a nominee from our troops in Norway.

'Please nominate officer to report back for duty at the Paris office,' was the purport of the signal. In normal circumstances an offer to serve, whatever the duty, in Paris at the Army's expense would result in an unseemly rush, perhaps with fatal consequences. But being in Norway in that glorious summer, carrying out fairly simple military duties and being the objects of much friendly hospitality, was not a normal circumstance. So the first signal and its repeat were ignored, but as the third showed considerable irritation and some threat of reprisals we decided to draw straws: the short straw would have to accept the assignment in Paris. I drew the short straw and, feeling a little depressed, prepared to fly back to the UK.

But before leaving I was approached by Ted Badger, a delightful colleague, much experienced, who had fought with the SAS in the Western Desert and Italy where he had been wounded and then commissioned. He looked worried and asked me if I had ever read a book called *Lost Horizon* by James Hilton. I said I had. He then asked whether I remembered that when 'those people' had left Shangri-La they 'fell apart', became old, 'the flesh dropping from their bones,' I remembered. So he asked me if, as I was now leaving

Norway, I could send a signal from England to tell him whether I was OK! Our time in Norway was not just recuperative, it was a short stay in Shangri-La!

The office in Paris was located in the Hotel Palais Royal, an establishment considerably less grand than its name suggested, not far from the Tuileries Gardens, but which housed also the office of a branch of the Secret Intelligence Services. At the head of our office and responsible for organizing these imaginative 'goodwill', and investigative, visits was the Hon. David Astor, a major in the Royal Marines who had headed a special mission into occupied France for which he was awarded the Croix de Guerre. His secretary was a Leading Wren, Joan Forty, who had worked first at Combined Operations HQ, then with the SAS, liaising between the Regiment and SOE, and latterly with the Free French Forces at their London HQ. Her presence was distinctive in two important ways: she was very attractive, and outside the Naval Attaché's office she was the only Wren in Paris. Inevitably she was the object of much admiring attention and of many social invitations from members of our teams. With the re-opening of the Officers' Club in the Rothschild mansion in the Faubourg St Honoré the social facilities were readily available. But it was a highly competitive situation, not easy to get a dinner date. Yet I was lucky enough to spend several happy evenings with her. And after the war when we got engaged and then married I decided that the short straw in Bergen was not a bad draw after all!

The re-visits to the operational areas were highly successful. In a spirit of joy and relief that the threatening cloud of occupation under which they had lived for so long had lifted, we were warmly welcomed and the letters of thanks and emblems very gratefully accepted, often with some emotion. Clearly nothing like these gestures had been expected by those people who had so bravely risked their lives, and some of whom had lost theirs and who no letter could reward, in concealing our presence and helping us where they could. Now able to meet people openly and talk without fear of discovery or suspicion of their allegiance, we learned of some of the later consequences of our wartime presence among them.

As far as my Section's operational areas were concerned there were no adverse consequences, just a happy meeting with many people, some of whom we did not know at the time but who were aware of us and did not betray us. Others we knew, like the Mayor and the Curé of Châtillon-en-Bazois, who, over the inevitable glasses of wine, told us how the Curé had allayed the suspicions of the German patrol that entered the town just after we had driven out the other end. And they told us, good-naturedly, as if it was a bit of a local joke, that we had nearly killed the patron of the bar-café on the outskirts of the town when we had set bombs on the German truck parked outside. He had come out for fresh air when the bombs exploded. He was shaken but fortunately unharmed.

Then there was the old farmer, a sun-tanned, wrinkled, moustachioed lion of a man who lived near Lac des Settons. He had hidden two of our men who had become separated from their Section after landing by parachute. He insisted I take *un verre* with him. It was a spirit he had distilled from rotting fruit. The first sip made me sweat and caused the hairs on the back of my neck to stand out stiffly. He told me of his 'secret' plan to dredge for a Jeep that had dropped into the lake, because his old horse was dying!

With some of the visits the happiness was tempered somewhat by sad memories of the price exacted by the enemy from the innocent solely because we carried out operations in their areas, like the visits to Dun-les-Places, Montsauche and Les Ormes, where civilians had been shot and homes destroyed because of our presence. Yet even there the reception was cordial and singularly lacking in recrimination. The spirit of resistance of those people was so strong that they accepted their losses as part of the price to be paid for eventual freedom from occupation. My admiration for the ordinary French citizen in the countryside, the villages and small towns is as strong now as it was then. Given some understanding of the awful choice between resistance or collaboration, often with the life of a loved one at stake, and of the scars left on the French national conscience, it could not be otherwise.

In the years since the war I have frequently re-visited those areas, often to attend, with other members of the Regimental Association, memorial services. We have always received the same warm welcome from the sons and daughters of those we knew as we did from their parents, and the bonds of friendship between those of us who are left and the survivors of the Maquis groups, particularly Bernard and Camille, with whom we fought, remain unbreakable.

A small incident on one of those visits illustrates how small gestures in those circumstances, probably in others too, can be the basis of a continuing friendship. We had attended a ceremony at Montsauche

171

which had been the object of German reprisals and the following morning I went into a newspaper shop to buy a paper. After serving me the proprietor asked if I was one of the *veteran Anglais* who had been at the ceremony. I said I had and he then asked if I would accept a small memento. I said I would, but it was not necessary. He insisted and, going to the back of his shop, produced a small tin and took out a wartime one franc piece and offered it to me. I thanked him and asked why. He said that he had been a small boy when some of our Jeeps came to liberate the town. He was standing at the edge of the pavement when one of the Jeeps stopped and the soldier in it lifted him up, stood him behind the guns and drove him round the town. He had felt so proud, was the envy of his friends and had never forgotten the kindness of that soldier, 'a typical Tommy' as he put it. I still have his one franc piece. I'm sure that that particular unknown soldier never thought he might be doing something memorable, simply a naturally thoughtful thing to do. Perhaps he had a son or a younger brother.

Another great benefit I gained from my time in Paris was when I was invited to take over the running of the office on David Astor's 'demob' from the Marines. This meant I was there for about three months, a formative time in France's post-occupation political and economic life, a time when one could mix socially with a variety of people closely involved in those developments. Some were former resisters, some were lawyers who had had to work under occupation law, some who just lived and worked under an enemy regime, listening when they could to BBC broadcasts, waiting for the promised liberation. For me it was a most educative period.

General de Gaulle, the brave former Colonel who had led an armoured counter-attack against the advancing German 'blitzkrieg' in 1940, by then leader of the Free French force and recognized by the Allies as the legitimate head of France's post-occupation Government, had in August 1944 made a triumphant entry into Paris to an enthusiastic welcome by the people. He represented, after all, the official spirit of French resistance and carried on his shoulders the hopes of most French men and women for the longed-for stability and much-needed reconstruction. Contrary to general belief, however, his carefully planned triumphant walk down the Champs Elysees from the Arc de Triomphe between cheering crowds was not entirely free of opposition. There was sniping from windows high above the Champs and more firing in Notre Dame. Some

Germans were still in hiding, possibly with a few committed 'Vichyites'.

There was no great damage and the incident was insignificant in the overall theme of the restoration of legitimate Government. But the incident was seen by 'the powers that be' as such a departure from the required scenario that the BBC correspondent who described it at the time, Robin Duff, a distinguished war correspondent, was so admonished that he left the Corporation and became the Paris correspondent of the *Daily Express*.

I learned this from him when we first met. Our introduction was made in an unusual way. I was staying at the 'Town Major's Hotel', the Hotel Scribe. There at breakfast one morning I was forced into conversation by a lady (of 'uncertain age') in a khaki uniform I had failed to recognize, not least because of the gaily coloured bows on the epaulettes and whom I had tried to avoid because I had noticed she was a keen conversationalist at breakfast which I was, and am, not. We were at the same table and I was hiding behind my copy of the Army newspaper when a buttery knife came over the paper, pressed it down and I was faced by a disapproving look and tart comment, 'Young man, you are ignoring me.'

I protested and introduced myself, as she did herself. That initially unwanted conversation was the first of many fascinating ones and many enjoyable meetings with a most interesting lady. She called herself Lady Moore-Guggisberg, which was a slight but excusable cheat because, while she was indeed the widow of Brigadier Sir Gordon Guggisberg, a distinguished WW1 soldier, she had introduced the 'Moore' because her maiden name was Decima Moore, one of two 'Gaiety Girl' sisters known in their day for their beauty and vivacity. Decima had followed a noble British theatrical tradition by marrying into the aristocracy. She was a person whose life was a mine of interesting experiences which she lived tirelessly, it seemed amid throngs of friends and acquaintances.

During the First World War she had opened in Paris, in the Faubourg St Honoré, the first all-ranks club for the British Army. She ran it with a team of volunteers. When the Second World War began in 1939 she went to Paris to re-open it. But that resumption of voluntary service to the Forces was shortlived. When the German Army broke through the Allied defences and closed on Paris she had to leave. She travelled on the tailboard of an army truck to a port in Brittany where she boarded a vessel for England. However, as soon

173

as Paris was liberated she returned to reopen the club once more. But times had moved on; it was the era of centralized control and the club came under the management of the Navy, Army and Air Force Institutes (NAAFI). In recognition of her pioneering role she was given an honorary position and that strange uniform with an absurd broad-brimmed hat with a flat crown, which she hated. So she decorated the uniform and the hat with bright ribbons.

At a later breakfast meeting she invited me to join a dinner party she was giving at the Officers' Club to meet someone she 'just knew' I would get on well with. I could not go to the dinner so she asked me to join the party for coffee. On arrival I was shown on to the terrace where the party, about ten in number, sat in a circle. The hostess was nowhere to be seen. I took the one vacant chair. The man on my left said that Lady Guggisberg was somewhere in the Club talking to other friends, which it seemed she did every few minutes during dinner. 'It's not surprising,' he said, 'she knows just about everyone in Paris.'

As quietly as I could I told him that I had been asked in order to meet someone special. He said he was there for the same reason. 'Who do you think it is?' I asked. Equally quietly he treated me to amusing, politely dismissive comments about each guest in turn. At that moment our hostess came along the terrrace, hands waving, breathlessly apologising for just *having* to go to ask someone a favour (which I am sure was granted). Then she came over, put a hand on my and my companion's shoulders and said, 'Oh, I'm so glad you introduced yourselves. So clever of you both to recognize who I meant.' Which of course we had not. 'I love making friendships,' she said.

And that is what she had done. That was how I met Robin Duff. For the rest of my time in Paris I saw a great deal of him and watched how he fulfilled his role as Correspondent of the *Daily Express* when it was enjoying a high reputation under one of the legendary editors of Fleet Street, Arthur Christiansen, whom I met when he visited Paris for a briefing on the political situation. Robin had a varied and interesting career after the war and my wife and I enjoyed his amusing and erudite company for many years.

Sadly it was around this time, October, that I heard from our HQ that the Regiment was to be disbanded! The Military 'top brass', who basically disapproved of the somewhat 'irregular' methods of the Regiment, in contrast to commanders in the field who had seen the value of them, had decided, it seemed, that SAS-type operations

174

were no longer needed in the British Army. By contrast the Belgian Army retained the Belgian SAS Regiment and the French Army retained their two French Battalions!

All members of the Ist SAS were to be returned to their former regiments, in my case the Parachute Regiment. I was to wind down our work in Paris and then seek further employment with the Paras! A final parade of the Regiment was held at the Chelmsford HQ, followed by a farewell ball; regretfully, I could not attend either. How short-sighted that decision was became evident when in 1947 a TA SAS Regiment was formed, merging with the Artists' Rifles and becoming the basis for a merger with the Malayan Scouts as a regular regiment to deal with the Communist insurrection in Malaya. Since then the SAS has been an indispensable, and very professional, element in the British Army's special forces operations, of which we are all hugely proud.

It was through Robin Duff that I had the privilege of meeting Thomas Cadett, the highly respected pre- and post-war BBC Paris correspondent whose short career with SOE ended when he roundly criticized their early lack of security. I also met Alan Moorehead, the Australian war correspondent whose later books about the war were widely acclaimed. The three of us spent many hours discussing political developments in France and the emerging disagreements between the Allied leaders that were to shape the uneasy power struggle between East and West. I particularly remember our meeting in a café the morning we heard about the atom-bombing of Hiroshima. We were stunned and shocked. Could the saving of Allied lives justify a mass killing? We tried to comprehend its meaning for the future of mankind: how could we control the power that had been released? Could there be a defence against it? Alan quietly observed, 'None; there is only one answer to it. It's God.'

Thus it was that I had the opportunity to observe at close hand how French social and political life evolved in the months following liberation, contrasting political manoevering and sophisticated attitudes in the capital with the more simple, basic focus on making a living free from fear in the countryside. I noted at the time that the overwhelming enthusiasm of the great majority of people for stability and normality was never completely free from feelings of guilt about the recent past and worries about how they could have let it happen. Those feelings were kept close to the surface by the staging of trials of collaborators, in which the evidence was an unhealthy reminder of what was done by some French to support the German occupation while others risked all to resist. Some had no option but to collaborate, but some did of choice; they and those who betrayed their compatriots were seen as traitors.

It was also evident that pre-war political rivalries were slowly reviving. There had always been a sharp division between right and left. When war broke out the Communist party was banned. Having to work 'underground', they already had a clandestine network and so were the first to resist. Members of the other parties followed, setting up their own undercover organizations. In the Maquis the different groups fought bravely side by side, political rivalries put on one side for the 'duration'. But even the overwhelming desire for peace and reconstruction could not allay many suspicions: suspicions in the south that any new Republic that was formed would be controlled by 'the north' and would not address the needs of the rural economy; suspicions that some collaborators were being shielded and would escape justice; suspicions (well-founded, as it later transpired) that some collaborators still occupied senior positions.

Nevertheless when elections were held for a new French Assembly – the first to be freely elected for over five years and a major step on the road to creating a new Constitution – all parties, including a strong and now legitimate Communist Party, declared their determination to work together for the reconstruction of France. One of the tasks of the Assembly was to elect a President, which was generally expected to be General de Gaulle. He was immensely popular and seen by most people as the spirit of resistance and of the new France. There was no doubt that he was determined to restore the self- respect and self-confidence of the French people and pride in the French State. Of course he meant this to be a State of his own creation. To this end he began persuading the people that their liberation was brought about by the French Resistance movement. Of course, though French Resistance, the Maquis groups, the SOE, the OSS and the SAS had all played important parts, it was the power of the Allied Armies, Air Forces and Navies that had freed France and other occupied territories. But he wanted to be sure he had a free hand in creating the kind of French State he wanted.

Ahead of the expected date of the election of the President by the Assembly, the parties wanted him to declare his policy intentions. They wanted him to agree to the policies they devised in return for

176

an agreement to elect him as President. He refused to discuss his own policy intentions before he was elected. It looked like deadlock and there was talk of postponing the election. The party leaders were worried about the power the General would have if he was elected without agreeing a political programme with them. But then they failed to agree a programme between themselves. Each sought a declaration of intent from the other! It was evident that, despite the popular wish for a settled future, suspicion between political leaders was rife in a wounded nation. The General lacked confidence in all the parties, but was especially suspicious of the Communists. He had complete confidence only in himself: '*L'État c'est moi*,' he is supposed to have said later, quoting Louis XIV.

In the event he was unanimously elected President of France in November 1945 and his task then to hand out the departmental portfolios in a way that would keep the peace between the political parties was bound to continue the inter-party bickering. Each party had its 'wish list' of the major portfolios. In the ensuing arguments de Gaulle played the 'back my choices or I resign' card with confidence. He knew that once elected there was no alternative to his Presidency. It was an uncertain start to the rehabilitation of that damaged nation.

Reflecting on the situation, a French lawyer, a centre-of-the-road patriot, told me, 'Our need to forget the shame of occupation and collaboration and to regain our pride will lead us along the path of a form of nationalism which will affect French policy for years to come.' It was a prophetic observation.

While all this was going on, the political landscape in Britain had undergone a transformation of its own with the surprise rejection in a general election of Winston Churchill, the inspiring war leader, and the election of the Labour Party under Clement Attlee. When later Churchill visited Paris, Thomas Cadett attended a dinner party for him. When asked about the election Churchill commented that the British people had taken leave of their senses and Cadett said that perhaps the electorate had distinguished between Churchill the war leader and Churchill the Conservative, to which Churchill replied, 'You don't know what you are talking about'. He was also asked whether he had said of the severely proper Stafford Cripps, 'There but for the grace of God goes God.' He said he hadn't but wished he had, and went on to comment, 'He has a red nose and doesn't drink. I drink and don't have one.'

Meanwhile there was much talk about disagreements between the Allied leaders over the way the occupation of Germany should be handled. Suspicion was rife here also. Had Roosevelt yielded too much to Stalin's requests? Was Stalin's view of the need to 'punish' the Germans (which had some justification in view of the tremendous Russian losses) compatible with the Anglo-US policy of rehabilitation? Was Stalin satisfied with half of Germany or did he want more? Could his ambition be contained?

By coincidence, while these issues were being discussed Francis Cammaerts arrived in Paris, heading for occupied Germany and a job in Berlin. When he learned that I was 'unemployed' he asked if I would like to join him as a liaison officer between the British and French military Government representatives. Another SAS colleague, Ronnie Grierson, would also be there. It was a lucky opportunity to learn something of the processes of military government. Without knowing anything about what the job might entail, it took me about two minutes to agree to apply for a posting there. I did and, with some helpful influence from Francis, it was agreed.

13

Berlin : Governing the Defeated

Those of us in the field at the end of the war in Europe knew little – and, I suspect, cared little – of the conferences of Allied leaders aimed at reaching agreement on the occupation of a defeated Germany and how it should be governed. These discussions began as early as 1943 and continued in Quebec and Moscow in 1944, and at Yalta in 1945. Although there was suspicion among the Allies, particularly between the Western Allies and Russia, about ultimate intentions, they agreed a plan and the mechanisms needed to fulfil it that could be put in place as soon as the fighting stopped and the surrender agreed. It was a tribute to Allied foresight and planning.

Whatever the strains that emerged in the process, it provided a workable framework, demilitarizing and governing Germany and controlling the revival of its economy, at least until the 'iron curtain' came down and half of it was taken under the direct control of Soviet Russia. Surely there was a lesson there that appears not to have been learned fifty-eight years later following the defeat of Saddam Hussein, when, if there was an agreed plan, it failed to foresee many of the consequences of releasing suppressed sectarian ambitions or to see the need for a quick transition. Because of this failure an efficient liberation deteriorated into a clumsy occupation.

Germany was divided into four zones, each under the control of one of the Allies, and Berlin, the shattered capital, into four sectors each also under the control of one of the Allies. Thus the British zone was the north-west of Germany from the Belgian-Dutch borders and up to the Danish border, and eastward to the Russian zone, the eastern border of which ran along the River Elbe. It had been agreed that, in recognition of the huge Russian losses during Germany's invasion of Russia and the Russians' determined fight back, they should take Berlin. They did, street by street, but then pushed on to a line along the Elbe. The French zone, which was agreed only by Britain and America giving up some of their allotted zones, was to the south. The American zone was to the east of the French and south of the British. Russia controlled the rest of Germany.

In Berlin the British had control of the western sector which included Gatow airport (which played a crucial part in relieving the later blockade of the city by the Russians) and had the Rivers Havel and Spree running through it. The French had the sector to the north, the Americans to the south of the British and the Russians to the east. Understandably, in view of their losses in the capture of Berlin, the Russians resented the western Allies' share of its occupation, but it had already been agreed.

The overall political authority for Germany was the Allied Control Commission, the Council of which at that time comprised the four senior military commanders: Montgomery, McNarney, Zhukov and Koenig, though there were changes later. The Commission worked through a Coordinating Committee of lesser Generals with civilian expert advisers. It was a brave and elaborate experiment in quadripartite occupation designed to placate the aggrieved feelings of the principal victims of Nazi aggression and satisfy their expectations as victors, while putting into the background for the time being the suspicions and irritations between them. It was an arrangement riddled with hidden difficulties, yet for a period, the important immediate post-conflict period, it worked.

The Regiment was disbanded in October, but it took until December for my 'movement order' to Berlin to come through, during which time I closed the Paris office. The interlude was a further opportunity to see more of the political struggles that characterized the acceptance of de Gaulle's Presidency and of the Government he wanted. His 'confrontation' with the Communists over their demand for a major departmental portfolio was ended by his seeking, and getting, a vote of confidence from the Assembly. While the motion was being debated the centre of Paris was paralysed by noisy student demonstrations and the sealing off by the gendarmerie of areas round the Chambre des Deputés. In the event a member of the Communist Party was made a Minister in the War Ministry, while de Gaulle himself took the portfolio of National Defence. Clearly he had got what he wanted.

However, many people to whom I spoke, some from the political left but also former resisters and people from the political centre, would have welcomed a radical appointment that might have opened to scrutiny the workings and manning of Ministries and regional administration where, they feared, former collaborators were being sheltered. Sadly the post-liberation enthusiasm was being tempered by political rivalry and suspicion.

I was due to leave for Berlin on 3 December, but there were delays which enabled me to share a farewell party with Robin Duff, the *Daily Express* correspondent who was leaving France, and journalism, for a job in the India. It was a wonderful gathering of the great and the good, and the poor and humble, of Paris representing the wide range of friendships he had made as a foreign correspondent, and I had made to a lesser extent in my short stay. We ran an 'open house' from 5.30 p.m. until 3 a.m. the following morning! The warmth of the expressions of regret at our leaving was rather humbling. When I left Paris the following day I left a city physically undamaged, grand and beautiful, that was in spirit, however, unsettled by political uncertainty. But I left still full of enduring admiration for the patriotic, friendly, practical attitude of the ordinary working-class Parisians, like Johnny's cousins and friends, of whom I had seen a lot, and the staunch *paysans* and *maquisards* with whom we had fought.

It was under a declining, pale, wintry sun that I drove out of Paris in an open Jeep (that had been overlooked when the Regiment was disbanded and its equipment dispersed) and headed for Metz. On the way I picked up a hitch-hiking GI who provided welcome company as we swapped war experiences and worried together about the future. We had a meal and slept in a bivouac area in Metz and left early next morning for Kaiserlautern in the French zone, where I left my GI companion whose parting words were 'Let's hope we've got this damn dictatorship thing settled for good', forgetting that there was still at least one in place! It became colder and colder as, under a threatening sky, I drove on to Mainz where I crossed the Rhine into the American zone. By the bridge I passed lines of shivering, hungry-looking refugees with their pathetic bundles of belongings, waiting, I assumed, to return to their homes, which, to judge from the general devastation, would provide them with little comfort.

By this time the cold had become intense and sleet and snow swirled round the windscreen into the Jeep which had a canvas hood but no side-screens. To add to my discomfort I only had a short Norwegian sheepskin jacket over my battledress. I was not enjoying the journey. Just outside Frankfurt I took the autobahn to Kassel, 110 miles or so of exposed windswept road. Kassel was a city of shattered buildings and rubble. There was no chance of finding a bed and I only managed a warming cup of coffee through the kindness of a couple of GIs standing by their truck in the shelter of a wall that had once been a building, so I pressed on to Brunswick where I slept fitfully in another, but much colder, bivouac area.

Next morning the sky was leaden and heavy with snow. The autobahn to Braunschweig, about a hundred miles farther on, was covered by ice and a layer of powdery snow that swirled here and there in the wind. When the wind dropped it snowed heavily. It was impossible to drive at any speed. I was losing a lot of time. What traffic I saw was American military traffic. It seemed that the weather kept all but essential movement off the roads. Beside being a cold drive it was a lonely one. When I eventually reached Braunschweig the scene was again one of devastation and destruction, made more desperate by the driving snow beneath a glowering sky. After a short stop to get my circulation moving again, I turned right to Helmstedt and the Russian zone.

Helmstedt was the gateway to the 'Magdeburg corridor' across the Russian zone, an autobahn which was the only road to Berlin allowed to us by the Russians. Before setting out on this 120-odd-mile stretch, on which it was advisable not to stop, one had to 'sign out' with the American border control, giving one's name and vehicle number and time of departure. This information was communicated to the American control on the border of their Berlin sector at the other end of the journey. It was a precaution against going 'missing', which, it was said, had happened to some people. It was a forbidding prospect as I passed through the checkpoint, heading east. The sky was dark, the driving snow swirling round the inside of the Jeep making it difficult to see, and it was very, very cold.

I had done about 100 eerie, lonely miles – I had seen no other traffic – when the need for a 'natural break' forced me to stop. As I got out of the Jeep my legs simply gave way under me; with only my battledress trousers to protect them, the circulation had become retarded. I lay beside the Jeep trying to rub them into use when I saw in the snow and mist ahead a Russian military convoy approaching. I thought of the Regiment, Britain and the Union Jack and decided

182

it would be an insult to all three for a British officer to be seen lying helpless on an autobahn by the Russian army. So I dragged myself under the Jeep and pretended to be doing a repair. At least I would be seen, I thought, as a competent member of His Majesty's Army. As the convoy went by I heard shouts and comments I could not understand, which I hoped were friendly Allied greetings, but which, I hate to admit, sounded very much like a barrage of jeers.

The final twenty miles or so passed without incident and I checked through the control point on my way to the British sector of Berlin. The devastation in the suburbs was as complete as any I had seen. Snow covered the stunted remains of bomb- and shell-shattered buildings and the piles of brick and rubble which lay spread across many of the streets, making them impassable. I passed pale and pinched-looking people, mostly old men and women, in old coats, shawls and blankets dragging sledges or pushing prams or barrows through the ruins, turning over bricks and pieces of masonry in their search for fuel and food. Where and how did they live? In the distance was the stark shape of the battered steeple of the cathedral on Kurfurstendamm. It was a ghastly as well as a ghostly picture of the retribution visited on the once proud capital of Germany, the once glamorous centre of the short-lived Nazi domination of Europe. It could have been the backdrop to a Gotterdammerung in the very citadel of the defeated Gods of evil, except that it was not a picture. It was terribly real.

In the course of that very uncomfortable journey I had seen at first hand the dreadful scale of the destruction of Germany's towns and cities and I had begun to appreciate the enormity of the task of Military Government in bringing some sort of order to the chaos and providing the basics of existence, an observation my subsequent experience there did nothing to dispel. The huge capacity of the coal mines and the steel mills in the Ruhr had been sharply reduced; electricity was in short supply and large parts of the rail network had been destroyed. The German people were not just defeated, they were bemused and, not surprisingly, they had lost the will so essential for recovery, retaining only the will to survive.

When I linked up with Francis I found we were to share a house in the Grunewald, a leafy up-market suburb which had been spared much of the destruction suffered by other areas, and we were assigned to a nearby Mess the president of which was a rather disagreeable Colonel. He once heard Francis and I discussing some of the radical policies being introduced by the new Labour Government in Britain in the fields of education and social security, and the proposals for a national health service. 'Socialist nonsense,' he said. 'Where did you two meet?' Without batting an eyelid, we said we had met in the Kremlin, without mentioning that it was actually a night club in Brussels. His reaction was a joy to behold. His complexion changed rapidly from healthily ruddy to deep crimson before he sort of exploded with the unoriginal and erroneous comment: 'Bloody communists!'

Ronnie Grierson, my old friend from the SAS, was also there as a liaison officer. He had recovered from a wound he suffered in Germany. Together we had penetrated the strict security arrangements surrounding the trial in Paris back in July of Marshal Pétain, the head of the Vichy Government in the unoccupied southern part of France until it too was occupied.

Our job as liaison officers between the British and French representatives in the Military Government was not very demanding. The atmosphere was friendly, often jolly, and I am sure the part we had played in the fight to liberate France was a great help in our relationships. But for me the job was not satisfying. My French was not good enough for me to participate fully in the many discussions we had on the areas of concern to our respective governments or our discussions of post-war politics. Francis and Ronnie on the other hand were fluent and it was natural that they led in these discussions, which were revealing, not least because of the emerging disagreement within the Allied community about how to promote yet control reconstruction.

On a visit to the newly opened Officers' Club in the French sector, I was surprised to hear at such an early stage much criticism of the Anglo-American attitude to German recovery. The French were suspicious that the policy of getting factories working, repairing the mines and railways to get coal moving to homes and to power stations, getting materials made for reconstruction, goods made available for consumption, thus providing work, would rebuild Germany's industrial strength which could again threaten the rest of Europe. While this was going on, they said, France lacked coal, electricity was rationed, French factories could work for only three days a week and French people were unemployed.

It was a finely balanced argument, though the French fears overlooked the fact that at that time teams of experts from Britain, France,

America and Russia were busy in Germany identifying machinery and materials they intended to remove as reparation for the damage done by German aggression. Yet, while it had not been the Allied intention then to restore Germany as a European power, later, after the Russians retired behind their iron curtain, policy turned to the strengthening of Germany as a buffer against possible Soviet aggression. This led to the anachronistic efforts, mostly by America, to provide German industry with new machinery and materials to replace those taken as reparations. So defeated Germany got the new stuff and the victorious Allies got the old! Funny old world even then!

Sadly, I also sensed in those conversations with the French an undercurrent of anti-Americanism, which of course became more pronounced later and caused someone to say, 'This is the doctrine of letting no good deed go unpunished'.

After a while changes in the administrative arrangements meant that Francis and I ceased to be Liaison Officers and became members of the British team in the Economics Division of the quadripartite Military Government of Berlin. Because of its significance as the capital of Germany but located deep in the Russian zone, Berlin was the only town in occupied Germany to be administered on a quadripartite basis. Overall control was in the hands of the Allied Kommandantura, responsible to the Control Commission's Council, working through the Military Government teams and, on the civil side, the local Burgermeisters.

The main policy objectives of the Allies were denazification, destruction of the war machine with measures to ensure it could not be restored, the introduction of effective government and the revival of economic and social life. In this they were largely successful, but when agreement on policy finally broke down Germany's division between west and east was a key issue in world politics for years to come.

In Berlin quadripartite committees were set up to be the authority in each aspect of the City's life: committees for finance, public utilities, transport, police, agriculture and horticulture, trade and industry for example. Each of the Allies had one or two representatives on each committee. The chairmanship of the committees rotated monthly to coincide with the rotating chair of the Commission's Council. It was customary for the nation in the chair to host entertainment in their sector for members of the committee and others involved in this intricately balanced bureaucratic administration.

185

Francis became a British representative on the Agriculture committee, which suited his experience of farming, and I was to be a representative on the Trade and Industry committee. No experience in my background fitted me for that task, apart from having been a junior clerk in a stock jobbers' office who laboriously read books on economics. However, in spite of the impressive title of my committee, the hope of achieving agreement on measures that would promote economic activity was more a political process than an economic one. It meant being clear about the British objective on each of the issues arising and their contribution to the overall aim of reviving the City's productive and commercial life. My co-representative on the British side of the committee was a rugged, taciturn Captain in the Canadian Army who had taken up his position, as had the others on that committee, before I arrived.

The work of the British representatives on all these committees was coordinated by an infantry Brigadier whose formation operated with such dash during the fighting that he earned the nickname 'Loony'. He had no more experience suitable for this role of ensuring that British policy was followed in all the committees covering such a spread of municipal activities than the rest of us had for our roles. Yet his approach to the problem was an ingenious application of a military principle. At a meeting of all our representatives he acknowledged, unnecessarily, what he thought was his inadequacy, and went on to say he knew only one way to tackle the problem: the 11th of May. This was the colloquial term for I.I.M.A.I., – information, intention, method, administration, intercommunication – the Army's 'drill' for the 'appreciation of a situation', in other words a 'trigger' for a sequential approach to the problem. Thus, in its military aspect, Information might be, for example 'Ridge ahead occupied by the enemy'; Intention – 'Take the ridge'; Method – 'Deploy sections 1 and 2 etc.'; Administration – 'What help needed'; Intercommunication – 'Who else should be informed?'

'Loony' decided that we should apply that 'drill' to our work on the committees. So we agreed to a procedure whereby before every meeting we would give him the background to the issue on the agendas: the likely approach of our Allied colleagues, what we believed the British objective to be, how that objective might be achieved, any help we needed and any special need to communicate with others. But he made it clear that he did not want written reports, that our debriefing reports to him after the meetings should be

186

verbal. It was a refreshing attitude to what was already a highly bureaucratic process.

But while it worked as a procedure for us amateur soldiers doing jobs we were never trained for, the major obstacle to getting agreement on the committees was the highly centralized Government of Russia. Neither their representatives nor their superiors in Germany were allowed to exercise any initiative. They were not empowered to take decisions. Every agenda item, every issue, had to be referred to Moscow. This severely delayed progress and was frustrating in the extreme to all the Western Allies. Important new issues requiring agreement were added to agenda that still held a number of matters not yet dealt with. At one time more than twelve items remained on the Trade and Industry agenda awaiting a response from Moscow. While our meetings were polite and conducted properly through interpreters and our social meetings remained convivial, the tone of the discussions became distinctly chilly.

It was particularly irritating to attend a meeting ready to seek agreement on some important new initiative, to develop trade say, then to be informed by the Russians that they were now ready to discuss the earlier items three and four on the agenda. There then ensued some chaotic moments while the 'western' representatives searched for their papers and briefs on those old items.

Another, and unexpected, obstacle to agreement was the unpredictability of the Soviet response to issues raised by the Allies. It seemed sometimes as if any excuse would do to oppose an allied initiative. Francis, on his Agriculture committee, in an effort to secure land for agricultural and horticultural production, proposed the setting up of a purchasing co-operative in land round Berlin. The Americans did not like the idea because it was 'kinda' socialist. The French thought it spoiled the Germans, but the Russians opposed it because it would 'interfere with private enterprise'!

Outside our place of work, away from the negotiating tables, life in Berlin for the members of the occupying powers was very pleasant. In the British sector there was a very well appointed and staffed Officers' Club. The staffing of Messes, Clubs and 'billets' was never a problem. Unemployed Germans were only too pleased to work in those capacities. They always behaved politely and correctly, often irritatingly too much so. We often wondered what had happened to the 'master race'. And at that time we were all following a determined 'non-fraternization' policy, so that between us and those who served us in the Mess, in the Club or in our billets, the relationship, if one could call it that, was very distant.

While 'non-fraternization' was probably an inevitable initial 'requirement' in our occupation of a country that had brought so much suffering to the rest of Europe, it was not sensible in practice when we were working to restore some degree of 'normality' to a destroyed and hungry nation, and blocked any relationship which might have led to a more helpful understanding. Inevitably it did not last long.

In addition to the more formal inter-Allied entertainment there was a great deal of informal 'partying' both between delegations and with newly found friends within one's own sector. They were truly international gatherings and, apart from being enjoyable, were usefully informative, enabling us and, no doubt, the members of the other teams to understand better their points of view and, therefore, their likely approach to foreseeable issues.

Our accommodation was comfortable enough and we were well looked after by a shared batman and the Frau, the former occupant of the house who now lived in the basement with her daughter. However, electricity supply was intermittent; sewage had to be collected and taken away; while there was water for washing and bathing, it could not be drunk. Drinking water was delivered by army tanker and transferred into whatever empty bottles were available. Usually these were empty alcohol bottles. A 'ration' of alcohol was delivered by the army once a month. We never knew what it would be, or how much we were allowed, until it was delivered. Always it was a strange mixture: a bottle of Bols gin, a bottle of kirsch, or cointreau, a bottle of whiskey, or vodka, for instance. Delivery of the ration was always the signal for a round of entertainment. And the mixture of it led to the concoction of some of the most exotic, and perilous, cocktails ever devised.

On one occasion the custom of putting drinking water into empty bottles nearly led to a death by drowning. It was the duty of our batman to put a bottle of drinking water in our bathroom, to be used mainly for cleaning teeth. One morning Francis, lying in the bath, wanted to quench his thirst. I was shaving. He asked for the water bottle. I passed it to him and he took a couple of mouthfuls. Unfortunately the batman had in error given us a bottle of another colourless liquid, kirsch! For a moment it was touch and go whether or not he could keep his scorching mouth above the waves.

Exercise formed an important part of our relaxation. The pre-war German pursuit of Aryan physical perfection meant that the necessary facilities abounded. There were squash and tennis courts, a fully equipped gymnasium complete with PT instructors and a fencing master, a stable of former officers' horses that needed exercising and there was sailing on the Havel. For occasional weekend breaks a Country Club provided for members of the Hitler Youth movement, a fine log and stone building on the bank of the Havel, was made into an Officers' Club. It had on the ground floor a dining room and kitchens and a lounge running the length of the building behind windows overlooking the water, and upstairs, along a gallery, a line of bedrooms also overlooking the Havel. If we had a weekend pass, we would telephone and make a reservation in the approved manner.

However, there was a difficulty with this welcome facility which without careful planning could curb the enjoyment of the occasion. The Club was run by the YWCA, the Young Women's Christian Association, and the only liquid refreshment offered was apple juice! The person in charge was a very pleasant but, we thought, unbending senior figure in the Association. As she often said, 'Rules are rules'. Between ourselves, we irreverently referred to her as 'the high priestess'.

An important weekend loomed. The birthday of Max, a delightful, amusing Australian whose 'party piece' at any lunch or dinner was to eat the flowers in the vase on the table. It would have been an insult to celebrate his anniversary with apple juice, especially as the occasion coincided with the delivery of the 'booze ration'.

So, having made our reservations at the Club, we arranged to carry some of our ration with us, leaving it in our parked Jeeps until, after a pleasant but sober dinner, we sat at a table in the lounge by the side of one of the curtained windows. We had bottles of apple juice on the table. At intervals one of us would 'retire' for natural purposes, go to the Jeep and take a bottle of alcohol round to the lounge windows. His departure was a signal for the rest of us to push our glasses up to the curtained window through which the hand of our friend would fortify the apple juice. This ploy worked well until it was the rather unsteady Max's turn to refuel. We waited with our glasses against the concealing curtain. Then, to our consternation we saw a hand push through the curtain of a table further along and empty some of the contents on to the table. Then followed a very audible oath. The

189

misdemeanour was repeated at the next and the next tables. Something akin to uproar ensued and the game was up. The 'high priestess' came to our table and asked whether any of us gentlemen had brought alcohol into the Club. Not exactly, we said, we know the rules. With great forbearance and patience, she then asked if we had any alcohol in the vicinity of the Club. We confessed – in our Jeeps. Was there still some in the Jeeps? Again we confessed – there was, but we would leave it there. Lowering her voice, she then asked if we might be good enough to bring what was left to her room after everyone had gone, as she hadn't had a drink for weeks! We did and had an enjoyable little party with her. From that moment we were prepared to worship in the temple of the 'high priestess' as often as we could.

The administrative HQs in our zone and sector were, as were the centres of the other Allies, the focus of much coming and going by 'visiting firemen'. These groups, who came regularly, were either reparation teams, Government Ministers and officials, inter-party parliamentary groups or the home Press, all anxious to see how political objectives were being attained and how the quadripartite machinery worked. It was a fairly constant part of our activity to meet them formally, show them round, explain and discuss, as well as meet them later informally. There was no doubt this was a burden, though a necessary one, on the administration: tours, meetings and receptions had to be arranged which frequently involved us as 'MilGov' representatives on the various committees. There was a public affairs section and a team of people whose job it was to provide answers to the endless Parliamentary Questions on denazification, demilitarization, inter-Allied relationships and the work of Military Government. This team was headed by a capable and determined civil servant known as 'the PQ queen' who was capable of bringing all work to a standstill while she sought the answer to a question that the Minister needed *immediately – repeat, immediately*.

I remember particularly one parliamentary delegation that included a newly elected Labour Party MP who had served in the Navy as a rating during the war. His name was Callaghan, James Callaghan. At the end of a reception for them, he, Francis and I, and one or two others, went off to one of our 'billets' and spent most of the night – the alcohol ration must have still been intact – discussing post-war problems in Britain and in the world generally and what could be done about them. Many years later when I was working in

190

the National Economic Development Office I attended an economic conference. Jim Callaghan was then Chancellor of the Exchequer and I happened to be behind him in the queue for the buffet lunch. I reminded him of that occasion in Berlin where we spent a whole night putting the world right. He remembered and observed dryly, 'We didn't make much of a job of it, did we?'

One of my many interesting experiences in that historic phase in post-world-war development, that commanded the contribution of so many eminent political leaders, prominent and successful military commanders, and skilled public servants, was to attend as observer some of the meetings of the Allied Commission's Coordinating Committee. This Committee met every five days to organize the implementation of the Control Commission Council's decisions and supervise the various aspects of quadripartite government. Its members were: for Britain General Sir Brian Robertson, advised by Sir Nigel Playfair, senior civil servant Sir William Strang and businessman Sir Percy Mills; for the USA General Clay, Mr Murphy and others; for France General Koeltz, advised by a M. Tasset and a M. Sergeant; for the USSR General Sokolovsky, advised by M. Sobolov and others.

The tone of the meetings was formal and polite, but, it seemed, the sessions were never easy. They were long and argumentative, while the perimeter bustled with minor advisers fetching papers and taking messages for senior advisers. The atmosphere was heavy with cigarette and pipe smoke. The Russians were heavy cigarette smokers. In one session when the Russians had refused to change their position on a particular item, Sokolovsky, smoking continuously from a large box of cigarettes in front of him, sent for another large box and said he was happy to sit there and smoke all the cigarettes until the matter was resolved.

This stubbornness called for great patience on the part of the other delegations. General Clay was inclined to get exasperated, while General Robertson was the epitome of courteous patience, which, when he was in the chair, helped to resolve many a difficult question. The core of the committee's difficulties was the different interpretation put on the Council's decisions by the different delegations. If a compromise had reluctantly been made in the Council's discussions in order to avoid a breakdown, the point could always be raised again and thrashed out at the implementation stage in the Coordinating Committee.

Britain was well served in these delicate political circumstances by the unusual combination of military commander, senior civil servant and business leader. I have often reflected since on the way in which so many of us found ourselves unexpectedly carrying out tasks, at the centre for some, on the fringe for others, of hugely important issues of politics, government and international relationships. Although I did not think it at the time, I realized later that it was a privilege to be involved in a minor capacity in those matters, the experience of which helped me a great deal later on when I worked with Government, businessmen and trade unions on issues of economic development.

There was a salutary moment when almost overnight the policy of non- fraternization became one of fraternization. In an effort to establish a more normal relationship we were now to make friendly contact with the defeated enemy with whom until yesterday we had dealt on polite but cool and distant terms. Of course the change was recognized as the practical need in the task of reconstruction for a better understanding of the people we were working with. But it was not easy to handle. We had been engaged in bitter combat with Germany for years. It had been the enemy. The Germans embraced the new situation enthusiastically, but we had difficulty in adjusting our attitude.

This became obvious when a number of 'MilGov' representatives were invited to a party given by Germans who were attempting to resume their lives as writers, journalists, artists and actors. Before we went we realized it was going to be a difficult evening, but we resolved to make a big effort to be conciliatory. At the party a colleague and I joined a small group standing in a corner. They spoke very good English and the conversation turned inevitably to the condition of Germany, the difficulties of being occupied and the danger posed by the presence of the Soviets. Discussing the incident later we were convinced we had listened sympathetically and made a genuine attempt to understand their point of view. But suddenly, in the middle of the conversation, came the salutary moment. One of the Germans – she was a writer, if I remember correctly, – said, 'It's no use talking to you two. You hate us so much, you just don't understand.'

Shocked, we protested.

'No, it's true' she went on, 'the hate and distrust is in you.'

We thought for a moment and then my companion said, 'It's not hate. Certainly we don't trust you. But you have to understand that we and others like us have two very good reasons this century for not trusting Germany, and we have good reasons, many of them very personal because of things you have done to friends and comrades, not to like you very much. You can't ignore that or pretend those things haven't happened.'

It was clear to us then, and must be clear to all of us now, that reconciliation is a very tender plant that grows very slowly.

If that incident was not enough to illustrate the deep damage war does to nations and their peoples, especially wars that with better preparedness and a willingness to resist aggression early might have been prevented and many limbs and lives saved, two other incidents brought it home to me. One was in the depth of the German winter, not long after I arrived in Berlin. We were told a re-formed German orchestra was to give a concert in the State Opera House, in the Soviet sector. We bought tickets. It was a bitterly cold Saturday afternoon and snow was falling. We knew the opera house had been damaged by bomb and shellfire and certainly there would be no heating, so we put on winter wear and took blankets. The sight that greeted us was unworldly. At least a quarter of the roof of the opera house was open to the sky and a part of one wall had been sliced open. We had been told that, as the orchestra's instruments had been destroyed in the fighting, they had borrowed from a variety of people what instruments they could get. We sat in the 'circle' and watched and listened with sympathy and admiration as the orchestra, accompanied by a choir, came in with shawls and blankets over their shoulders, knitted balaclavas on their heads and mittens on their hands. Snow flakes were falling through the open roof on to the audience and players alike as they played and sang Beethoven's ninth symphony, the Choral.

At such a time of uncertainty and in such bleak, almost hopeless, conditions that song of brotherhood and freedom was performed passionately by this group of poor, cold and probably underfed musicians. It was spellbinding. It may not have been the greatest performance of all time, but to us it was a deeply emotional and memorable one. It suggested that Germany might be able to find again the soul it had for too long rejected. I see and hear clearly that performance even today. And when I hear and enjoy a performance of the 'Choral' that occasion always comes to mind.

The other incident was in the Spring, April, when I was ordered back to the UK to be 'demobbed'. My time was up. A couple of days before I left I attended my last Trade and Industry Committee meeting and explained to my colleagues that it would be my last meeting as I was returning to England and to civilian life. There were courteous and generous expressions of regret and good wishes from my colleagues in the other delegations. But the one I remember most was the Russian tribute because of what it told me about conditions in Russia, that had suffered so much from the mad German attempt to conquer it. The Russian representative, I remember his name well, was a Colonel Panfilov who as a young man had been a Tsarist officer, but who had then seen the (red) light and joined the Soviet army. He was a courteous, almost old-worldly, man. He stood up at the table and said something like this, 'Captain Close, when you return home I hope you find your house still standing and your family still alive. I hope you will find the means to keep them and that you find some satisfactory work.'

This said not much about my situation but much about conditions in Russia and the Russian army. He did not realize that I had regularly received from and sent mail home. I knew my (parents') house was standing. I knew they were alive and I knew they had the rationed means of survival. I deduced that those in the Russian army did not know these things, that they had not enjoyed regular mail and information from their homes. In those circumstances the endurance of the Russian soldier, and civilian, was something to be admired. This feeling was reinforced years later when I was on a business mission to the Soviet Union. 'You must remember,' they kept saying, 'we suffered twenty million war dead from the German invasion.' The scale and effect of that is hard to comprehend even today.

A few days later I was in Britain attending a demobilization depot somewhere near Woking to draw my 'demob' clothing. We stood in a long line and shuffled towards a Staff Sergeant who 'sized' us for our clothing. 'Suit or jacket and slacks, Sir?' I chose the jacket and slacks, and the trilby that went with them. He looked me up and down and called out something to the people behind a long counter who selected the appropriate items from shelves behind them and stuffed them into a bag. The man in front of me turned and said wrily, 'Yesterday I was Colonel Stevens. Today I'm told I'm "short, portly and square". Funny, isn't it?'

So ended my six-and-a-half years in army uniform. I stood for some moments at the door of the depot clutching the last travel warrant I would receive from His Majesty's War Office. Buses waited to take us to the railway station. But it was a time to pause for a moment and think briefly about what that phase of my life had meant to me.

A time to recall that callow youth of 19 who, excited and wondering, was mobilized in 1939, who in 1940, carrying a WW1 weapon, became one of thousands in a badly defeated army, who, caught in a morass of terrified civilian refugees while firing defiantly if not very effectively at attacking aircraft, trudged to Dunkirk and on to the beaches where they were miraculously saved to fight again, who watched helplessly from the ground the great victory in the air that saved us all, who, then experiencing restless boredom and self-doubt, took part under new leadership in the metamorphosis of the British armed forces on the way to greater adventures with the SAS, fighting the enemy behind his own lines and then on his own territory in a huge victory that more than made up for the earlier defeats and who, finally, at a crucial time in post-war relationships, was privileged to take part in a well-planned, broadly successful experiment in military government to control and also revive the defeated enemy.

Certainly they had been formative years. One had overcome many fears, coped with long periods of frustration, tried to fill the gaps in one's education, felt the senses sharpen in times of action, learned the life-saving value of good discipline, enjoyed the elation of victory and experienced the comfort of unrepeatable wartime camaraderie forged by serving together in a common cause which formed lifetime friendships.

But now what? If the youth of 19, on mobilization, poorly equipped, looked ahead with wondering uncertainly, so also did the ex-soldier of 26, though happily conscious he was returning to a still free country, realizing that he faced a future in difficult postwar conditions for which he was again singularly ill prepared.

Epilogue

In September 2004 the author was one of a small group of SAS 'veterans' who returned to the areas where they had operated in enemy-occupied central France in 1944 on a 60th Anniversary visit of Commemoration and Remembrance organized by the Regimental Association. They were accompanied by some of the next of kin of those who were killed on those operations. Together with local French authorities and villagers they held twenty-five cermonies of remembrance, travelling 2,000 miles, and laid wreaths and Regimental crosses on the graves and places of execution of former comrades in Brittany, the Morvan region and the Vosges. These were the places where fierce fighting had taken place between members of the SAS and their Maquis friends against the German occupation forces.

Most of the graves rest in village or town cemetries where they are carefully looked after by the local people, often by their children. In Saint Sauvant Forest where thirty-one SAS were captured, executed and buried in a mass grave only discovered after the war, the place where they were shot is kept clear, planted with flowers and looked after by the small daughter of a nearby villager. At Dun-les-Places, alongside officials from the town and 'veteran' Masquisards who had fought in the area, the group laid a wreath at the memorial to more than twenty men taken from their homes in the town and shot as a reprisal for local resistance activity, and they paid their respects at the graves in the town cemetery. In a forest in the hills above the small town of Ouroux at the secret camp once occupied by an SAS Squadron, the group attended a touching ceremony at the graves of some members of the SAS and a Maquis group, and the crew of an

RAF bomber shot down nearby, which, despite the distance from the town and the difficult location, are still kept scrupulously neat and tidy. And in the town itself the visiting 'veterans' were warmly welcomed and entertained to lunch by 'veterans', and their families, of two Maquis formations with whom they had fought. Here they met old comrades and renewed friendships forged in the fight against occupying forces, lasting bonds epitomized by the often-repeated promise of the Maquisards, 'We will never ever forget what you did for us'.

Further on they visited the graves of Maquisards executed near Bains-les-Bains and the graves of thirty-one SAS murdered by the Gestapo after they were captured near the town of Moussey in the Vosges mountains. Because of intense SAS activity in that area 220 men, the entire male population of the town, were deported to Germany from where only seventy returned after the war. In spite of this troubled background, here, as elsewhere, the townspeople welcomed the visiting group with warmth and affection. After the war the Commonwealth War Graves Commission wanted to rebury the remains of the SAS soldiers in an official cemetery, but the people of Moussey refused to let them go, insisting that they belonged with the community with whom they had fought, mirroring the feeling of all the communities where members of the Regiment had been killed.

Also in the Vosges mountains, at Natweiler-Struthof, the site of the only German concentration camp on French soil, a wreath was laid at the memorial to those who perished there, in honour to the memory of four women members of the SOE and a member of the SAS whose bodies after execution were fed to the ovens. The group visited Villequiers where the villagers had rescued the body of an SAS soldier killed there and buried him in one of the family vaults in the cemetery. They did this, in spite of the presence nearby of German patrols, by the whole village population surrounding the coffin as it was carried through the streets to the cemetery.

One of the highlights of this visit of Commemoration and Remembrance was a ceremony at Sennecy-le-Grand attended by both French and British Ministers and senior Military representatives, and by the Princess Royal and her husband. Wreaths were laid by British and French authorities, by the Princess Royal and by 'veterans' from both countries at the memorial to the 551 officers and men of the SAS Brigade, comprising the British, French and Belgian Regiments, who were killed in the fight to liberate France.

To describe this 60th Anniversary return to the scenes of the Regiments' actions in occupied France as memorable would be a grave understatement. It was an opportunity, of which there will be few others, for those who are left both to honour the memory of those who did not return and to reaffirm the friendships created so many years ago between those who fought together and those civilians who suffered the indignity and the terrors of enemy occupation – something we in Britain have, happily, been spared.

Appendix 1

The SAS Regimental Collect

O LORD who didst call on thy disciples to venture all to win all men to thee, grant that we, the chosen members of The Special Air Service Regiment, may by our works and our ways dare all to win all, and in so doing render special service to thee and our fellow men in all the world. Through the same Jesus Christ our Lord, Amen.

Appendix 2

We are the Pilgrims, master; we shall go
Always a little further : it may be
Beyond the last blue mountain barred with snow
Across that angry or that glimmering sea,

White on a throne or guarded in a cave
There lives a prophet who can understand
Why men were born : but surely we are brave,
Who take the Golden Road to Samarkand.

Verses by James Elroy Flecker from *Hassan*, frequently quoted in
SAS Commemoration and Thanksgiving Services.

Appendix 3

(Adaptation by an unknown SAS member after Rudyard Kipling)

If you can read a map and find your way
    And trust your compass and follow where it may,
If you can trust yourself when we all doubt you,
    And make allowance for our doubting too;

If you can walk and not be tired by walking
    Or being lost and late don't deal in lies
Or when silent don't give way to talking
    Nor talk too big nor look too wise;

If you can hump a bergen nor mind the weight
    And care for it as tho' it were your life,
If you can fight alone yet basha with a mate
    And work with him yet never come to strife,

If you can force your heart and nerve and sinew
    To serve your turn long after they have gone
And so hold on when there is nothing in you
    Except the will which says to them 'hold on',

If you can talk with trogs and keep your virtue,
　　Or walk with 'brass' – nor lose the common touch
If neither we nor Pen-y-Fan deter you
　　If all men count with you but none too much;

If you can fill the unforgiving minute
　　With sixty seconds' worth of distance run,
Yours are the wings and everything that's with it,
　　And, which is more – you're SAS my son.

Appendix 4

Lili Marlene

(SAS Version, composed by a member of L Detachment,
the original formation of the 1st SAS)

Out in the desert in 1941 L Detachment SAS was formed to
     fight the Hun,
We used to hear a soft refrain,
A lilting strain each night again,
Of poor Lili Marlene, of poor Lili Marlene.

Then back to Cairo we would steer, and drink our beer with
     ne'er a care,
And poor Lili Marlene's boyfriend will never see Marlene.

Check your ammunition, see your guns are right,
Wait until a convoy comes creeping through the night
Then you have some fun my son,
And blow the Hun to Kingdom come,
And poor Marlene's boyfriend will never see Marlene.

Then back to Cairo we would steer and drink our beer with
     ne'er a care,
And poor Marlene's boyfriend will never see Marlene.

Driving into Fuka thirty planes ahead, belching ammunition
and filling them with lead,
A flamer for you a grave for Fritz,
Just like his planes he's shot to bits,
And poor Marlene's boyfriend will never see Marlene.

Then back to Cairo we would steer and drink our beer with
ne'er a care
And poor Marlene's boyfriend will never see Marlene.

Africa Korps has sunk into dust, gone are his Stukas, his
tanks have turned to rust,
No more will we hear that soft refrain,
I heard this strain each night again,
And poor Marlene's boyfriend will never see Marlene.

Index

Berlin, 178, 179, 180, 181, 182, 183, 185, 187, 193
Bernard, Maquis, 115, 132, 134, 135, 171
Bond, Major 'Dick', 156, 157, 158
Borrie, Tpr. Alec 'Boy', 116, 123, 163
Boston (Lincs), 8
Bothwell, 60
Boulogne, 41
Bourbon-Lancy, 120, 131
Boxmeer, 147, 148
Brassy, 116, 120
Braunschweig, 182
Bray Dunes, 30, 31
Brighouse, 53
Bristol, 55, 57
B.B.C., 111, 121, 172
British Expeditionary Force, 14, 29, 69
Britain, 33, 37, 43, 44, 127, 128, 130, 134, 170, 180, 184, 190, 192
Brittain, Freddie, 11, 31, 33, 35
Brittany, 173, 197
Browning, General 'Boy', 142
Brussels, 138, 139, 141, 142, 143, 144, 145, 146, 149, 152, 153, 184

Cadett, Thomas, 175, 177
Calais, 41
Caldwell, Tpr. 'Fred', 163
Callaghan, James, 190
Calvert, Brigadier 'Mad Mike', 158
Camille, Maquis, 115, 132, 134, 135, 171
Cammaerts, Francis, 144, 178, 183, 184, 186, 187, 188, 190
Canadian 4th Armoured Div., 156, 158, 161, 163
Canterbury, 42
Capo Murro di Porco, 95
Castiglione, 67
Cercy, 119
Chalaux, 115, 116, 133
Chamberlain, Neville, 2
Champlatreux, 130
Chartham, 42, 48
Chartres, 109
Château-Chinon, 109, 121
Châtillon-en-Bazois, 118, 121, 124, 126, 127, 130, 1311, 171
Chelmsford, 154, 155, 165, 167, 169, 175
Cherbourg, 15
Chesterfield, 73, 78
Chilham, 42, 48
Christiansen, Arthur, 174
Churchill, Odette, 144